With gratitude for your partnership and support of our ministry,

Stephen A. Macchia, President
Evangelistic Association of New England

OUR GOD IS AWESOME

TONY EVANS

Renaissance Productions

MOODY PRESS
CHICAGO

ISBN: 0-8024-6187-5

3 5 7 9 10 8 6 4

Printed in the United States of America

This book is gratefully dedicated to:

Rev. John McNeal, who taught me about
the holiness of God,

Dr. Howard Dial, who gave me a love for
the Word of God,

Dr. B. Sam Hart, who led me into
the service of God,

and my father,
Mr. Arthur S. Evans, who led me into a
relationship with God

CONTENTS

FOREWORD

Writing a book about God, His character and work, can make an author feel like our family feels when going on vacation: We know we're forgetting something, but we're not exactly sure what it is! Many authors would rather let the challenge pass.

My good friend and colleague in ministry, Dr. Tony Evans, has accepted the challenge. Dr. Evans is recognized in the evangelical church around the world for his unique gifts. The result of his gifts expressed in this work deserves a place at the top of your "must read" list.

Tony acknowledges up front that it's hard to know where to begin when your subject is God Himself. But as you read the book, you will agree with me that Tony started at the right place. I am struck by his clarity and strategic emphasis that knowing God is the foundation and motivation for everything else in the Christian life.

The pressing priority of pursuing the knowledge of God, in the sense of both intimate fellowship and correct information, is confirmed by the words of the apostle Paul, who pulled out the "scrapbook" of his personal pedigree and accomplishments, thumbed through it, and then told the Philippians: "But whatever things were gain to me, those things I have counted as loss for the sake of Christ. More than that, I count all things to be loss in view of the surpassing value of knowing Christ Jesus my Lord" (3:7–8).

This hunger marks Tony's life and ministry, and this commitment shines through on every page of *Our God Is Awesome*.

This is a passionate book, written by someone who believes that the knowledge of God's perfection and His ways is the most important study that could occupy our minds and hearts. If you've heard Tony on his nationwide radio program "The Urban Alternative" or in conference ministry, you know that he teaches God's Word with an irrepressible energy that stirs a response in one's soul.

Our response to the knowledge of God comes right to the front in *Our God Is Awesome*. That's one of the reasons this book is so valuable. Tony is not content to give us a mini-course in theology. Truth always demands a response—and Tony is at his best when he calls God's people to act on the truth they've learned. Each chapter concludes with very practical steps to help us do just that.

Thankfully, Dr. Evans doesn't pretend to explain everything about God. That would be an unending task. Instead, he reverently and thoroughly seeks to help us understand God better that we might love Him more.

It's a pleasure for me to recommend this book. In doing so, let me echo Tony's prayer for his readers, which is that by the time you finish this book, you will know a little bit more about our great God . . . and have a greater desire to enjoy, obey, and serve Him.

Dr. Joseph Stowell, President
Moody Bible Institute

PREFACE

Discoursing about the attributes of God can be a dull and listless enterprise. Especially if one pursues the task as "a clinical examination of a supernal being" (even the sound of this evokes drowsiness). In my many years of theological training, I have read countless theological works which sought to explain God by using words with more than three syllables or nine letters.

The doctrine of God is not presented in Scripture as a set of well-organized theological tenets unrelated to the realities of everyday life. God has determined to reveal His character in the contexts of peace and pain, joy and sorrow, grace and wrath, birth and death, love and hate, and countless other real life situations. We learn about God's law from a murderer named Moses. We learn about God's worship from an adulterer named David. We learn of God's sovereignty from a sufferer named Job. We learn about God's grace from a rebel named Peter. These and many others reflect the down-to-earth context in which God chose to reveal Himself to mankind. And just as these repentant people of old were used to communicate God's truth to men and women today, even so repentant men and women today can personally come to know the wonder of the awesome God of whom they spoke.

An academic study has its place and is helpful to the minister and student of the Bible, but it's hard to get to know God on such a formal and academic basis. It is somewhat like having a relationship with the postmaster general on the basis of one's ability to lick a stamp. Hardly a life-changing experience.

After all, this is the God who allowed His Son to die for our sake. Also, because of the close relationship we share with God via our adoption through Jesus Christ, He wants us to call Him "Daddy." Paul says in Romans 8:15, "For you have not received a spirit of slavery leading to fear again, but you have received a spirit of adoption as sons by which we cry out 'Abba! Father!'" The word *Abba* is the Aramaic (the language spoken in first-century Palestine) equivalent of "Daddy." It is certainly a term of respect, but it is also a term of endearment. Every child of God should get to know his or her heavenly Father.

When I decided to write this book, I wanted to present God in all the splendor and majesty that befits Him. The likelihood of realizing such a lofty goal is slim. However, I did not want my readers to think that God was on the outer edge of the universe, nor did I want to treat Him as though He belongs in a specimen jar. God will forever transcend the reasoning of man, but through Christ and through His Word, the Father has drawn near to us. This book celebrates God's self-revelatory grandeur, up-close and personal. It also seeks to address the appropriate response as we encounter our great God.

By knowing God, we can better understand how we are to live. How can a person imitate God when he or she does not understand what to imitate? We do not carry adjectives and descriptions to God hoping He will fit one of them. Rather, we go to God to find out what the adjectives mean. A study of the words *power* and *authority* is a vain pursuit without pursuing God for the true understanding. What is *holiness* apart from the holiness of God? How can we speak of omnipresence apart from God?

How many times a day do you think one person tells another, "I love you"? Husbands and wives say it all the time, but do they know what it means? First John 4:16 declares, "We have come to know and have believed the love which God has for us. God is love, and the one who abides in love abides in God, and God abides in him." John also wrote, "We love, because He first loved us" (v. 19). Apart from God, what is love?

Understanding who God is provides us with understanding and insight for living. Far too many Christians live in what I would call a state of unconscious Christianity. They have no idea as to how the world works from a Christian perspective. When trials come their way, they are caught totally off guard and unprepared to wage war against the spiritual forces of wickedness.

How a person lives his or her life is a function of how he or she thinks. If a person's mind constantly feasts on earthly, everyday things, that person's source of strength and encouragement will be limited to the resources of the natural world. When people in the Bible considered the attributes of God, their contemplation of God's character gave them comfort and assurance. Many biblical references to the attributes of God emerge from prayer and from praise.

These moments of intimate adoration of God gave birth to some of the most profound theological truths. Yet this theology was not an academic theology, but a theology of passion. When David's soul ached from despair and despondency, he cried out to the Lord in anguish. Inevitably, somewhere amid his tears and distress he would remember that God was his audience. When he focused upon the power and grace of God, David's gloom became gladness. Psalm 13 is a perfect example of this. The "unfailing love" of God allowed David to redirect his heart and mind:

> How long, O Lord? Wilt Thou forget me forever?
> How long wilt Thou hide Thy face from me?
> How long shall I take counsel in my soul,
> Having sorrow in my heart all the day?
> How long will my enemy be exalted over me?
> Consider and answer me, O Lord, my God;
> Enlighten my eyes, lest I sleep the sleep of death,
> Lest my enemy say, "I have overcome him,"
> Lest my adversaries rejoice when I am shaken.
> But I have trusted in Thy lovingkindness;
> My heart shall rejoice in Thy salvation.
> I will sing to the Lord,
> Because He has dealt bountifully with me.

I pray that this book will lead you on a journey to understand and encounter our great God and Savior, just as David did; so that when you understand Him, in His many and diverse attributes, He will become both your joy and your "refuge and strength, a very present help in trouble."

With Gratitude

A special word of thanks goes to my friend, Mr. Phil Rawley, for his excellent editorial assistance in the preparation of this manuscript, and to Greg Thornton, Cheryl Dunlop, and the Moody Press publishing family for their partnership in ministry and their dual commitment to biblical integrity and technical excellence.

PART ONE

THE SUBJECT OF GOD

1
THE STUDY OF GOD

t's hard to know where to begin when your subject is God Himself, a subject more important than anything else we could ever study. Everything else in life emanates from the knowledge of God.

Even coming up with a title for this book was difficult, because nothing can fully express the subject, especially since God is more than the sum total of His attributes. David said, "Such knowledge [of God] is too wonderful for me" (Psalm 139:6). But God invites us to know Him. He wants us to contemplate all that He is, because nothing else matters without Him.

In order for life to be meaningful something must be big enough to warrant our commitment and our affections. The only thing that fits this qualification is God Himself, not only because of who He is, but because *knowing who He is defines who we are.* Much of the confusion about day-to-day living comes because we only see the trees and miss the forest of the great God whom we serve.

I like what the great English preacher Charles Spurgeon told his church one Sunday:

> I believe . . . that the proper study of God's elect is God; the proper study of a Christian is the Godhead. The highest science,

the loftiest speculation, the mightiest philosophy, which can ever engage the attention of a child of God, is the name, the nature, the person, the work, the doings, and the existence of the great God whom he calls his Father.[1]

I pray that by the time you put down this book, you will agree with Spurgeon—and more important, you will know a little bit more about our great God.

My purpose in this opening section is to set the stage, so to speak, by considering some important and foundational truths about God. In Part Two, I want to deal with the perfections of God, known as His attributes or His characteristics; that is, *Who is God and what is He like?* Knowing this is critical: If you misdefine God you've misdefined everything else, because everything emanates from God. You can literally make sense of *nothing* if you have not first made sense of God.

No study of God can be said to be comprehensive for three reasons: The first has to do with the sheer limitation of the human mind. A finite mind cannot fully grasp an infinite being. Second is the moral problem. The presence of sin even in our converted state has limited our capacity for understanding spiritual truth. Third, we have a resource problem. God has simply not told us everything about Himself. What He has told us we can know, but He has not revealed everything.

Because of the greatness of our subject, I will be taking you to many portions of Scripture. But due to the limitations of space and my own finiteness, we will neither exhaust the subject nor be able to give equal attention to all of these Scriptures. I hope that this study will be sufficient to help you taste and see that the Lord is good. I will not be spending time trying to convince atheists of the existence of God. This book is not the setting for that.

As I begin I feel a little bit like the late Art Linkletter, who saw a little boy drawing a picture and asked, "What are you doing?"

The boy replied, "I'm drawing a picture of God."

Mr. Linkletter said, "Well, I thought that no one knew what God looked like."

The boy looked up confidently and said, "They will when I get through."

1. Quoted in J. I. Packer, *Knowing God* (Downers Grove, Ill.: InterVarsity, 1975), 13.

THE STUDY OF GOD

It's true that we don't know what God looks like, but I hope by the time we finish I will have painted a picture of God both definable and defensible. My thesis in this introductory chapter can be stated simply: The study of the knowledge of God is the most important pursuit in life. Absolutely nothing is more important.

Of all the things that matter in your life and mine, to know God through a purposeful study of His nature, His character, and His perfections should be our driving force. Only then will we be able to define everything else accurately. But let me make three clarifications right now before we get into the heart of this chapter and the book.

More than Awareness

First of all, when I talk about the study of the knowledge of God, I am not referring to an awareness of God. Simply to say there is a God doesn't say a whole lot about Him, because it would be hard to miss Him entirely when you understand that He is an all-encompassing Being. So when I talk about knowing God, I mean more than that you are aware He exists.

More than Information

Second, when I talk about knowing God, I mean more than that you have information about God; that is, knowing that He is the Creator or powerful or big or grand or majestic. Those are all true, but they're not sufficient when we talk about knowing God.

More than Religion

Knowing God also means more than having a religious experience with God or saying that we feel Him. It is valid to have an emotional and religious experience with God, but to know Him involves more than that.

Knowing God involves more than awareness, more than information, more than a religious experience. To know God is to have Him rub off on you, to enter into relationship with God so that who He is influences who you are. One of the great tragedies today is that you can go to church and be aware of God; you can go to church and have information about God; and if your church has a great choir, you can even go to church and "feel" God; but you can leave church with Him never having rubbed off on you.

So when I talk about knowing God, I am talking about having the awareness, the information, and the "religious experience" rub off on you and become part of who you are. With this in mind, I want to communicate four things about the study of the knowledge of God.

LIFE'S MOST MEANINGFUL PURSUIT

The study of God is the most meaningful pursuit in life. Jeremiah 9:23–24 expresses the importance of knowing God better than I ever could:

> Thus says the Lord, "Let not a wise man boast of his wisdom, and let not the mighty man boast of his might, let not a rich man boast of his riches; but let him who boasts boast of this, that he understands and knows Me."

The Right Kind of Bragging

It's amazing how many things we brag about. Some of us can brag about our educational achievements. We've gone through school and we've done well. We've got a bachelor's degree. We've earned a master's degree. Perhaps we even graduated *magna cum laude*. We get recognition for that achievement. People call us by name, they give us titles, and, if we are not careful, we might boast about that.

THE KNOWLEDGE OF GOD AFFECTS YOUR SELF-INTERPRETATION. GOD SAYS, "IF YOU ARE GOING TO BRAG, BRAG THAT YOU KNOW ME."

Perhaps you started on the bottom rung of the ladder at your company. You've grown up through the company and now you've become a supervisor, you've "graduated" to become a manager. You own your own business, your own success. Now extra money is in the account. The home looks nice. The cars are modern. The suits are authentic. All the data necessary to indicate that you are successful might tempt you to brag.

But God says, "If you are going to brag, if you really want something to shout about, can you brag that you know Me? Because if you can't talk about that, then it doesn't matter how much money sits in your account, what degree hangs on your wall, or what position you hold in the company. You don't have much to brag about."

A lot of us have pride about the wrong thing. Pride is like growing a beard. It just keeps growing and needs to be shaved daily. Every day, you and I need to get up and look at our degrees, our careers, our money, and then say, "If it were not for the grace of God. . . ."

The fact that we don't do this means we don't really know God, because if we knew God we would understand that we have the ability to get up in the morning, go to work, and spend money only because God is God. The knowledge of God affects your self-interpretation.

Hitting the Right Target

A man once went to visit a farmer and noticed something very odd. On the side of the farmer's barn were a number of targets with holes dead center in each bull's-eye. Evidently, his farmer friend was an excellent shot, a tremendous marksman. The visitor said, "My goodness! Every single hole is right in the center of every single bull's-eye! I didn't know you were that good."

His farmer friend said, "I'm really not."

"Wait a minute. I see a hole in the center of every single bull's eye. How could you not be that good and shoot that well?"

The farmer replied, "It's like this. I shoot the hole into the barn first, then I draw me a bull's-eye."

That's the way a lot of us live our lives. We shoot for riches and then draw the meaning of life around it. We shoot for power and draw the meaning of life around it. We shoot for education and draw the meaning of life around it. Then we go around saying, "I hit a bull's-eye!" We give the impression that we know how to shoot, making our friends think we know what we are doing, making the people we come in contact with think we have been successful, when in actuality we don't know what in the world we are doing. We are as confused as those around us. Why? Because we hit a bull's-eye shooting at the wrong target.

Having the Right Focus

But God says, "If you are going to brag, can you brag on the fact that I have rubbed off on you; that My thinking has become your thinking; that My way of living and walking and moving and functioning has become your way? Only when that happens can you say that you know Me."

So the question is simple. Can you brag that you know God? Can you brag that not only have you come into a relationship with God, but that you *know* Him, that you have entered into intimacy with Him, that He has rubbed off on you? That's the question, and I want you and me to experience God in such a way that He rubs off on us. Then we'll have something to brag about.

I like the story of the woodpecker who was pecking on a tree. Just as he flew away, lightning hit the tree and split it right down the middle. The woodpecker heard the noise, turned back, and said, "Look what I did!"

A lot of us are spiritual woodpeckers. We are like King Nebu-chadnezzar, a man we'll run into in a later chapter. We say, "Look at this Babylon I have built. Look at this home I've built. Look at this car I drive. Look at this school I went to. Look at this job I have. Look at what I have done." But the only reason we have anything is that God let lightning strike. So God says, "Brag that you know Me, the God of lovingkindness."

The Hebrew word translated *lovingkindness* in Jeremiah 9:24 is *hesed*. It means "loyal love." It means, "I have hung in there with you. You didn't hang in there with Me. I stuck with you. I am a God of justice, I rule in fairness, and I am righteous. I have a standard on earth and I delight in these things."

OUR BRAINS ARE TOO SMALL, OUR KNOWLEDGE TOO LIMITED, OURSELVES TOO FINITE TO LIVE LIFE THE WAY IT WAS MEANT TO BE LIVED APART FROM THE KNOWLEDGE OF GOD.

You see, the knowledge of God always rubs off in history. He delights in displaying His lovingkindness, justice, and righteousness on earth. Therefore, you cannot say you know God unless it's rubbed off in your history; unless it has affected how you treat your husband or your wife, how you raise your kids, how you spend your money, and how you relate to people. Unless the knowledge of God has changed you, you don't know Him.

LIFE'S MOST AUTHENTIC PURSUIT

The study of God is not only the most meaningful pursuit in life, it is also the most authentic pursuit. I want to look at John 17, Jesus' high priestly prayer in which He prays on behalf of His disciples, including you and me:

> These things Jesus spoke; and lifting up His eyes to heaven, He said, "Father, the hour has come; glorify Thy Son, that the Son may glorify Thee, even as Thou gavest Him authority over all mankind, that to all whom Thou hast given Him, He may give eternal life. And this is eternal life, that they may know Thee, the only true God, and Jesus Christ whom Thou hast sent." (vv. 1–3)

Authentic Life

According to Jesus, authentic life is eternal life. Please do not misread me here. Jesus is not referring to everlasting life; that is, He is not talking about how long you are going to live. He's talking about a *quality* of life in verse 3. Eternal life means knowing God. Life can never be what it was intended to be for you or me unless that life consists of God's life being lived out in us.

Jesus says in verse 3 that the only way you will get eternal life experience in this life is in the knowledge of God. Do you see that to know God is to live life authentically? To know God is to live life as it was meant to be lived. That's why Jesus said He came to give us life and to give it to us more abundantly. Life can never be lived like it was meant to be lived without the knowledge of God.

Yet many of us attempt to live our lives our way, using our puny brains to figure things out. We want a quality life without a quality God dictating it. We can't have it. Our brains are too small, our knowledge too limited, ourselves too finite to live life the way it was meant to be lived apart from the knowledge of God.

When my daughter was growing up, she liked to work puzzles. So one day, I gave her a thousand-piece puzzle. But she came back sometime later, very frustrated. I asked her, "What's wrong?"

She said, "Dad, this puzzle has too many pieces. I can't put it together."

Life, like that puzzle, has too many pieces. It looks too difficult. Well, I can tell you someone who can put the puzzle together: the

Puzzle-Maker. God is the Puzzle-Maker who knows what protrusion matches with what indentation so as to connect the parts of the puzzle.

To understand this, you have to understand a very simple principle: Eternal life, or the quality of life that God has intended for us, equals the knowledge of Him. Jesus makes a comparative statement in John 17:3. If you want to live, He says, don't go looking for life. Look for the knowledge of God, because authentic life means knowing Him. If you are not succeeding in life, it is because you are not succeeding in the knowledge of God. What you need is not to look for life, but to look for Him who can locate life for you.

Many of us who are alive have never yet learned how to live. We think living is wrapped up in the things I've already mentioned —money, education, prestige, or power—when living really should be about the knowledge of God. That's why studying the Scriptures is so important. In John 17:17 Jesus prays, "Sanctify them in the truth; Thy word is truth."

Telling the Truth

Only one standard of information clarifies what life is all about, and that standard is the Word of God. If we are going to live life authentically, we need someone who will tell us the truth. We don't do that with each other. We don't tell people the truth because we don't want to offend them. We don't tell them the truth because we don't want them mad at us. We don't tell them the truth because people like being lied to. No woman wants to ask, "How do you like my new dress?", and get this response:

"Worse thing I ever saw in my life."

Even though we may think a piece of clothing or a hairstyle must be the worst we have ever seen, we aren't about to say so because people don't want the truth. Therefore, our relationships are often shallow and never get to where they are supposed to be.

You don't have that problem with God. God calls it as He sees it. He will not tell you, "I'm OK, you're OK." He tells you, "You were dead in your trespasses and in your sins, and you lived according to the flesh, according to the lust of this age." He's not going to make it comfortable or convenient for you. He doesn't even worry about damaging the "self-esteem" you've built apart from Him. He will tell you the truth, like a good doctor. He's going to tell you that you are sick so you will know what treatment you need.

The Real You

That's the downside of our study. When God unveils who He is, the knowledge will also unveil who we are. We're faced with the problem Peter had when he ran into Jesus Christ and found out who he was. The revelation of Jesus Christ made Peter fall on his face and say, "I am a sinful man" (Luke 5:8).

The prophet Isaiah saw the Lord and cried out, "Woe is me!" (Isaiah 6:5). Why? Because if you want the real deal, if you really want the truth, God will give you the truth, the whole truth, and nothing but the truth, and some of it will not be pleasant.

That's why not all church services and sermons are designed to make you shout. Shouting has its place, but some sermons should make you cry, gnash your teeth, and fall prostrate on your face before God. Because when you see God as He is, when He unveils Himself, when the true knowledge of God is revealed, it shows you for who you are.

The Real World

The knowledge of God also shows the world for what it is. People spend much time analyzing our world. Philosophers analyze society because people want answers to the fundamental questions of life such as, Who is man? Where did man come from? Where is he going? People dissect the thought of great philosophers like Schleiermacher, Hegel, Kant, and the philosophical thinkers of our age, as they study the development of man and how he relates to the universe in which he finds himself.

So people sit on the floor with their legs bent and their eyes closed, trying to get into a metaphysical state to come to a philosophical understanding of who they are. But when you have the Word of God, you can bypass all that.

Other people pursue the social analysis of man: how man functions in communication and communion with others, how people relate to each other, how people can stop themselves from hurting one another, and how they can live in peace with one another. The result is often political attempts to make the world right. But when you have the Word of God, you understand the rules of society because God tells the truth about the world.

God also tells the truth about sex, about money, and about all the ingredients that relate to life. He tells the truth about who you are. He is the greatest psychologist in the world, for He knows what makes you tick (John 2:25). And so who you are, where you came from, why you are here, and where you are going all come from the knowledge of God.

We have many college graduates in our church in Dallas. This means they spent twelve years in primary education and four years in college. We also have a number of people who have their master's degrees. Depending on the type of degree, that was two to four more years of study. Still others have their doctorates, which means another two to four years. That's anywhere from twelve to sixteen years studying to be what they intended to be for the rest of their lives, and everyone along the continuum said, "It's absolutely necessary."

When you thought about dropping out of high school, some mother, father, aunt, or uncle said, "You can't do that. Boy/girl, get your education."

When you didn't want to go to college, the person said, "No, if you really want to get a decent job, you've got to go to college."

Then in college you saw how little you really knew, so you went on to get more information. And if you're like me, with a doctorate, you are downright ignorant because you find out how much you have yet to learn. If we are willing to spend that kind of energy to have a decent career, isn't it more important that you spend time knowing God so you can have a decent life?

And by the way, you won't discover the knowledge of God just by going to college. When we took our daughter, Priscilla, to a major secular university in Texas, she walked into her dormitory room and began to meet some of her dorm mates. After about twenty hours on campus, she called the hotel where my wife and I were staying and said in her own inimitable way, "Daddy, I'm in hell."

The very first person she met said, "There is no God. There has never been any God. If there is a God, I am he." What a great introduction to college!

The first class she attended, one of her professors announced, "I want to serve notice on you right away that the idea of God is obsolete."

So while you won't necessarily find the knowledge of God on a college campus, it still needs to be your lifelong pursuit.

You'd better get used to it down here, because the knowledge of God is the focus of heaven. Let me tell you something about heaven. Only one thing happens there: People get to know God. You will spend eternity in heaven getting to know God.

You may say, "How boring."

I say no, how exciting. You see, there's only one difference between earth and heaven. Heaven holds the perfect knowledge of God, while the knowledge of God keeps getting interrupted down here. For example, you have to go to sleep. So for eight hours, you are not conscious of God. Or you have problems that distract you from God. In heaven God takes away all the negatives so that you have uninterrupted knowledge of Him.

In fact, you will be part of so much activity in heaven related to the knowledge of God that He won't even let you go to sleep there. Heaven has no night. God will not give you eight hours to take off, but He will give you a brand new body that won't get tired so you won't miss sleep and you won't miss anything. Unlike a good TV program that gets interrupted by the commercials, in heaven no "commercials" will interrupt the excitement of God's revelation of His knowledge.

I'll see you at the corner of Gold Street and Silver Boulevard and you will say, "Hey! Do you want to know what I found out about God just now?" Heaven will be the uninterrupted knowledge of God. But He wants us to get in practice before we get there by making the knowledge of Him our priority in life.

LIFE'S MOST BENEFICIAL PURSUIT

The study of God is not only the most meaningful and the most authentic pursuit in life, it is also the most beneficial. Nothing will benefit you more in day-to-day living than the knowledge of God. Daniel 11:32 says this: "The people who know their God will display strength and take action."

Daniel was a captive in Babylon, an ungodly nation that was turned over to the Medes and the Persians. Daniel was constantly under oppression. He was constantly being victimized, but he says, "The people who know God even in the midst of a bad situation will know the right steps to take in confronting the issues of life."

Confidence

The knowledge of God gives the ability to make the correct response to the circumstances of life. The people who know their God shall be strong. They will have the confidence and ability to do the right thing. You see, the problem today with people who want to correct the social or political order, who want to change this and

27

fix that, is that they want to do good things, but they don't know the right way.

But the people who know their God shall be strong, move forward with confidence, and take action. Knowledge of God is not passive. It's not something you do on the sidelines. It really frees you up to do something, but to do the right something.

Simply because of the size of our church and the exposure God has given my ministry, I'm constantly being called on to get in this or that movement, to endorse this person, to stand with that cause, to march on this thing and to do that thing. Many of these things are fine, but some are not consistent with knowing God. So I have to say, "That's not consistent with the biblical approach."

I have to say that because some people don't want to hear that there is a biblical approach, or that their approach is wrong. I'm saying that when you know God you can be confident about your approach. You don't have to waffle back and forth and be inconsistent and in and out and up and down and go with what everybody thinks.

The world is filled with ideas, but the people who know their God can stand firm, be confident, not be budged, and at the right time, take action. But only the knowledge of God produces that kind of confidence in the circumstances of life. Earlier in the book of Daniel, his Hebrew friends Shadrach, Meshach, and Abednego got thrown into the fiery furnace. The Babylonian officials came to these three and said, "Look, if you don't change your view, if you don't bow, then you are going to burn."

WISDOM MEANS THE ABILITY TO TAKE A DIVINE, SPIRITUAL PERSPECTIVE AND TURN IT INTO AN EARTHLY, FUNCTIONAL APPLICATION.

But these three men knew their God, so their answer was, "O Nebuchadnezzar, we do not need to give you an answer concerning this" (Daniel 3:16). In other words, these men were saying, "We will not take a lot of time to debate this. We know you are the king and the head of the company, and we know you can fire us (literally!), and we know you can make life really bad for us, but let us explain something to you. The God whom we serve can protect us."

These guys were speaking to an unregenerate leader, but he was the greatest political power of the day. When you know God, you can be strong even if it's with the president. While I would respect the president's position because God calls us to, I would have no problem telling the president that he's wrong on this and on that because God said so. Why? Because when you know God, you can be strong. You can be confident. But with that strength and confidence comes proper humility—after all, you are merely passing along what God said, not your own ideas.

So these three Hebrew young men said to Nebuchadnezzar, "Our God whom we serve is able to deliver us" (v. 17). They knew that because they had studied Moses and the Red Sea. They figured any God who could open up the Red Sea could take a little water and put out Nebuchadnezzar's fire. They knew their God, so they were strong and took action, and God honored that action.

Many of us are spiritual wimps because we don't know God, so we don't know the right thing to do. Many men can't lead their families because they don't have the divine grit to take hold of a biblical approach. Many women are spiritual wimps too. They don't have the divine wit to believe that God can do more to change men through wives on their knees than women can do with their words.

Security

The knowledge of God also gives security in life. Look at Psalm 46:1–3:

> God is our refuge and strength, a very present help in trouble. Therefore we will not fear, though the earth should change, and though the mountains slip into the heart of the sea; though its waters roar and foam, though the mountains quake at its swelling pride.

The psalmist says that even when earthquakes shake things up, those who know God will take courage. They will be secure. When the ground under you starts shaking, there isn't much around you to hold onto. Just ask the people who have survived California earthquakes.

Wisdom

The knowledge of God not only gives security, but it gives wisdom. Paul prays in Ephesians 1:17 "that the God of our Lord Jesus Christ, the Father of glory, may give to you a spirit of wisdom and of revelation in the knowledge of Him." Wisdom is spiritual insight for earthly application, the ability to know what God wants and the know-how to apply it where you live. Wisdom is to truth as a shoe is to shoe leather. Wisdom means the ability to take a divine, spiritual perspective and turn it into an earthly, functional application. Wisdom brings the application of truth to life. Paul says the knowledge of God gives wisdom.

Proverbs 9:10 puts it this way: "The fear of the Lord is the beginning of wisdom, and the knowledge of the Holy One is understanding." Solomon says God will show you how to live a wise life. A lot of us have book sense, but we don't have common sense. A lot of us are smart, even brilliant, getting all A's on our report cards, yet in life we go from failure to failure.

It's not that we don't have information, it's just that we don't have wisdom, the ability to apply the knowledge we have. But the knowledge of God can give us wisdom, Proverbs says, the ability to make the right decisions in life.

Order

The apostle Peter says the knowledge of God can give you a well-ordered life:

> Grace and peace be multiplied to you in the knowledge of God and of Jesus our Lord; seeing that His divine power has granted to us everything pertaining to life and godliness, through the true knowledge of Him who called us by His own glory and excellence. (2 Peter 1:2–3)

Peter says the knowledge of God will give you *grace, peace,* and *power.* What more could you ask for? A grace life, a peace life, and a divinely powerful life is a pretty good life! It's a well-ordered life, but Peter says it only comes by the true knowledge of God.

As God rubs off on you—not just as you become more aware of Him, not just as you get more information about Him, but as He rubs off on you—He gives you grace, peace, and power for all of life.

Spiritual Fruit

Not only that, but if in fact you allow God to work in your life; if you allow Him to transform your life, He will give you spiritual development. Colossians 1:9–10 are two verses worth memorizing:

> For this reason also, since the day we heard of it, we have not ceased to pray for you and to ask that you may be filled with the knowledge of His will in all spiritual wisdom and understanding, so that you may walk in a manner worthy of the Lord, to please Him in all respects, bearing fruit in every good work and increasing in the knowledge of God.

Paul says that the knowledge of God will change the way you walk. The familiar gospel song puts it this way: "I looked at my hands, my hands looked new. / I looked at my feet and they did too." That's what these verses talk about. When you know God you walk differently. You move differently. You act differently. You think differently. Why? Because you are filled with the knowledge of God. With this knowledge comes the knowledge of His will, and the knowledge of His will transforms your life. As He transforms your life, you bear spiritual fruit.

Fruit has two characteristics. First, it always reflects the character of the tree of which it is a part. When you bear spiritual fruit, you begin to look like Christ. Second, fruit is never borne for itself. It is always borne so someone else can take a bite. When you start bearing fruit, other people want to take a bite out of your life. Other people want to be like you, because you are a productive person for the purposes of God. That's spiritual development.

LIFE'S MOST CHALLENGING PURSUIT

Finally, the study of God is the most challenging pursuit in life. Look at the following verses:

> Oh, the depth of the riches both of the wisdom and knowledge of God! How unsearchable are His judgments and unfathomable His ways! For who has known the mind of the Lord, or who became His counselor? Or who has first given to Him that it might be paid back to Him again? For from Him and through Him and to Him are all things. To Him be the glory forever. Amen. (Romans 11:33–36)

An Eternal Challenge

Do you want a challenge? Decide to get to know God. It's a challenge for a number of reasons. It's a challenge first because verse 33 says getting to know God will never end. God is never, and will never be, fully comprehensible to man, not only in time, but in eternity. Do you know why you will live with God for eternity? Because that's how long it takes to understand Him.

Any married person can relate to this. You can live with a woman or a man for fifty years and still discover new information. Now if you can do that with another person over a lifetime, think about our infinite God. It will take eternity and then some to understand Him. The knowledge of God will always be a challenge because you will never learn it all.

A Revealing Challenge

Second, the knowledge of God challenges us because getting to know someone demands that he reveal himself to us and grant us the privilege of that knowledge. It's like a guy who comes up to a lady and says, "My name is John. What's your name?"

Now John may want to get to know her, but another question stands on the floor. Is she as interested in knowing his name as he is in knowing hers? In other words, the knowledge of another person is not just contingent on one person's desire to have that information, but on the other's desire to reveal it. God has made it very clear that He has a passionate desire to reveal Himself to us. In Hosea 6:6, God Himself says that He desires us to know Him more than He desires our offerings.

So if you do not come to know God, it is not God's fault because He has made Himself available to be known. And although we can never know God exhaustively, we can know Him intimately. That's challenge enough! Anyone who has ever dated and gotten serious with someone knows that as two people get to know each other, a growing process of intimacy develops. A transformation occurs over time. That's what happens with God. As you come to know Him, you will discover a growing process of intimacy, a closeness where you feel that you know Him and you want to know Him more.

A Priority Challenge

Knowing God is also a challenge because it must be your priority. Deuteronomy 4:29 says that you must search for God with all your heart if you would find Him. The sage says that the knowledge of God is like a man searching for silver (Proverbs 2:4). Where can silver be found? Underneath the ground, so dig.

Why has God not made it easy? Because He wants to know, "How serious are you? You get up and work out because you're serious. But when you've got to get up and spend time with Me, you're too tired. You need that extra fifteen minutes of sleep. Are you serious? You have time to watch your favorite TV show, but you are always too tired to spend time with Me. Are you serious?"

Getting to know God is a challenge because it's hard work to make it a priority. So where do you start? First of all, you must start with a desire to know God. Moses said in Exodus 33:13, "Let me know Thy ways, that I may know Thee."

David said, "As the deer pants for the water brooks, so my soul pants for Thee, O God" (Psalm 42:1).

Paul said his greatest longing was "that I may know Him" (Philippians 3:10).

Jesus said, "Blessed are those who hunger and thirst for righteousness, for they shall be satisfied" (Matthew 5:6).

All of them say the same thing. God only feeds hungry people. If you are not hungry, you are spiritually starved. You might say, "I want to be hungry, but I'm not. How do I get to be hungry?"

The Place to Begin

That's easy. Just hang around food. No matter how recently I've eaten, I always get hungry when I'm around fried chicken. I'm certain that when Mary and Martha fed Jesus and the disciples, they served some fried chicken. It's just logical. They couldn't eat chitlins or pig feet. Chicken was easily available, and after all, they were preachers!

If you want to get spiritually hungry, even if you are not hungry now, get around someone who's cooking something. Get around someone who preaches and teaches God's Word faithfully. Get around someone who feasts on God, and you'll get hungry.

So it has to start with an appetite. Not only that, but you can't enter into the knowledge of God until you have accepted His Son, the Lord Jesus Christ, as your personal Savior. Unless you are a Christian, unless you have faith in Christ, you can never get to the knowledge of God. You can only be on the awareness and information level.

If you are not a Christian, if you've never received Jesus Christ as your only Savior—as the only One you are depending on to give you a relationship with God—you can never know God. Once you are a Christian, relationship is going to require time with God. You never get to know anyone without spending time with him.

The Scripture says, "Be still, and know that I am God" (Psalm 46:10 KJV). Knowing God requires time alone with Him. Back up from the frantic rat race and "be still." The biblical word for being still is *meditation*. It means reflecting on who God is, what He has said, and what He has done.

That's why prayer is so hard sometimes, because prayer involves entering into another realm that we are not used to going into. But we've got to be still. We've got to spend time with God. During the preaching of these messages and the writing of this book, I asked God to help me get to know Him.

I can't fully explain what it means to know God. I can use the terms, but it's like defining a kiss. Webster has the terms. He calls it "a caress with the lips; a gentle touch or contact." But anyone who has kissed someone knows that a kiss is really much more than that. You can't fully explain it, but Lord have mercy, it's good when you get it! I can't fully explain what getting to know God will feel like, but I know that you will like it when it happens.

Responding to the Knowledge of God

Since it's true that nothing else in life will come into proper focus until you understand and know God, it is never too early to begin aligning your life with Him. Here are some ideas to help you start the process:

1. As I said above, the true beginning point in knowing God is entering into relationship with Him through the Lord Jesus Christ. If you have never trusted Christ as your Savior, or if you are unsure of your standing before God, all you need to do is admit that you are a sinner (see Romans 3:9–10, 23) and cannot save yourself (Acts 4:12). Acknowledge that Jesus paid for your sin on the cross (Romans 5:8), and put your faith in Him alone to save you. Call upon Him to save you today (Romans 10:13), receive Him as your Savior (John 1:12)—and welcome to the family. Be sure to tell your pastor or a Christian friend about your decision.

2. All of us cling to things that give us a sense of identity and importance, whether job titles, family heritage, bank accounts, or material possessions. List three of the things that are most important to you, and ask yourself what would happen if you lost them. Could you give them up and still say things are OK because you know the true God and that's enough? It's worth thinking about as you read this book.

3. Perhaps you know a step of obedience and faith that God wants you to take, but you're holding back for fear of what people will think or what the outcome might be. If so, remember that the people who know their God can be strong and take action. Take that needed step, and trust God for the consequences. He will bless you for taking Him at His Word.

4. Speaking of the Word, there's no better way to know God than to hide His Word in your heart and mind. Proverbs 9:10 would be a great verse to memorize over the next few days or weeks: "The fear of the Lord is the beginning of wisdom, and the knowledge of the Holy One is understanding." It captures the theme of this book. If it helps, write it on a card and carry it with you for review until you know the verse well.

2
THE NATURE
OF GOD

Once upon a time a scorpion needed to cross a pond. Wondering how he would get to the other side, he noticed a frog nearby. "Mr. Frog, will you please hop me across this pond?"

The kind, gentle frog said, "Certainly, Mr. Scorpion. I will be glad to do so."

So Mr. Scorpion jumped onto Mr. Frog's back as Mr. Frog hopped from pod to pod, bringing Mr. Scorpion to the other side of the pond. But just as the frog said, "Well, Mr. Scorpion, here we are," he felt an excruciating pain in his back. Mr. Scorpion had stung him.

As Mr. Frog lay dying, he looked up at Mr. Scorpion and said, "How could you do this? I brought you from one side of the pond to the other and now you sting me so that I die."

Mr. Scorpion looked at Mr. Frog and said, "I can't help it. It's my nature."

It's important to know the nature of the one you are dealing with. If you think you are getting one thing, but when you get it it's not what you thought it was, you could be in trouble. That happens today with a lot of errant teaching about who God is. God has been so misdefined, tragically redefined, and even dismissed that people do not understand His true nature.

Then they begin operating on this misinformation, thinking that they know the true God when in fact they know something totally different than who and what the true God is. Knowing the nature of God as He reveals Himself, rather than how we wish He were, can save us from a life of confusion and defeat.

Bunnies hop because it is their nature. Cows moo because it is their nature. Lions roar because it is their nature. Cats catch birds because it is their nature. Dogs chase cats because it is their nature. That's just what they do. You don't have to prod them to do it, you don't have to encourage them to do it, you don't have to teach them to do it. It's part of what they are.

When we talk about the *nature* of something, we mean what is intrinsic to its being. When we talk about the nature of God, we speak of characteristics intrinsic to His being. What does He do naturally? To some people God appears a tyrant, so they are waiting for their next whipping. To others, He's a joke. To still others, God seems like a nice grandfather with a long, white beard, kind of gentle to be around but with very little influence. Or He's just a bigger, better version of man.

But if we are going to have an intimate walk with God, we must understand what makes Him tick—His true nature. That's what I want to do in this chapter, consider the character of God, His nature, by looking at five areas that will help us grasp the greatness of our God.

GOD IS A TRANSCENDENT BEING

God exists above His creation. A key passage for this wonderful truth is Isaiah 40:

> To whom then will you liken God? Or what likeness will you compare with Him? As for the idol, a craftsman casts it, a goldsmith plates it with gold, and a silversmith fashions chains of silver. He who is too impoverished for such an offering selects a tree that does not rot; he seeks out for himself a skillful craftsman to prepare an idol that will not totter. Do you not know? Have you not heard? Has it not been declared to you from the beginning? Have you not understood from the foundations of the earth? It is He who sits above the vault of the earth, and its inhabitants are like grasshoppers, who stretches out the heavens like a curtain and spreads them out like a tent to dwell in. He it is who reduces rulers to nothing, who makes the judges of the earth meaningless. . . . "To whom then will you liken Me that I

THE NATURE OF GOD

should be his equal?" says the Holy One. Lift up your eyes on high and see who has created these stars, the One who leads forth their host by number, He calls them all by name; because of the greatness of His might and the strength of His power not one of them is missing. (vv. 18–23, 25–26)

When we say that God is transcendent, we mean that He is totally distinct from His creation. The word *distinct* is a synonym for transcendent. God is unique. He is one of a kind. You can make no comparison that will give you an understanding of God unless He grants that comparison, because there is nothing you can compare Him to.

That's the problem with coming up with your own idea of God. If it's your idea, the idea is probably wrong. The only understanding you can get of God's nature is the understanding He gives you, because nothing else in the universe is like Him.

Distinct in His Thoughts

The Bible declares that God is distinct from us in His thoughts. In Isaiah 55 the Lord says:

"My thoughts are not your thoughts, neither are your ways My ways," declares the Lord. "For as the heavens are higher than the earth, so are My ways higher than your ways, and My thoughts than your thoughts." (vv. 8–9)

Many times you hear people say, "Well, I don't believe God will do that." How do they know, if His thoughts are not like their thoughts? God is transcendent in His thinking. He does things totally differently than the way we do things. He operates in a totally different way than anything we've ever seen before. Therefore, if you are going to think right, you've got to think God's thoughts because His thoughts and your thoughts don't match. His thoughts are transcendent, distinct.

Distinct in His Person

As we just saw, God asks, "Who will you liken Me to? Who is like Me?" Psalm 50:21 says that God is totally unlike man. He looks at man and says, "I am not like you." So when you deal with God, you are not dealing with an elevated man. The great French agnostic Voltaire said, "God created man in His own image, and man returned the favor." God created man, and we've reduced our unique God to just a Superman. But He remains totally, utterly, absolutely transcendent.

Distinct in His Deity

Psalm 97:9 says, God is "exalted far above all gods." He is also "exalted above all the peoples" (Psalm 99:2). God is absolute deity, and He cannot be compared with anything you've ever seen or known before. That truth contains heavy implications relative to the transcendent nature or distinctiveness of God. Let me show you what I mean from the Ten Commandments.

The first commandment says we are to have no other God because there is only one true God. Then the second commandment says:

> You shall not make for yourself an idol, or any likeness of what is in heaven above or on the earth beneath or in the water under the earth. You shall not worship them or serve them; for I, the Lord your God, am a jealous God, visiting the iniquity of the fathers on the children, on the third and fourth generations of those who hate Me, but showing lovingkindness to thousands, to those who love Me and keep My commandments. (Exodus 20:4–6)

God says, "Because I am unique, you are to make no likeness of Me." What does that mean? It means we must not paint pictures of God. Now let me explain. I'm sure you are familiar with those photo booths they have in the malls. You go in, put in some coins, sit down, and draw the curtain. The light comes on, you get in your pose, and the pictures snap. Some ugly pictures come out of those machines, don't they? Those photos may be good for the passport office, but not for trying to win friends and influence people.

Someone says to you, "Show me a picture of your girlfriend (or wife or husband)." You dig in your wallet or purse and pull out the picture, and then you always say, "This isn't a good shot. If you really saw what she looks like in real life, you would understand. This just gives you a general idea."

We apologize for a bad picture. God says, "Don't make any likeness of Me, because anything you come up with will make Me look bad." We are to make no likenesses of God to enable us to worship Him other than those He prescribes. When people paint pictures of God—or even Jesus, since we don't know what He looked like— and then use those pictures as objects to enhance worship, that's idolatry. When we put up crosses to help us worship God better, that's idolatry.

Anything you create to help you see God more clearly, other than what God has prescribed, is idolatry because it's a poor rendering. It's a bad picture. God says that He is jealous to protect His glory. He does not want bad photographs taken of Him, so He says, "Don't make any image of Me."

Now if you want to buy something to decorate your wall, or because you enjoy its artistic value or because it's just jewelry to you, that's one thing. But you cannot use any emblems or symbols to enhance your worship other than the ones God prescribes, like the bread and wine. These are designed to show forth the death and resurrection of Christ, and they are legitimate parts of corporate worship because God prescribes them. Otherwise, He says, "You cannot create, on your own, likenesses of Me because I am totally distinct and you would limit My glory if you did that."

WE APOLOGIZE FOR A BAD PICTURE. GOD SAYS, "DON'T MAKE ANY LIKENESS OF ME, BECAUSE ANYTHING YOU COME UP WITH WILL MAKE ME LOOK BAD."

God does not want His glory either limited, localized, or leveraged. He doesn't want it limited because He doesn't want us to come up with anything that doesn't fully reflect Him. He doesn't want it localized because He doesn't want anyone to feel that unless he is in a certain place with a certain object, he can't worship. And God doesn't want His glory leveraged because He doesn't want it used to free you up to do things that He doesn't prescribe.

Many of us feel free to do the things we do and to live the way we live because we have made God so small that He just winks at what we're doing. He OK's it. That's what happened in Exodus 32 when Moses went up to the mountain and seemed to be taking too long. The people said to his brother, Aaron, who was supposed to be the one making sure that the people stayed with God, "Moses has been gone too long. We need a god we can see" (v. 1).

So Aaron said, "Bring all your jewelry and let's make God something real nice. Let's make Him a molten calf." So they melted down their gold and formed it into a calf. This was really kind of a compliment from a human standpoint. After all, the people expressed value. They gave their gold to make it. They also expressed strength, because the bull is one of the strongest of God's creatures. But the people were really saying, "Until Moses comes back and tells us something from God, we will make a representation of God we can see and touch."

And the Bible says that when God saw what they were doing, He was hot with anger because they had reduced Him to a golden calf. Not only that, but they leveraged His glory because they used the occasion as an excuse to have an orgy. They "rose up to play" (Exodus 32:6). They became immoral.

When you reduce God to something you're comfortable with, it frees you up to do what you want. That's why God does not want likenesses that limit or localize or leverage Him. Some people say, "When I pray, I don't see anything." That's good. You are not supposed to. Because if you see something, it isn't God. That leads to a second truth about our great God.

GOD IS A SPIRIT BEING

During Jesus' encounter with the Samaritan woman in John 4, He makes a very, very important statement about His essential nature. They are talking about worship, and Jesus says, "An hour is coming, and now is, when the true worshipers shall worship the Father in spirit and truth; for such people the Father seeks to be His worshipers. God is spirit . . ." (vv. 23–24a).

Please notice that "spirit" has no article. God is not "the" Spirit, God is *spirit;* that is, spirit is His essence, who He is. This phrase comes at the front of the sentence in Greek for emphasis, so Jesus is saying, "I want to emphasize why you must worship God in spirit and truth."

God Is Immaterial

"God is spirit." What does it mean to say something is spirit? First of all, it means that God is nonmaterial. He is immaterial; that is, He does not have a body. Jesus said in Luke 24:39 that spirits don't have bodies.

You say, "But Jesus has a body."

Jesus does have a body, but that's because He became man, not because of His eternal essence. God's essence is immaterial. Now, the God of the Bible knows that we have trouble with that because we function in a world that needs bodies for us to understand things. So the Bible contains many *anthropomorphisms,* a word for your theological dictionary. This term is made up of two Greek words: *anthropos,* which means "man"; and *morphos,* which means "form."

In other words, God speaks to us in "man-forms." The Bible may say, "The hand of the Lord is mighty to save," or, "The eye of the Lord can see." The Bible may talk about God's back, His face, or His ears. Those are anthropomorphisms, the use of human descriptions to help us relate to a spirit being we could not relate to otherwise.

But even though God allows Himself to be described in human terms, when it comes to worship He says, "You must worship Me in My essence." God is spirit. He is immaterial, even though He speaks and uses material objects to make clear who He is. That is why what you do with your body is not God's first concern. What you do with your heart is His first concern, because what you do with your body will be a *result* of what you do with your spirit, your inner being.

God Is a Person

The second thing you need to know about God as spirit is that He is a Person. John 4:24 says, "Those who worship *Him*" (italics added). God is a Person. When I say this, I mean that He has the three attributes of personhood: emotions or feelings, intellect or the mind, and will or the power to choose. Those three things make people distinct from the rest of creation. God is a Person because He feels, thinks, and chooses.

So when I speak of God as spirit, I do *not* mean that He's not a Person. He is an immaterial Person. The classic statement of God's personhood is His answer to Moses in Exodus 3:14. Moses wanted to know what he should tell the children of Israel when they asked who had sent him. God's response was, "I AM WHO I AM. . . . Thus shall you say to the sons of Israel, 'I AM has sent me to you.'"

God Is Invisible

If God is spirit, not only is He immaterial, not only is He a Person, but He is also invisible: "No man has seen God at any time" (John 1:18). That verse means just what it says. No one has ever seen God. Moses once prayed, "Show Me Thy glory" (Exodus 33:18). But the Bible says that God had to hide Moses "in the cleft of the rock" lest Moses see God and die (v. 22).

That's why when you go to heaven, you must have a new body. This body can't stand the heat. I know some people run around saying they have seen God. No, they just had too much pizza. "No man has seen God at any time." The only revelation of God in terms of full visibility—although clothed in humanity—is the Person of Christ.

But that's also why prayer gets boring unless your spirit is growing, because you can't see anything. Your spirit can see because prayer is spirit to spirit, but if you're not developing spiritually, you won't have much dynamic with God because He does not exist as a physical being, someone you can see. Some people might object, "Wait a minute. How can you worship someone you can't see?"

The same way you can know it's windy. Tell me, what does the wind look like? What are its component parts? How does it feel? No one can describe wind because it's invisible, even though you know it's there. You can say, "It's a windy day." Why? Because its effects are clear. Limbs bend, hats blow, umbrellas turn inside out. It's obvious when it's windy, not because you can see the wind, but because its effects are without question.

You see the reality of God in what He does, not in what He looks like. So if God never blows any wind in your direction, you will not know He's real. But if you are growing in your faith and He's blowing in your direction, even though you can't see Him you will know He's all around you. God is invisible, yet His effects can be seen.

At least two very important implications for your life and mine come out of the fact that God is spirit.

1. *Knowing that God is spirit frees you from materialism.* Many of us don't have a real life because we are trying to find life in all the wrong places. We look for the meaning of life in material things, the things our five senses hold onto, whether relationships, money, prestige, or power.

But God is spirit, and if you are ever going to find the meaning of life and make it work, your spirit must be in touch with His Spirit regardless of circumstances. Politicians want their names remembered in the history books; athletes want their names remembered in the record books; businessmen want their names remembered because of their economic achievements. All of these things are quickly forgotten, broken, or lost; but the reality of the knowledge

THE NATURE OF GOD

of God at work in your life cannot be lost. If you are not developing a spiritual relationship with God you cannot know Him, for God is spirit.

2. *Knowing that God is spirit means that you are complete in Him (Colossians 2:9–10).* Everything you need for everything He has called you to be is located in Him. Listen to what Paul says in Acts 17:24–25:

> The God who made the world and all things in it, since He is Lord of heaven and earth, does not·dwell in temples made with hands; neither is He served by human hands, as though He needed anything, since He Himself gives to all life and breath and all things.

Do you see what Paul is saying? He says that God is so comprehensive and so complete, He is self-generating. And you are spiritually complete in Him if you will do as Jeremiah 29:13 says: "You will seek Me and find Me, when you search for Me with all your heart." You can go to church every Sunday and yet never find God, because your heart must be in it. If your body is in church but your heart is not in it, you won't meet God. You may tap your feet to the music and clap your hands at the sermon, but you will not meet God.

God demands your heart. He is spirit, and unless your heart is in your worship, you will be no different twelve months from now than you are today. But when your heart connects, when you come before the Lord in worship and in your day-to-day walk with Him and say, "Lord, you are spirit; my heart goes out to You," He's ready to talk.

GOD IS AN ETERNAL BEING

A third truth we need to know about the nature of our great God is that He is eternal. Moses declared:

> Lord, Thou hast been our dwelling place in all generations. Before the mountains were born, or Thou didst give birth to the earth and the world, even from everlasting to everlasting, Thou art God. (Psalm 90:1–2)

He Has No Beginning

"From everlasting to everlasting"—that's a long time! When did God begin? From everlasting—but if you exist from everlasting you have no starting point. To put it another way, there has never been a time when God was not. Now don't try to figure that one out or it will drive you stark raving mad. I remember when I was a young Christian, I just stood in my room one day thinking about the fact that God has no beginning. But how can something not have a beginning?

The evolutionists say that out of nothing a beginning happened. They give a lot of different reasons such as the "Big Bang" or cosmic energy or primordial slime. But they try to argue that something came out of nothing. I'll stick with God because everyone has the same problem: *Who's the first cause here?*

God existed from everlasting. There never was a time when God was not, and there will never be a time when God will not be. It is very important to realize that God is forever. This truth has a fundamental implication for us: With God, *there is no such thing as the succession of events.* History is a meaningless concept to Him.

We are creatures of history because we are linear creatures. By that I mean we go from point A to point B to point C, from one to ten. We go from this event to that event to the next event, one after the other. We are creatures of the past, the present, and the future. We are linear, successive creatures, but that is irrelevant to God. He knows about history because He's the God of history, but history doesn't control Him. Remember that He told Moses, "I AM WHO I AM."

That verb *AM* is very important because it means that God forever lives in the present tense. He has no past. He has no future. The problem with talking about God is coming up with analogies that make sense because we are dealing with Someone who is transcendent, but let me try.

All of us have attended a parade, which we see as a succession of events. We stand on the curb and watch a float pass by, then a band, followed by a drill team, one after the other. At best, you can look down the street and see two or three successive events at a time. But you can't see around all the corners or see the full length of the parade because it is linear. It moves down the street from point A to point B.

However, if you were to go aloft in the Goodyear blimp, it would be a new deal. From overhead you can see the whole parade in one grand sweep. The succession of events becomes irrelevant from the blimp because you are so high up looking so far down that it's all one event.

You and I live from today to tomorrow to next month to next year. But God sits in the Goodyear blimp. He sees the whole thing as one because He's from everlasting to everlasting, always in the present tense, no past, no future. What does that mean? It means if God's telling you something about what's going to happen tomorrow, you'd better believe it because He's already been there and back. God says there's a heaven and a hell—things you don't want to wait to find out for yourself.

God says, "If you obey Me, I'm going to honor you. If you disobey Me, you will run into problems. It's all present to Me. I'm watching the whole parade."

But what do we do? We say to God, "Show me. Let me see what the next float looks like."

He Is Independent

The eternality of God also means, as we've seen already, that God is independent. Everything created needs something outside of itself to exist. But God depends on nothing outside Himself to exist. He is self-generating. Now I've got good new and bad news. The bad news is God does not need us. He did not create us out of any need or lack in His Person.

Before there was earth or anything else, God was. When the earth was created, God had already existed millions of years. In fact, even that is an understatement, since one can go back into eternity forever and never find a time when God did not exist. How did He make it that long without us? Because God needs nothing outside of Himself to be Himself or to be complete. He is totally self-generating. He is totally fulfilled within Himself.

The good news is that God created us so we could get in on what He is enjoying: Himself. He created us so that we can enjoy Him, benefit from Him, and participate in His world, not to make up for something that was lacking. God does not need man, and so man can't threaten Him.

GOD IS AN IMMUTABLE BEING

God is not only transcendent, eternal Spirit, He is also immutable. Immutability means not having the ability to change. "Every good thing bestowed and every perfect gift is from above, coming down from the Father of lights, with whom there is no variation, or shifting shadow" (James 1:17).

Changeless in His Person

God cannot, does not, will not change. That makes Him unlike everything else in creation. The second law of thermodynamics says that every transformation of energy is accompanied by a loss of available energy, so that future use of that energy is no longer available to the same degree. In other words, people change, clothes change, seasons change, times change, hair changes, and shoes change—but God does not change. His Word does not change. Psalm 119:89 says, "Forever, O Lord, Thy word is settled in heaven."

Changeless in His Purpose

The writer of Hebrews testifies that God's purpose is unchangeable (immutable, incapable of change), and to prove it God swore "by two unchangeable [immutable] things, in which it is impossible for God to lie" (Hebrews 6:17–18). God's character does not change. Neither does His love (Jeremiah 31:3). The Son of God does not change, for "Jesus Christ is the same yesterday and today, yes and forever" (Hebrews 13:8). God's plans do not change (Psalm 33:11), and His knowledge is the same today as it was on the day He created the world.

Do you get the point? God does not, cannot, and will not ever change! Let's go back to James 1:17. "Father of lights" means that God is the Father of the moon, the stars, the sun, the lights in heaven. He's not one of the lights. We don't worship the moon. He is the lights' "Daddy." He made them. Then James throws in a wonderful line about God: "with whom there is no variation, or shifting shadow." That's sweet.

Every day, we've got to deal with shadows because the earth rotating on its axis around the sun shifts the light of the sun every twenty-four hours. We have a shadow on our side of the earth at dusk because of the earth's rotation. Several hours later, that shadow will turn to darkness. If it were not for the lights up in the heavens (and, in modern times, artificial light), you would be able to see virtually nothing at night.

But then the next morning, that shadow will disappear again. It will be daylight here and night somewhere else, a never-ending process. But God is not like our twenty-four-hour time period. He does not move from dark to light, from night to day. He is constant. That's why heaven has no night, no "shifting shadow." It will not be light today and dark tomorrow because God's nature is consistent. He is immutable.

Changeless in His Character

Whenever we talk about God's immutability, someone always says, "Wait a minute. The Bible talks about God changing His mind. In fact, He changed His mind about destroying Israel after Aaron built the golden calf."

That's true as far as it goes. The Bible does say that God was going to destroy the people for their sin (Exodus 32:10). But Moses pleaded with God not to do it, "so the Lord changed His mind about the harm which He said He would do to His people" (v. 14).

THERE IS ONLY ONE TRUE GOD, NOT THE GOD OF THIS OR THAT RELIGION. YOU ARE EITHER RELATED TO THE ONE TRUE GOD, WHO IS TRANSCENDENT, SPIRIT, ETERNAL, AND IMMUTABLE, OR TO NO GOD.

Let me add another one to that. God also changed His mind concerning Nineveh (Jonah 3). He said that He was going to destroy the city in forty days (v. 4), then He changed His mind. So we've got a problem here. If God doesn't change, how can He change His mind?

Although God's character does not ever change, His *methods* may. Here's what I mean. God's character is constant; however, if a change on man's part affects another part of God's character, God is then free to relate to that person out of that part of His character rather than out of the previous part of His character.

For example, God was going to destroy Nineveh because of its sin. God does not change His mind about sin. But what changed was that the people of Nineveh repented. When they did, they appealed to another part of God's character, His grace. God was dealing with them from one part of His character, His wrath against sin. But their repentance brought them under another part of His character.

So God "changed" only in that He allowed the Ninevites' actions to pull in another part of who He is. God doesn't change in

His essence, but He changes in His methods based on our willingness to adjust. It's not God who adjusts. He reacts to our adjustment. When you get right with God, you appeal to another aspect of His character—but that character never changes, because it is already perfect.

By the way, God has given us proof that He will never change: the rainbow. The rainbow was God's promise to Noah that He would never destroy the earth by water again. Destroying mankind in the Flood hurt God so bad that He said, "I'll never do it again, and to let you know I'll give you a rainbow as a sign in the heavens." Every time you see a rainbow, you need to say, "Thank You, Lord. You don't change. You are constant." God is immutable. He does not change.

GOD IS A TRIUNE BEING

This is the final and most difficult truth we want to examine. Let me set the parameters to begin. There is only one God. Deuteronomy 6:4 affirms, "The Lord is our God, the Lord is one." God Himself declares, "Besides Me there is no God" (Isaiah 45:5). Paul says the same thing: "There is no God but one" (1 Corinthians 8:4). There is only one true God, not the god of this or that religion. You are either related to the one true God, who is transcendent, spirit, eternal, and immutable, or to no God.

One God in Three Persons

However, this one God is made up of three distinct Persons: Father, Son, and Holy Spirit. The word we use for this is *Trinity.* This word does not appear in the Bible, but the teaching of the "threeness" of God shows up all through the Bible. This is difficult for many people to understand, so a lot of people make a joke of the Trinity.

But it shouldn't be any problem for us. Do you know why? Because God is transcendent. He's not like us. Many Bible teachers have struggled to illustrate this. Some use water, which can be liquid, ice, or steam, but all three have the same two parts hydrogen, one part oxygen. Others try to illustrate the concept of the Trinity with the egg. An egg has a shell, a white, and a yolk, but it's all one egg.

I appreciate these efforts, but none of them really catches the essence of the Trinity. We have to come back to the point where, as someone has said, if you try to explain the Trinity you will lose your mind. But deny it, and you will lose your soul.

The Trinity in Creation

But we still need to consider this important doctrine, and the Bible gives us a lot of information. First of all, we see the plurality of God in creation. "In the beginning God created the heavens and the earth" (Genesis 1:1). The Hebrew word for God here is *Elohim,* a plural word. Even in the first sentence of the Bible, God lets us know that He is plural even as He is singular.

He shows this in the creation of man, because in Genesis 1:26, God says, "Let Us make man in *Our* image" (emphasis added). But then the very next verse says, "God created man in *His* own image" (emphasis added). The text moves freely from plural to singular and back to plural. Why? Because our one God is made up of three Persons.

The Trinity Throughout Scripture

We also get a glimpse of the Trinity in Isaiah 48:16, where the pre-incarnate Christ says, "The Lord God has sent me, and His Spirit," associating God the Father with the Son and the Holy Spirit. That's why you can have Jesus on the cross saying to the Father, "Why hast Thou forsaken Me?" They are two different Persons. The Father is not the Son; the Son is not the Spirit. But the Father is God; the Son is God, and the Spirit is God. All three are equal in essence as part of the singular Godhead while remaining distinct from each other in their personhood.

The plurality of God also appears in the descriptions of God. The Father is called God (Galatians 1:1, 3; Ephesians 1:2–3). The Son is called God (John 20:28). The Holy Spirit is called God (Acts 5:3–4). In fact, in Hebrews 1:8 God the Father calls God the Son "God."

The Bible says all three Persons of the Trinity are at work in salvation (1 Peter 1:1–2). Paul tells us in 2 Corinthians 13:14 that one member of the Trinity gives us grace, one member loves us, and another unites us in fellowship. These are not mutually exclusive ministries, of course. All three members of the Trinity are working together to sanctify us.

The Bible ascribes creation to God (Genesis 1:1), to Jesus (Colossians 1:16), and to the Spirit (Genesis 1:2; Psalm 104:30). The Trinity is active in prayer (Ephesians 2:18) and in the blessing of the believer (2 Thessalonians 2:13).

Thus all three act in unity, one God in three Persons, equal in essence though distinct in function. The best illustration of the Trinity is the family: a woman and a man who are one, and children who bear the same essence as mom and dad. That's the best we can come up with. When God created us in His likeness, the first thing He did was make a family.

But even that can't fully explain the Trinity. What makes the cross so horrible is that on the cross, Jesus looked up and said, "My God, My God, why hast Thou forsaken Me?" In some unexplainable way, God the Father broke ranks with God the Son. Some kind of interruption took place in the Trinity. I don't know how that happened, but in some extraordinary way God turned away from God without ceasing to be God.

So how do we conclude? With 1 Timothy 1:17, where Paul writes to this young preacher: "Now to the King eternal, immortal, invisible, the only God, be honor and glory forever and ever. Amen."

I don't know what's going on in your life, but if you get to know this God, He will be an anchor for your soul. It won't stop the hurricanes and tornadoes of life from hitting you and making the billows roll. But with this God—not "the force"; not some anemic God you conjure up; not some deified man—as your anchor, your boat's going to stay afloat.

Responding to the Nature of God

L et me say it again. If the transcendent, spirit, eternal, immutable, triune God is your God and you get to know Him, the anchor of your soul will hold. Try these ideas to help you get your anchor set firmly in Him:

1. Let God be God. This may sound elementary, but we often fall into the trap of trying to confine God to our perceptions of Him. One sign of this common malady is thinking, or saying things like, "God would never allow that," "I can't see how God could bless that person," or "I don't believe God will hold us responsible for that." If this is a problem for you, go to the Lord in prayer and give Him permission to be Lord in your heart.

2. Related to our tendency to box God in is our inclination to make bargains with Him. They may be well-meaning bargains, and sometimes they are even unspoken, but we cannot put God on a performance basis. We can't say, "I'll give to Your work with the understanding that You will bless my finances." God may want to bless you anyway, but He doesn't do deals. Got any "deals" working with God right now? Cancel them.

3. Sometimes we turn things around the other way and put ourselves on a performance basis, figuring that the better we are, the more God will love us. But Colossians 2 says you are already complete in Christ in terms of your standing before Him. You don't have to work harder to make yourself more acceptable to Him. Rejoice in that wonderful truth, let it sink deep into your soul. Then enjoy the fact that you are free to serve Him out of love and gratitude, not because it's your duty.

4. If you want to make knowing God a priority in your life, it means you're going to have to say no to some other things, even good things. Have you said no to anything lately so you can say yes to God's invitation to know Him intimately?

PART TWO

THE ATTRIBUTES OF GOD

3
THE SUFFICIENCY
OF GOD

T he very thought of God supercedes your wildest dreams. Job put it best in Job 26:14. When
he looked out on the creation, he was so awed
he said, "These are the fringes of His ways; and
how faint a word we hear of Him!"

Job was saying, "Men know so little about God. Even when people look as far as they can into the solar system, they've really seen
just the fringes of God." What a metaphor for our study in this second and by far the largest section in this book: the attributes of
God.

We begin with the attribute known as God's sufficiency. This
attribute of God means He is totally and absolutely complete within
Himself. Nothing can be added to or taken away from God. That
thought defies comprehension because we don't know anything
else like that in our universe. But that explains why the Bible says
nothing compares to God.

It frustrates autonomous men that they can't put a limit on God.
They can't box Him in. The test tubes don't work when it comes to
Him. The mathematical formulas don't equate when it comes to
God because His sufficiency means that all that makes God who He
is already resides within Him.

That doesn't mean we Christians have God figured out either. Trying to comprehend the subject of God overwhelms us because it only reveals how little we know. Sometimes I think it's better if I don't study it so I won't know how ignorant I am. The study of God can be intimidating because it lets us know how great He is, and in the process it lets us know how small we are.

ALL THE THINGS THAT MAKE LIFE WHAT IT IS PROVE THAT WE HAVE AN ALL-SUFFICIENT GOD AND THAT NONE IS LIKE HIM.

After we built the Family Life Center at our church in Dallas a few years ago, I would often come through and meet one particular gentleman who would always "woof" at me. He would tell me how he wanted to whip me on the Ping-Pong table, and I would always say, "No, I don't have time."

He would reply, "Pastor, why don't you just say you can't play?"

Well, after a while I got a little tired of it and said, "OK, I'll play."

So I put my Bible down and took off my jacket, and while he was "woofing" and telling me what he was going to do and how bad he was going to beat me, the game began. He scored the first point, the second point, and the third point. Soon it was 16–0, his favor. I looked at him and without smiling said, "The game is over." Then I started. Soon it was 16–10, then 16–15. I tied him at 16, and when the score reached 21–16, the game was over.

By this time, all the men in the Family Life Center had lined up, about fourteen of them as I recall, and each of them suffered the same fate as the first guy, the embarrassment of losing to his pastor on the Ping-Pong table.

Then they started woofing me at the pool table. I unhooked my tie this time and went over to the pool table. They were quite shocked to see me take the cue behind my back and call the shot. They were very surprised to see me put two balls into two different pockets with one shot. They were stupefied to see me shoot from one end of the table, make the ball come back on the other side at the other end and drop in the pocket. I ended the day's activity by saying, "Don't mess with me."

You see, the reason these men were woofing was because they had put me in a box. They looked at me only as a pulpiteer. They were not aware of the many years I spent in the Boys' Club. They didn't know about my background in the YMCA. They were unaware of a lot of the data associated with me, but after that personal "conversion" experience, they had a new appreciation for their pastor.

The point is, the more you get to know about someone, the better you can appreciate him. When we come to know God in His sufficiency and superiority, when we are exposed to things we didn't know before, it can be downright intimidating. That's how I feel as I approach the study of God, but He invites us to know Him. So I want to observe four truths about the sufficiency of God.

GOD IS RESPONSIBLE
FOR HIS CREATION

The sufficiency of God means that He is totally responsible for all of creation. Colossians 1, in a reference to the second Person of the Trinity, puts it so clearly:

> And He is the image of the invisible God, the first-born of all creation. For by Him all things were created, both in the heavens and on earth, visible and invisible, whether thrones or dominions or rulers or authorities—all things have been created by Him and for Him. (vv. 15–16)

Creation Reveals His Person

These verses tell us that the glory of God's all-inclusiveness can be realized by all the variety that exists within His creation. If you want to see how glorious God is, He invites you, "Look at what I have done." If you really want to know how sufficient, how good, how complete something is, look at what it produces. If it produces glorious results, then the one responsible for that production must be more glorious than the thing produced. All of us can look at nature and see that "The heavens are telling of the glory of God" (Psalm 19:1).

That's why God does not spend time trying to prove His existence to atheists. Only a fool would reject the existence of God after looking at a creation as complex and orderly as this world. All the things that make life what it is prove that we have an all-sufficient

God and that none is like Him. God asked Job, "Where were you when I created the universe?"

God was saying to Job that by virtue of His creation, the greatness of who He is becomes evident. The Bible declares that God is responsible for creation, which of necessity means that God preceded creation. God could precede creation because He "has life within Himself" (John 5:26). God has self-generating power, His own internal battery, so to speak, by which everything exists. Why did God create this universe? Not of necessity, but simply because it brought Him pleasure to do so.

Creation Reveals His Pleasure

Do you ever do anything just because it makes you feel good? You don't have to do it. You have no need to do it, but you just enjoy doing it. God created the universe out of His own good pleasure. In fact, Ephesians 1:5 says that God does all things out of Himself simply because it pleases Him to do so. God's self-sufficiency shows in the fact that when He wants to do something, He does it.

ALL THAT GOD IS HE ALWAYS WAS. ALL THAT GOD IS AND ALWAYS WAS HE ALWAYS WILL BE. YOU CANNOT OFFER ANYTHING THAT WILL ENHANCE HIM, NOR CAN YOU TAKE ANYTHING AWAY THAT WILL DETRACT FROM HIM.

Now this crosses the doctrine of the sovereignty of God, what He chooses to do and not to do, which we will consider in chapter 5. Suffice it to say here that God has a patent on creation because creation comes from Him. God can create because He is sufficient within Himself to produce anything He wants to exist.

And when God creates, He only has to speak the word. He doesn't have to go through trauma, draw up blueprints, or form construction companies. Within Himself He holds the power to pull off anything.

This explains precisely why knowing God becomes so important. When we know Him, we will want what pleases Him. And when what we want pleases Him and is according to His will, He speaks the word and brings something out of nothing. God's sufficiency means that He's totally responsible for all of the created order, and He can be responsible because He is sufficient within Himself to produce anything His heart desires.

GOD IS INDEPENDENT
OF HIS CREATION

One of the great passages of Scripture is Paul's sermon to the Greeks in Athens as they were groping after the true God:

> And Paul stood in the midst of the Areopagus and said, "Men of Athens, I observe that you are very religious in all respects. For while I was passing through and examining the objects of your worship, I also found an altar with this inscription, 'TO AN UN-KNOWN GOD.' What therefore you worship in ignorance, this I proclaim to you. The God who made the world and all things in it, since He is Lord of heaven and earth, does not dwell in temples made with hands; neither is He served by human hands, as though He needed anything, since He Himself gives to all life and breath and all things." (Acts 17:22–25)

In this classic passage Paul explains to people who want to know the true God, the God who created heaven and earth and everything in it, that this God is independent of His creation. By independent I mean that God does not need anything from His created order to enable Him to continue being God. God does not function out of necessity.

No Outside Influences

All of us can explain who we are by virtue of the influences in our lives. I can describe where I am today by pointing to the influence of my parents. I can tell you the schools I went to that educated me, expanded my vocabulary, and gave me a perspective of different sciences. I can explain the clothes on my back by talking about someone who took animal skins or pieces of cloth and stitched them together. I can explain everything related to me by virtue of other entities that influenced me.

But God has no such explanation. No influences have ever made God what He is. All that God is He always was. All that God is and always was He always will be. You cannot offer anything that will enhance Him, nor can you take anything away that will detract from Him. All that God is He is because that's who He is.

No Necessary Relationships

This understanding can enhance our worship of God, because while God has a voluntary relationship to everything, He has a necessary relationship to nothing. In other words, God relates to His creation because He chooses to, not because He needs to. For example, if you show up for worship at your church, that's good and God is glad to see you. But He will not be worse off if you stay home. He's not going to panic. Now I might be ticked as your pastor, but God will be no less God because your worship is not a necessity for Him.

Several reasons may help explain this. First, God's worship is within Himself. God adores Himself already. He's not like people, who want compliments. One time my wife told me, "You didn't say anything about my new dress." I didn't see her new dress. I didn't even know it was a new dress.

God does not need to be noticed. He does not need recognition. It is not God's privilege that we get to worship, but our privilege. We come to worship God because He's asked us to, not because He needs us to. You do not add to God, because if you don't worship Him, someone else will.

In Isaiah 6:2–3, the Bible tells us absolutely clearly that God has beings in heaven who worship Him twenty-four hours a day. That's all the seraphim do, and guess what? They're tickled to death to do it! They don't sleep, they don't slumber, all they do is exalt the name of God.

No External Needs

So God does not need you or me. We need Him. God is sufficient, complete within Himself. He does not need anything in His created order to make Him feel better about being God. Job 22:2–3 says that God receives no benefit from man.

Job underscores that again by reminding us that man at his best offers nothing of benefit to God (Job 35:7–8). Jesus said that even our best, when it's placed against God, makes us "unworthy slaves" (Luke 17:10). This is true for entire nations too. "The nations are like a drop from a bucket . . . a speck of dust on the scales" to God (Isaiah 40:15). He simply blows on them and they cease to exist.

God's self-sufficiency also means He is answerable to no one. He does not need our permission to do what He plans to do. Our complaints don't make a difference either. All of us face this with our children. Sometimes our kids want us to get their permission to be parents. But that's not how it works, so sometimes we have to tell our kids, "No, I'm Mama (or Daddy) and you are the child. You don't tell me. I tell you."

God says, "I'm God. You are man. You don't tell Me. I tell you." It's the same principle. God can do this because He is the self-sufficient, independent, self-existent God who has life within Himself. Since nothing is greater than God that could produce God, He is the greatest Being that has ever existed.

And since there is nothing greater than God that you could ever call God, there must be only one God—the God of the Bible who never had a starting point. So of necessity, God ought to be worshiped because in the universe we can find nothing like Him. He ought to be worshiped because He is unique. We ought to jump out of bed to go to church on Sunday morning. Why? Because no one else is worth jumping out of bed for!

Some Implications

What are the implications of God's independence? First, it means that you cannot help God out. God will do what He is going to do no matter what you do. Therefore, He cannot be intimidated. You can't threaten Him.

Second, God does not need to be defended. He can defend Himself. He can move people and nations. He can shut down and raise up things. That's why the Bible says, for example, " 'Vengeance is Mine, I will repay,' says the Lord" (Romans 12:19). He says, "I can do things you haven't thought about."

Third, God's independence means that He does not depend on us. He enjoys us and wants our worship and fellowship, as we will see. But when you come to know God, you have to bank on Him, not the other way around.

WE ARE DEPENDENT ON GOD'S SUFFICIENCY

Here we see the other side of the equation. God's creation is *not* independent of Him. Let's look again at Paul's sermon in Acts 17:

He made from one, every nation of mankind to live on all the face of the earth, having determined their appointed times, and the boundaries of their habitation, that they should seek God, if perhaps they might grope for Him and find Him, though He is not far from each one of us; for in Him we live and move and exist, as even some of your own poets have said, "For we also are His offspring." Being then the offspring of God, we ought not to think that the Divine Nature is like gold or silver or stone, an image formed by the art and thought of man. (vv. 26–29)

Our Reference Point

In God we move and have our being. Paul makes the point that we cannot know ourselves apart from God. You will never know who you are, where you came from, why you are here, or where you are going apart from God. No self-definition will help you make sense of time and space and reality apart from God. In Him, you live. In Him, you move. In Him, you have your being. God appointed when you were born, and He has appointed when you will die. I don't care how much you jog, you will not postpone that date. It is determined and appointed by God.

God says all of life is to be lived in relationship to Him. But autonomous, sinful man rebels against this. Sinful man can be compared to a rebellious teenager who doesn't want Mom and Dad to rule over him anymore. Men have decided they will live independently of this great God, and so they have rebelled against Him.

Our Inescapable God

But when men rebel against God, they only create an environment where, instead of enjoying His love, they must endure His wrath. You see, even in hell men will not get away from God. You can do nothing to get rid of God. I figure if you can't beat it, join it. Since you can't beat God, since you can't get away from Him, rather than resisting God, why not be a cooperator under Him so that you can enjoy His benefits? We are all dependent on God.

Even if you couldn't see it, the sun would still shine. You can't get mad at the sun and say, "I can't see you, sun, so stop shining." The sun will shine because that's what the sun does. God is going to be God because that's what God does. We must choose whether we want to see Him, acknowledge Him, recognize Him, and submit to Him, but God is going to be God.

If you don't believe in God, if you reject Him, He's still God. If you don't want Him to be God, He's still God. If you curse Him, He's still God. If you don't acknowledge Him, He's still God because God is not dependent on us, we are dependent on Him. If anyone has to jump, we have to jump—not God.

Before I go to our last point, let me summarize. God is sufficient within Himself. He is responsible for everything we see, all of creation, yet He is independent of His creation. He can do whatever He wants. By virtue of the fact that we live, move, and have our being in Him, we are utterly dependent on Him. All that we are is because of all that He is. My last point is the logical and very practical next step.

WE FIND OUR
COMPLETENESS ONLY IN GOD

I don't know of any more important statement I can make than this: God's sufficiency means that we can find our completeness only in Him. This truth appears all through the Bible, but I want to take one of the most beautiful poetic passages in Scripture to make this final, all-important point.

David wrote Psalm 23 while reflecting on his old occupation as a shepherd. David knew God. The Psalms reflect his intimacy with God and his knowledge of God. God Himself said that David was a man after His own heart. As he reflected, David realized that what he as a shepherd was to his sheep, God was to him. God was a shepherd over him.

So David wrote, "The Lord is my shepherd, I shall not want" (v. 1). He says that if you really come to understand who God is; if you begin to live in the light of who God is rather than who you think God is; if you simply let God be God, you will have no lack. Many of us are failing in our lives because we want to make God into a man. David is saying, "Let God be God."

When sheep try to make shepherds into sheep, the sheep are going to be confused. But as long as sheep let the shepherd be the shepherd, they will have someone to lead them where they ought to go. Sheep cannot take the place of shepherds, and shepherds do not want to become like sheep.

Stop trying to get God to be like you, and simply let God be God. When you do that, He will let you be you as you ought to be. David says, "I shall not want." He then takes the other five verses to explain that if the Lord is your shepherd, He will meet every category of need.

Spiritual Needs

"He makes me lie down in green pastures; He leads me beside quiet waters. He restores my soul" (vv. 2–3a). David says if the Lord is your shepherd, He will meet your spiritual needs. He is not referring to drinking water or eating green grass here, because if you were drinking the water it wouldn't be quiet. And if you ate the grass, the pasture wouldn't be green but bare.

No, a carpet of green grass and quiet waters is a picture of rest. David's point is that God gives you back your life. Life is full of frustration. But if you will let God be God even in the midst of life's pressures and pain, when you submit who you are to who He is, He gives you back your soul. He gives you spiritual rejuvenation. God can take a messed-up day and turn it into a glorious week. He can take a messed-up month and turn it into a beautiful year. He can turn a tragedy into a triumph.

The Bible tells us about two roads. The broad way leads to destruction. The other way is narrow and leads to life. Fundamental differences appear between these two roads. The broad road is crowded. A lot of parties happen on that road. A lot of traffic comes down that road, a lot of good times. But no filling stations can be seen on the broad road. When you run out of gas, you are finished. You have to pull over to the side.

The narrow road looks less pretty and less crowded. You don't have as much fanfare, but Jesus Christ moves up and down the narrow road. Yes, you might have to pull over in a ditch, but He refuels your tank so you can keep on keeping on. You don't have to quit, you don't have to give up. He restores your soul. He meets your spiritual needs.

Directional Needs

David continues, "He guides me in the paths of righteousness for His name's sake" (v. 3b). When David led sheep, every now and then a dumb sheep would wander off on the wrong road. David would leave the flock and find that one sheep, pick it up, put it on his shoulder, and take it by the right path back to the fold.

What David did for sheep God does for His sheep; that is, He can take a lost sheep and make it found. He can take wrong decisions and make them right. He can take you going down the wrong road in life, and if you will reconnect with Him, put you on the right road. He can take a bad situation and make it good.

If the Lord is your shepherd, not only does He meet your spiritual needs, He meets your directional needs. He guides you in life. I didn't know I would be in Dallas. I had plans to go to another city, but through a set of circumstances in which God led me, I wound up in Dallas. I didn't know some of the things in my life would happen, but that's the way God led me.

Maybe you didn't know you would be where you are today, but the Good Shepherd knows the right road for His sheep. If you will simply let God be God, He will restore your soul. If you will let Him be the sufficient, independent God, stop giving Him advice and simply do what He says, He will direct you down the right road.

If the Lord is your shepherd, He will meet your spiritual needs. He will meet your directional needs. Why? "For His name's sake," so that when you get to where you are supposed to go, you will give Him the credit because only He knew the road you should take.

Emotional Needs

David then says if the Lord is your shepherd, He will meet your emotional needs. "Even though I walk through the valley of the shadow of death, I fear no evil; for Thou art with me; Thy rod and Thy staff, they comfort me" (v. 4).

IF THE LORD IS YOUR SHEPHERD, HE CAN KEEP FEAR FROM OVERWHELMING YOU.

When sheep get lost, they come between two mountains or two crevices and if it is the right time of day, the sun casts a shadow over the path. Not being very smart, the sheep see the shadow and think night is coming. Of course, sheep are afraid at night. David says that when the shadows of life come over us and we think things are bad; when the shadows of life come over us and we think we have no hope; when the shadows of life come over us and we think things are out of kilter, God stands by us with His rod and staff.

The rod was a club the shepherd had designed to pulverize the hyenas and foxes that tried to prey on the sheep. The staff was a long stick with a hook on it so the shepherd could reach into the bushes and pull a sheep out when it got caught in the thicket.

David had gotten caught in the thickets of life because of his immorality. He had committed adultery with Bathsheba and murdered her husband. He was all tangled up. The shadow of death came over him, but when he dealt with his sins and returned to God, God's rod protected Him. God's staff pulled him back in, and God's grace covered him. If the Lord is your shepherd, He can keep fear from overwhelming you.

There's a lot to be afraid of today, especially in cities like Dallas. Everybody has a gun. Gangs seem out of control. People have gone crazy. But when you live in God's hand, you can be in the worst part of any big city and be safer than a person outside of God living in a house in the suburbs with bars on the windows.

When the Lord is your shepherd, He takes care of your emotional needs. As the psalmist puts it, "He giveth his beloved sleep" (Psalm 127:2 KJV). He gives you the ability to sleep regardless of the circumstances around you. God will meet your emotional needs so that you can say, "I will fear no evil."

Physical Needs

God will also meet your physical needs, according to verse 5: "Thou dost prepare a table before me in the presence of my enemies; Thou hast anointed my head with oil; my cup overflows." Inside the belt shepherds wore was a little cloth and a pouch.

In the pouch were fodder and grains, so whenever David found a lost sheep he would spread the cloth on the ground and put the food from his little pouch on the cloth. That was the "table" for the sheep. Foxes and hyenas hung around, but not only could they not eat the sheep, they could not eat what the sheep was eating because of the shepherd's presence.

He would also take a cup that he carried on his belt, dip it in water, and as he walked over to the sheep the water would splash out the top of the cup. The cup would be running over, letting the sheep know that there was going to be more than enough water to satisfy his thirst.

God is saying that what David was to his sheep, He is to His children. He is so sufficient that the running over of your cup does not depend on what the economy does. It does not depend on recession or inflation. It does not depend on who is laying off or who is hiring. When you stay in God's will and God's way, He gives you your daily bread. He meets your needs.

In fact, God does not stop meeting the needs of His children before it's time to die. When Israel went camping in the wilderness, they got corn flakes from above. Manna floated down to earth. God supernaturally supplied them because He was their shepherd. When the Lord is your shepherd, He is sufficient for your spiritual needs, your directional needs, your emotional needs, and your physical needs.

Eternal Needs

Finally, God is sufficient for your eternal needs. "Surely goodness and lovingkindness will follow me all the days of my life, and I will dwell in the house of the Lord forever" (v. 6). God is good not only for time, but for eternity. If you know Jesus Christ, He's sufficient!

If you are down, He's what you need to lift you up. If you don't know which decision to make, He's who you need to direct your path. If you are afraid about how the world is going, He is able to give you sleep. If you are confused about how you are going to make ends meet, He's all you need to pay the bills. If you are not sure about where you are going to live forever, He's all you need to get your eternal destiny straight.

Now I have a question. Is there any issue in your life that doesn't fit into one of these categories? Your needs are either spiritual, directional, emotional, physical, or eternal. God is sufficient for all of them. Everything you need can be covered by the sufficiency of God as you live under His authority, according to His will, and in concert with His Word. If you come to know Him and live in Him obediently, willingly, and voluntarily, God will demonstrate to you His sufficiency.

You may ask, "Then why does God let me go through trials?" So that you will know how *in*sufficient you are and how utterly sufficient He is. Some people are very independent. They don't need man or God. They can do it by themselves. They are sufficient within themselves. They pay cash.

If that's the way you approach life, I can guarantee you God will humble you. If you try to live independently of God, it may not be today and it may not be tomorrow, but one day God will make you lie down. He's going to put you in a situation where only He can get you up.

Some diseases doctors can't heal. Some jobs you won't be able to find. Some bills you won't be able to pay. Some people you won't be able to make like you. Some fears you won't be able to overcome. And when God puts you flat on your spiritual bed, directional bed, emotional bed, physical bed, or eternal bed, you will look up and say, "Lord, have mercy!"

And God will say, "Do you believe I'm sufficient?"

If the Lord is your shepherd, He is sufficient for all your needs. But none of this matters unless you experience it for yourself. Nothing I write in this book will mean anything unless you submit to the independent, sufficient God, saying not, "Lord, this is what I want from You," but, "Lord, what do You want from me? I give You my life."

So the only question on the floor is, *Is the Lord your shepherd?* Only if you let Him be your shepherd will you learn that He is sufficient for your needs. God is sufficient by virtue of His creation. God is sufficient by virtue of His independence. God is sufficient by virtue of our dependence. Therefore, we can find our completeness only in Him.

Responding to the Sufficiency of God

I s the Lord your shepherd? If not, you can make Him your shepherd by submitting to His leadership, by saying, "Dear God, not my will, but Your will be done. I submit to You." Here are some suggestions to help you make this commitment real:

1. How long has it been since you thought about the fact that God created you out of His good pleasure? He *wanted* to create you. You are incredibly valuable to Him. Thank the Lord that He loves you so much—and ask Him to help you see other people in this light.

2. List the three biggest trials or challenges you're facing right now. Beside each trial, write down at least one way that you know God is sufficient to meet your need. Ask Him to deal with each need in the way He sees best.

3. Maybe you're the independent type. Can you find any area of your life where you've excluded God, even unconsciously, because you feel perfectly capable of handling that area? Give this question some prayerful, heart-searching thought, and be prepared to respond to whatever God shows you.

4. Take the psalmist-shepherd's advice and find a carpet of green grass and quiet waters. In other words, take a retreat to get alone and commune with God—whether it's a day away from the routine, an early-morning walk, or just a few minutes alone in your office or bedroom where you pull the blinds and shut the door for a brief time of uninterrupted solitude.

4
THE HOLINESS
OF GOD

ast fall, we had a problem with our television picture. Both sets transmitted a lot of fuzz. I got it looked into, and the repairman told me we had a reception problem. Our antenna and wiring were just not doing the job. I about had cardiac arrest when the repairman told me what it was going to cost for the rewiring we needed to get good reception. So every time I watch TV, the focus is not that clear. It's not sharp. It's somewhat distorted, and I'm sure you know how irritating that can be.

That's what may happen when you try to study God. If your antenna is not working right, you won't get a clear picture. He won't come in clear. He won't be sharp, not because something is wrong with Him, but because something has gone wrong with your receiver.

Since Adam's fall, our ability to pick up the "God channel" has been greatly disturbed. As a result, we stare into the picture of the "Holy Other," our great God, but somehow He just doesn't come into clear focus. Even after you are saved, tuning in to God can be quite difficult because as I have already stated, He is unlike anyone you will ever come into relationship or contact with in all of your life.

Of all the things about God hard for us to focus on, one of the most difficult is His holiness. That's what we want to look at in this chapter. Holiness is one of those uncomfortable attributes because it reminds us how much unlike God we are. Let's start with a definition: The holiness of God is His intrinsic and transcendent purity, the standard of righteousness to which the whole universe must conform.

God does not conform to any standard created by others. He is the standard. Therefore, He demands that His creation conform to His standard. Some atheists say there could not be a God, given the existence and prevalence of evil. Actually, the opposite is true. You can call evil evil only if there is a God against whose standard you can measure evil.

HOLINESS IS THE CENTERPIECE OF GOD'S ATTRIBUTES. OF ALL THE THINGS THAT GOD IS, AT THE CENTER OF HIS BEING, HE IS HOLY.

Bad wouldn't be bad unless you had a standard that made it bad. You can only call something evil because you have a standard—a good and holy God. We can't say everything possible about the holiness of God in one chapter, but I want to tell you five things about this great subject.

GOD'S CENTRAL ATTRIBUTE

Holiness is the centerpiece of God's attributes. Of all the things that God is, at the center of His being, He is holy. Exodus 15 shows a great picture of God's holiness as Moses and the "sons of Israel" sing about their deliverance from Pharaoh and his army.

Majestic in Holiness

In verse 8, the singers begin reciting what we might call poetic anthropomorphisms. We have already talked about this figure of speech, which uses human language to define God since we don't have spirit language that makes sense to us. Moses says, "At the blast of Thy nostrils the waters were piled up," describing the parting of the Red Sea. God doesn't have nostrils, of course. Moses was saying in a poetic fashion that when God blew, when He snorted, so to speak, the waters parted.

Verse 10 also uses this language to picture the great deliverance Israel had experienced: "Thou didst blow with Thy wind, the sea covered them; they sank like lead in the mighty waters."

Having recited Israel's great deliverance, Moses then says, "Who is like Thee among the gods, O Lord? Who is like Thee, *majestic in holiness,* awesome in praises, working wonders?" (v. 11, italics added). Moses says that if you want to understand the majesty, the distinctiveness, the uniqueness of God, you have to understand it in concert with His holiness.

The Key to God's Nature

God's holiness unlocks the door to understanding and making sense out of everything else about Him. This attribute infiltrates all the other attributes. His love is holy love. His omniscience is holy omniscience. His omnipresence is holy omnipresence. Everything has been infiltrated by this defining attribute of God called holiness.

God even calls Himself by that name. Throughout the Old and New Testaments He is called "The Holy One." When Mary was reciting her praise to God at the news that she would be the mother of the Savior, she said in Luke 1:49: "The Mighty One has done great things for me; and holy is His name."

God's holiness is central to understanding who and what He is. Nowhere in Scripture is God called "love, love, love"; "eternal, eternal, eternal"; or "truth, truth, truth." He is never emphatically called by any name except one: "Holy, Holy, Holy, is the Lord of hosts" (Isaiah 6:3). Whenever you see three words like this, you are reading an emphatic statement meaning that this is a centerpiece, this is key, this is something you don't want to miss. At the heart of who God is, is His holiness.

God swears by His holiness (Psalm 89:35). Why? Because it is the fullest expression of His character, because it fully explains who He is. The Bible declares that God's law is holy (Romans 7:12), and that God is holy in all of His being (Leviticus 19:2). Holiness is the centerpiece, the defining point, the heart of the matter of who God is.

GOD'S HOLINESS
SEPARATES HIM FROM CREATION

The prophet Isaiah writes:

> For thus says the high and exalted One who lives forever, whose name is Holy, "I dwell on a high and holy place, and also with

the contrite and lowly of spirit in order to revive the spirit of the lowly and to revive the heart of the contrite." (Isaiah 57:15)

God says He dwells on high in a holy place because He is the Holy One. The Hebrew word *holy* means "separate." It's the same root word from which we get the words *saint* and *sanctified*. All three of these carry the meaning "to be separate or distinct." Because God is separate and distinct from His creation we must humble ourselves before Him. Because He is so high in where He dwells and who He is we must bow low.

Perfect in Holiness

That's why God told Moses at the burning bush, "Remove your sandals from your feet, for the place on which you are standing is holy ground" (Exodus 3:5). When you come to understand how high and holy God is, you will come to understand how little we are. A "Mr. Big Stuff" attitude not only reveals a misconception of yourself, but a terrible misconception of God.

The Bible makes clear in Romans 10:3 that people are ignorant of the holiness of God. They do not understand that "God is light, and in Him there is no darkness at all" (1 John 1:5). He is perfect in holiness. James 1:13–14 says that God cannot sin, He cannot even be tempted to sin, and He cannot tempt someone else to sin. The very idea of sin either in God or coming from God is inconceivable because of His purity.

We must understand this because we get really confused here. We grade sin by degrees. We say, "He's a bad sinner, a murderer, a rapist."

Then we climb the ladder a little bit and say, "Well, he's an OK sinner. He's not all that hot, but he's not like that bad sinner."

Then we climb up a little higher and come to the "good" sinner. He's a nice guy. He's not perfect, but he's cool.

Finally, we come to the "excellent" sinner. That's where most of us think we stand. We say, "Yeah, I'm not perfect, but Lord have mercy, I'm good!"

No Degrees of Sin

We make these measurements, but God recognizes no such measurement. He has no degrees of sin. Now don't misunderstand me. There are degrees of consequences. Every sin doesn't deserve the same penalty, but evil does not have degrees. The man on death row is no different in the sight of a holy God than the person who goes through all of his life and tells one lie. This is fundamental. God does not have a grading system for sin because He is totally, absolutely perfect in all of His ways. He knows no gradations of sin.

That ticks us off. We don't like a God who puts us on the same level as a criminal. We may not like it, but we'd better understand it. It's critical that we understand this in order to have a right view of God and a right view of ourselves.

If you were high above the earth and saw one man standing on a mountaintop and another standing in a valley, they would look to you as if they were standing side-by-side. You would be so high that the small matter of a mountain would be irrelevant. God is so high that while one person may be living better than the dregs of society, from God's separate, unique, high position, all stand on level ground. That's why the Bible says, "There is none righteous, not even one" (Romans 3:10). "All have sinned and fall short of the glory of God" (v. 23).

YOU DISCOVER YOU ARE NOT WHAT YOU THOUGHT YOU WERE WHEN YOU SEE GOD. WE DO NOT TAKE LIVING THE CHRISTIAN LIFE SERIOUSLY ENOUGH BECAUSE WE DON'T KNOW WHO GOD IS.

The great naturalist and writer, Henry David Thoreau, epitomized most people's attitude toward sin. Near the end of his life, Thoreau was urged to make his peace with God. "I did not know that we had ever quarreled," was his response.

There has been a quarrel, all right! God has a quarrel with us, because we have all offended His holiness. All men need to be saved because everyone has the same problem.

Someone might object, "But that's not fair."

Sure it is. Suppose you were sick, and as the doctor was getting ready to operate on you, he said, "All my scalpels are dirty. I've got one that I just picked up out of the mud. It's real dirty. I've got another one here that I cleaned, but I smeared some of the dirt on it. It's a little better, but it's still dirty. But I've got this one scalpel that's just got a little spot of dirt on it. So I think we can chance this operation on you with this scalpel that has only a little spot."

But that little spot can be as bad as the thick dirt. Why? Because it only takes a few germs to contaminate your whole body. You want to make sure that the doctor's scalpel has been sterilized. You want absolute cleanliness when it comes to cutting you open. God is so holy, His scalpel so absolutely clean, that He is as offended by an evil thought as He is by murder. While there are differences in the consequences of sin, there is no difference in essence.

Encountering a Holy God

That's how holy God is, how totally unlike us. We have to do the adjusting. He's not going to change. When you come to understand the holiness of God, something has to happen. When the prophet Habakkuk ran into the holiness of God, he said, "My inward parts trembled . . . my lips quivered. Decay enters my bones" (Habakkuk 3:16). He had a different view of himself.

When Job encountered the holiness of God, he cried out, "Behold, I am insignificant . . . I lay my hand on my mouth" (Job 40:4). "I repent in dust and ashes" (42:6). And Job was a good man. God said so (see Job 2:3).

When Isaiah beheld God's holiness, he could only say, "Woe is me!" (Isaiah 6:5). Here was a great prophet, but all he could say was "Woe is me!" Isaiah was announcing a curse on himself. He was saying, "Cursed am I." Then he said, "I am ruined," or undone. The word *ruined* means to unravel. Isaiah said "I'm coming apart" because he saw God in all His awesome holiness.

When you come face-to-face with God, He affects your self-esteem. You discover you are not what you thought you were when you see God. We do not take living the Christian life seriously enough because we don't know who God is. As I said earlier, kids sometimes forget who is the parent and who is the child. When they forget that, they will try anything. So every now and then parents have to remind their children who's who. We are like children at times. We forget who God is, so we try anything.

If we are going to be serious about walking with God, we have to understand who He is and who we are in light of Him. We must go low because He sits high. We must hallow His name. We must worship Him seriously. We must stop playing church, stop playing Christianity. Most people hurry to get to work on time because they don't want to upset the boss. But they come to church saying, "As long as I get there before the benediction, I'm on time."

When God sees us treating our bosses better than we treat Him, He says, "You don't know who I am. I am the Holy One."

GOD'S HOLINESS
AND SIN

The holiness of God demands that He judge sin. This is repeated all through the Bible. God has always judged sin, and He has a future judgment in store, which is the Great Tribulation:

> And I heard a loud voice from the temple, saying to the seven angels, "Go and pour out the seven bowls of the wrath of God into the earth." And the first angel went and poured out his bowl into the earth; and it became a loathsome and malignant sore upon the men who had the mark of the beast and who worshiped his image. And the second angel poured out his bowl into the sea, and it became blood like that of a dead man; and every living thing in the sea died. And the third angel poured out his bowl into the rivers and the springs of waters; and they became blood. And I heard the angel of the waters saying, "Righteous art Thou, who art and who wast, O Holy One, because Thou didst judge these things." (Revelation 16:1–5)

Natural and Necessary

God judges man and creation because a holy God cannot skip over sin. He couldn't skip over it if He wanted to because of His holy nature. God's holiness means sin must be taken seriously and always will be judged. Even health and holiness go together. The Bible says some Christians who live a rebellious life get sick (1 Corinthians 11:30; James 5:13–16). On the other hand, unholiness and decay go together. Where there is unholiness, there is decay.

When we talk about the wrath or judgment of God, we do not mean mere emotional outbursts. We get mad because someone ticked us off. We get mad because we're having a bad day. God doesn't have bad days, and He doesn't just blow up. God's wrath is His natural and necessary reaction to anything and everything that is opposed to His holiness. It's natural to Him, and it's necessary because of who He is. So we are not talking about outbursts of rage. If God had outbursts, we'd all be dead.

Comprehensive

God's judgment against sin is also comprehensive. The Bible declares that God has judged and will judge Satan, and He will judge men. In fact, the Bible puts men and Satan together under judgment in Matthew 25:41. There Jesus says: "Then [God] will also say to those on His left, 'Depart from Me, accursed ones, into the eternal fire which has been prepared for the devil and his angels.'"

God did not create hell for people. He created hell for the devil. Then why do people go there? Because they choose to follow the devil. If you choose to reject God and His salvation, you get the curse and the wrath that has been assigned to Satan. And by the way, Satan is not the "ruler" of hell, as most people think. He will be the lowest being in hell, the most severely punished. If you follow him you follow a total loser!

God is so holy that He even judged His Son. Men crucified Jesus "by the predetermined plan and foreknowledge of God" (Acts 2:23). God's holiness is terrible. It's terrible in the Old Testament. It's terrible in the New Testament. The Bible says, "Our God is a consuming fire" (Hebrews 12:29). Not *was,* as in the Old Testament, but *is.* Our God is right now "a consuming fire." He cannot be trifled with.

We are dealing with a very holy Being who demands to be taken seriously and who stands distinct from anything that is impure. Think about it. For one sin, Adam was put out of the Garden. For one sin, Cain and his progeny were cursed. For one sin, Moses was kept out of the Promised Land. For one sin, Elijah's servant got leprosy. For one sin, Ananias and Sapphira were killed. That's "a consuming fire."

God must always have by nature a judgment for sin. A lot of people think, for example, that David got away with his sin. They say, "David sinned grievously, and God was gracious." That's true. David did sin and God was gracious, because David should have been executed. But did God skip over David's sin? No, He just took the lives of four of David's children in his place.

In other words, David lived because someone else died. After David sinned with Bathsheba, the baby died. I know that's hard to swallow because it is so unlike what we think God ought to be like. But that's making God in our image. God is holy by nature. The tension comes when we wrestle with the reality that God judges sin while simultaneously loving the sinner. We have to keep that tension in perspective here.

God Loves the Sinner

God does not wipe us all out because while He despises and judges sin, He is intensely in love with the sinner. God wants to destroy the sin without destroying the sinner. Anyone who has ever had cancer understands this. You want to nail that cancer, but you want to be able to walk away. You want to put the radiation on the cancer and wipe it out, but you want to be set free.

So God's holiness is directed against sin, but He loves the sinner. The problem is He cannot overlook the sinner in judging the sin, because the sinner is the one doing it. The seriousness of this business of God and His holiness should shake us down to our socks. The Bible says that when God came down to the children of Israel, Mount Sinai shook. He had not even said anything yet. Just His holy presence made the mountain shake violently (Exodus 19:16–18).

Then God told Moses, "Go down, warn the people, lest they break through to the Lord to gaze, and many of them perish" (v. 21). God said, "If these folk hang around the foot of this mountain, they are going to be in trouble. If they even try to take a peek at Me, they shall surely die." That's our holy God.

When God moves, mountains shake. How come we are not shaking? If mountains shake when God moves, why don't we quiver at the thought of God? Why are we not reverential toward God? Why don't we hold Him in awe? Because we have forgotten who He is. We must take God seriously!

GOD'S HOLINESS
AND HIS TERMS

The holiness of God means that we can only approach Him on His terms. That's what the Book of Hebrews is all about. Hebrews spends a lot of time contrasting the old covenant with the new covenant. The old way of approaching God and the new way of approaching God are contrasted most graphically, in my view, in Hebrews 9. Verses 21–22 sum it up:

> In the same way he sprinkled both the tabernacle and all the vessels of the ministry with the blood. And according to the Law, one may almost say, all things are cleansed with blood, and without shedding of blood there is no forgiveness.

The fundamental principle is this: The only thing that can satisfy the demands of a holy God is "the shedding of blood." I cannot explain why that is so. I do not have all the data. I know there must be restitution. I know God requires a sacrifice, but why He chose this arrangement, I cannot fully say. All I know is that this is what God says. The very first thing that happened when Adam and Eve sinned was that God killed an animal to provide them a covering, physically and redemptively.

God is jealous for His holiness. We saw this earlier in Exodus 20:5. That's why He said, "Don't make a likeness of Me because I'm unlike anything you have ever thought of. Don't even think about it. I am a jealous God. I don't want you painting Me any less than who I really am, so just take me at My word."

Israel's Tabernacle

In the Old Testament, God established a comprehensive and somewhat complicated system of worship because people could not just barge into His presence. Some years ago, when George Bush was president, I was invited to the White House along with others for a briefing from the president. Can you picture me going into the White House doing my little Dallas thing and saying, "Is Mr. Prez in? I need to see him now."

They would say, "I'm sorry, sir, you can't see him."

"No, you don't know who I am. Tony Evans of Dallas, Texas. Pastor of Oak Cliff Bible Fellowship Church. We've got a radio program. I'm sure you've heard it."

They would say, "No, *you* don't understand. No matter who you are, he's the president."

Because of who the president is and what he represents you don't just barge into his office. You come by invitation and by permission only. It's the same with God. You don't barge into His presence. You only come because He has allowed you entrance.

God established a place and a process of worship for Israel called the tabernacle. The tabernacle was designed to let Israel know who God was; to let them know that He was distinct from them, yet He wanted to be present with them. He was different from His people, yet He wanted to be in touch with them.

The tabernacle had three different compartments, divided by three curtains. One curtain hung across the outside entrance into the court. Another curtain covered the entrance into the holy place where the sacrifices were made. The third blocked entrance into the "holiest of all" where God's presence was. Only the high priest was allowed to go in there, and only once a year.

But even the high priest couldn't just skip past the outer portions of the tabernacle to enter God's presence. Imagine him saying, "Look, I want to see God and I want to see Him now." So he pushes past the first curtain, walks by the altar at the second curtain, and pulls back the curtain to the "holiest of all." The second he crossed that threshold, he would be utterly obliterated. He would be remembered no more. And do you know why? Because he skipped the altar.

> ## *I*F YOU FEEL LIKE YOU ARE A WORSE SINNER NOW THAN YOU WERE LAST YEAR, IT MAY BE BECAUSE YOU SEE MORE OF GOD THIS YEAR THAN YOU SAW LAST YEAR.

That's how serious God's holiness is. You see, unless blood was on that altar covering your sin, you'd better not try to go past that curtain because sinful men cannot waltz into the presence of a holy God. He doesn't allow it.

Our Tabernacle

You say, "But wait a minute. How come we don't have a tabernacle?" We do! Listen to the writer of Hebrews:

> For Christ did not enter a holy place made with hands, a mere copy of the true one, but into heaven itself, now to appear in the presence of God for us; nor was it that He should offer Himself often, as the high priest enters the holy place year by year with blood not his own. (9:24–25)

But he goes on to say in verse 28: "So Christ also, having been offered once to bear the sins of many, shall appear a second time for salvation without reference to sin, to those who eagerly await Him." Do you know why you can waltz into God's presence today? Because Jesus put His shed blood on that altar for you. You couldn't approach God any way you wanted in the Old Testament, and you can't approach Him any way you want in the New Testament.

The only reason you can approach God today is that Jesus Christ split the curtain separating us from the holiest of all. Christ opened the way so that now we have access to God through Christ (Ephesians 2:18). When God sees you coming before Him, He only lets you come into His presence because He sees you through the lens of Jesus. God's condition for approaching Him is a blood sacrifice, and Jesus made that sacrifice for us.

GOD'S HOLINESS
AND OUR LIFESTYLE

Finally, the holiness of God demands that Christians reflect His character in their lifestyles. First Peter 1 puts it so well: "As obedient children, do not be conformed to the former lusts which were yours in your ignorance, but like the Holy One who called you, be holy yourselves" (vv. 14–16).

Pleasing Our God

God says, "Because of who I am, that is who you should strive to be." The holiness of God demands that holiness be the goal of the believer. Paul says, "Let everyone who names the name of the Lord abstain from wickedness" (2 Timothy 2:19). Hebrews 12:10 says that God is so eager for our holiness He "spanks" His children "that we may share His holiness," just like we spank our children that they might be partakers of our rules and regulations and guidelines.

If you know Jesus Christ, if you have been saved, your actions should be pleasing to Him. You won't always pull it off. You will fall on your face at times because we are all just saved sinners. But when you fall, God will forgive you if you confess your sins (1 John 1:9).

If you fall, get up in the name of Jesus Christ. His blood not only saves you, it keeps you in contact with God. The Bible says that anyone who says he has no sin is a liar (1 John 1:8). When you come into the holy presence of God, you see more of your sin, not less of it.

If you feel like you are a worse sinner now than you were last year, it may be because you see more of God this year than you saw last year. You've seen His holiness, so now things you didn't think were wrong you recognize as wrong because they're measured against His holy standard. God wants us to build on our salvation by pursuing holiness.

Pursuing Holiness

You don't build a chicken coop on the foundation of a sky-scraper. However, many Christians build junky lives on the foundation of the cross. Remember the Susan B. Anthony dollar? It was designed to give women a presence in the currency system, but people wouldn't use it because it looked too much like a quarter and they kept getting them mixed up.

A lot of us Christians are worth a dollar, but we look like a quarter. We have a high spiritual value, but we live like "chump change." We build chicken coops on the foundation of the cross. You can't excuse sin. You can't say, "Oh, everyone does it." No, you don't know who God is.

You can't say, "Well, it was just a mistake." No, you don't know who God is.

You don't just pass it by or ignore your sin. You fall down like Isaiah and say, "Woe is me! I am undone! I am a man/woman of unclean lips. Woe is me!" When Isaiah did that, an angel took a coal from the altar and put it on his lips. God cleaned Isaiah up.

Getting Clean

Have you ever been real dirty and stepped into a nice, hot shower? You are filthy, but you get in that shower, turn on the hot water, and say, "Ahhhhh!"

God will tell you that you are dirty. If you will just admit you are dirty and stop thinking you are clean, He'll come alongside you and scrub you up so you can walk away clean, saying, "Ahhhhh!"

But not only that, after God has cleaned you up, He will fix you up so that He can use you up. That's what happened to Isaiah, and that's what God will do with you if you come clean with Him.

So our prayer must be like that of David: "Create in me a clean heart, O God" (Psalm 51:10). In other words, "Lord, give me a clean heart. I'm dirty. I'm sinful. I've messed up, but if you will scrub me, I will be clean. Then you can dress me and send me on my way."

Do you know who God is? If you are not a Christian, you must come to Christ because He is your tabernacle; He is your way to get to God. In fact, the Bible says, "There is salvation in no one else; for there is no other name under heaven that has been given among men, by which we must be saved" (Acts 4:12).

Christ is your mediator (your go-between), your tabernacle, your only way to get to God. You must express complete faith in

His finished work on the cross, where He shed His blood for your sin. If you will do that, if you will trust the Lord Jesus Christ alone as your Savior, God will make you His child.

If you are a Christian, your job is to keep short sin accounts with God and to walk always wanting Him to clean you up. You know what cleansing you need even today. Go before God right now and ask Him to use some "spiritual detergent" to clean up the dirt that may have accumulated in your life.

Responding to the Holiness of God

God's holiness is awesome to consider. It's even more awesome to realize that we live and move as His children in the atmosphere of His holiness and that He expects holiness of us. I hope these applicational ideas will encourage you in your desire to be holy as our great God is holy:

1. How's the "God reception" in your home and family right now? Is He coming in clear or fuzzy? Here's an interesting experiment you can perform to help you get a handle on things. Over the next few days, sit down and listen to your home. By that I mean take note of the conversations, the level of the electronic noise coming in, things like that. You may discover that a lot of "atmospheric interference" blocks your family's ability to hear and respond to God. If needed, make some adjustments to eliminate and tune out some of the static.

2. If you are holding other people accountable to live up to your mental list of do's and don'ts, tear up that list and set those people free to respond to God as He leads them. Remember: God's standards seldom match ours.

3. Here's an idea you can use in your witnessing as people throw out their objections to believing in God. Many will say, "God isn't fair." Instead of challenging that and putting yourself on the defensive, agree. "You're right, God isn't fair, and I'm glad. If He were fair, you and I wouldn't be here today. We'd be in hell. What we really need is not God's fairness, but His mercy."

4. Since holiness is such a foreign concept to the human heart, ask God to help you live each day in a healthy awareness of His awesome holiness. Pray that God will make the truth of 1 Peter 1:15–16, "Be holy yourselves also in all your behavior; because it is written, "You shall be holy, for I am holy," a reality in your heart and life.

5
THE SOVEREIGNTY
OF GOD

The God most of us worship is too small. The God of most Christians seems anemic, weak, and limited. He does not have the capacity to make a difference, to turn things around. The God most of us serve resembles more the flickering of a candle than the burning of the noonday sun.

One reason for this is that we do not understand God's sovereignty. We have allowed God to be everywhere but on His throne, and we have paid dearly in our own spiritual failure and weakness and limited power because the God we talk about has little to do with the sovereign God of the universe.

GOD'S ABSOLUTE RULE

God's sovereignty concerns His absolute rule and control over all of His creation. God rules absolutely over the affairs of men. He sits on the throne of the universe as Lord. Everything that happens comes about because He either directly causes it or consciously allows it. Nothing enters into history or could ever exist outside of history that does not come under the complete control of God.

Only when you understand that this is the kind of God with whom we have to do will you take seriously the issue of His authority. I know that many people do not like the doctrine of God's sovereignty. They don't want a sovereign God. Certainly non-Christians, and unfortunately many times we as Christians, don't want a sovereign God because we don't want anyone ruling over us. We want to be autonomous.

Perhaps you have teenagers in your home like that. When they get to a certain age, they want to be free. I remember as a teenager telling my dad whenever I wanted to do something and he said no, "But Dad, I'm almost a man." Now, I wasn't crazy. I would always say "almost" because I wasn't ready to pay rent and make car payments!

In the same way, people do not want to be under the authority of God. They want a "jack-in-the-box" God who will pop up whenever they call Him. But until they need Him, they say, "Don't call us. We'll call You."

Satan knows this propensity well. He has it himself. He did not want to serve God, but he wanted to be autonomous. When he tempted Eve in the Garden, Satan said, "God knows that the day you eat of this fruit, you will be like Him—autonomous. You'll be able to think your own thoughts, go your own places, and be your own person. Stop letting God stifle you. Become autonomous."

But once you understand God's sovereignty, you realize nobody can be autonomous from Him. You and I function in a universe over which He has absolute control by causing or by allowing everything. When we know that kind of God, it will graphically change the way we think, act, and live. I want to say four things about our sovereign God.

GOD DOES WHAT HE PLEASES

The sovereignty of God means that He exercises His prerogative to do whatever He pleases with His creation. God can do whatever He wants to do simply because it's all His. "The earth is the Lord's, and all it contains, the world, and those who dwell in it" (Psalm 24:1). By virtue of His ownership, God can do whatever He wants to do whenever He wants to do it.

God Rules

Suppose you came into my home and said, "Evans, I don't like your furniture. I don't particularly appreciate the art on your walls. The way you've got your bedroom organized is really an eyesore to me. You need to move this vanity over here, the bed over there. Your kitchen utensils, plates, and saucers really don't fit my taste. I wish you would do something about it."

I would only have one response to you: "When you start buying the furniture and paying the bills, then we can entertain your viewpoint. But as long as I'm spending the money, your viewpoint carries no clout in my house."

When you start making universes, creating planets, and giving life, perhaps then you can start dictating how God ought to run the universe. But until and unless you get that divine clout, you cannot exercise that divine prerogative. The prerogative always belongs to God, never to us, and He does whatever He chooses. Let me show you that this does not just appear as a fleeting thought in the Bible, but as an overwhelming doctrine.

Job says that "what [God's] soul desires, that He does" (Job 23:13). Job 42:2 puts it this way: "I know that Thou canst do all things, and that no purpose of Thine can be thwarted." That is, you can't overrule God.

According to Psalm 115:3, "Our God is in the heavens; He does whatever He pleases." Psalm 135:6 tells us, "Whatever the Lord pleases, He does, in heaven and in earth, in the seas and in all deeps."

Listen to Proverbs 16:4: "The Lord has made everything for its own purpose, even the wicked for the day of evil."

And in Isaiah 45:7, God says He is "the One forming light and creating darkness, causing well-being and creating calamity; I am the Lord who does all these."

The New Testament does not remain silent either. Paul says in Ephesians 1:11 that God works all things "after the counsel of His will." Romans 11:36 testifies, "For from Him and through Him and to Him are all things. To Him be the glory forever. Amen."

Not even evil and unrighteousness can escape the all-controlling hand of God. I love Revelation 19:6, which says, "For the Lord our God, the Almighty, reigns." God rules! Even when it looks like He's not ruling, He's ruling. When chaos appears, He's ruling the chaos. When things are falling apart, He's ruling the falling apart of those things.

God Decides

Our God is sovereign. That means there's no such thing as luck. The word ought to be expunged from the dictionary, or at least from any serious usage. You are never lucky or unlucky. Under God, no chance happenings occur. Anything that happens to you, good or bad, must pass through His fingers first. There are no accidents with God.

I like the story of the cowboy who applied for health insurance. The agent routinely asked him, "Have you ever had any accidents?"

The cowboy replied, "Well no, I've not had any accidents. I was bitten by a rattlesnake once, and a horse did kick me in the ribs. That laid me up for a while, but I haven't had any accidents."

The agent said, "Wait a minute. I'm confused. A rattlesnake bit you, and a horse kicked you. Weren't those accidents?"

"No, they did that on purpose."

That cowboy had the right idea. Things don't just happen. Everything that occurs, occurs under the hand of a sovereign God. Once you understand that, all of life takes on a different shape and perspective. In a universe controlled by a sovereign God there can be no chance happenings, no luck, no mistakes; good and bad fall under His control.

YOUR CHOICES WILL NOT DETERMINE WHETHER GOD WINDS UP WHERE HE WANTS TO GO. HE WILL ARRIVE AT HIS DESTINATION . . . EITHER THROUGH YOU, AROUND YOU, OVER YOU, BY YOU, OR IN SPITE OF YOU.

A great example of this comes in Exodus 4, where Moses tried to tell God, "I can't talk. I stutter." Look at God's answer in verse 11: "Who has made man's mouth? Or who makes him dumb or deaf, seeing or blind? Is it not I, the Lord?" God knew all about Moses' speech impediment. God gave it to him.

Our Decisions

Not the smallest detail of our lives escapes Him—*none.* That creates a problem for us, because this question must now be answered: If in fact God is this kind of God, then why do my decisions matter? If He is sovereign and has already determined everything that will happen according to what pleases Him, then why do I need to choose? Why not just sit back, relax, and let Him do what He's going to do since He's going to do it anyway?

Here we find our traumatic tension, if you will. Let me try to explain. In theology we call this an antinomy; that is, parallel truths which run side by side and do not appear to cross each other. On the one hand, we have a sovereign God. On the other hand, I get to choose. But if I get to choose, then how much is He really in control? And if He's really in control, why do I need to choose?

I don't propose to have the last word on the subject; however, I do have a word on it. Suppose I were to go downtown in Dallas, with my destination being city hall. That is my determined purpose, but I am not limited to just one option for getting there. I could take the direct route to downtown Dallas by jumping on Interstate 35 and arriving at my destination.

However, for one reason or another I may choose not to go that route. That choice will in no way impede me from getting to city hall because I know at least two other courses. While my goal remains the same, I can keep my options open.

God has determined in His sovereign will where He's going to wind up. But within the context of His will, He has many ways of getting there. He allows you to make choices. Your choices will not determine whether God winds up where He wants to go. He will arrive at His destination, but your choices affect which route He takes. God is going to get there either through you, around you, over you, by you, or in spite of you. When it is all said and done, however, even the route you choose will be the one He sovereignly planned to use in order to achieve His intended purposes.

You get to participate in choosing the route God takes. Does He run over you? Does He remove you? Does He bless you? Does He curse you? You will not stop God from getting where He wants to go. The question is, how will you look once He arrives?

For example, God has determined that in all eternity, men will bring Him glory. That is, one of the ends toward which God moves is that all men who were ever created will for all time give glory to His name. Some of us will be giving glory to God's name in heaven for all eternity as we live with Him in the joyousness of His kingdom.

Another group of people will be doing the very same thing in hell, giving God glory forever and ever. Hell has no atheists. Nobody there doubts the existence of God. No one does not call on His name. All men will, for all time, do exactly what God has ordained men will do. But He has given them a choice as to which route they will take.

Sovereignty and Prayer

What about prayer? God has determined what He's going to do, but He will not do certain things until we make the choice to pray. "You do not have because you do not ask" (James 4:2). It's like a mother who has a very sick child. She knows when she puts the child to bed that she's going to have to get up in the middle of the night to minister to the child, and she determines to do so.

But she won't get up until the child calls out. The child's call does not make the mother do something. She had already decided she was going to do it, but in her sovereign choice she decided not to do it until the child called. So when she hears "Mama," the mother will do what she had already planned to do.

God has determined what He's going to do, but on some of those things He says, "I won't do it until I hear 'Daddy.'" When we call on Him, He responds.

So God has given us options within His sovereignty to determine how we will fit into the outworking of His sovereignty. No one will thwart the plan of God. All we can do is cooperate with it.

Created for Him

The sovereignty of God means first of all that He exercises His prerogative to do with His creation whatever He chooses. Consider 1 Corinthians 8:6, which says:

> For us there is but one God, the Father, from whom are all things, and we exist for Him; and one Lord, Jesus Christ, by whom are all things, and we exist through Him.

You exist for God. That is why you were created. You were not made just to get a good job, to live happily ever after, to get married, and to have kids. Those you call bonuses. You were created to bring God glory and to accomplish His purposes on earth. That's why you will find no rest in life until you find your rest in Him.

GOD'S GLORY AND WILL

The sovereignty of God involves the exercise of His attributes in order to maintain His glory and accomplish His will. I said it already, but let me say it again. Men do not want to submit to God and have often tried to do a coup d'etat against God. That can never work because of God's attributes, which guarantee that no one will knock Him off His sovereign throne.

Forever Sovereign

As we will see in upcoming chapters, God is omnipotent; there is nothing He can't do. God is omniscient; there is nothing He does not know. God is omnipresent; there is no place He does not exist. God is free. No one can box Him in or limit Him since He is infinite in nature. We saw in chapter 4 that God is holy; He is totally apart from all sin.

GOD'S ATTRIBUTES GUARANTEE HIS SOVEREIGN RULE. NO ONE CAN THWART IT, AND NO ONE CAN REBEL AGAINST IT.

God will always be sovereign because He always has these attributes to guarantee it. You can't plan a revolt against Him because He's all-powerful. He can put down the revolt. You can't get in a secret room and plan to knock Him off His throne because He's all-knowing. He's in the room at the meeting with you while you plan to get rid of Him.

You can't plan to do something in one place to catch Him by surprise somewhere else because He's omnipresent. He's at both places at the same time. You can't box Him in, you can't confine Him, because He's independent. God's attributes guarantee His sovereign rule. No one can thwart it, and no one can rebel against it.

A Great Example

We see a great lesson of this in Daniel 4. This is a sweet chapter because sometimes we get the big head. A song from the sixties began "Mister Big Stuff, just who do you think you are?" Well, old Nebuchadnezzar thought he was God's gift to creation.

According to verses 29–30, he was walking on the roof of his royal palace in Babylon when he looked around and said, "Is this not Babylon the great, which I myself have built as a royal residence by the might of my power and for the glory of my majesty?" Nebuchadnezzar was saying, "I am the man!"

95

The only problem with verse 30 is that verse 31 follows: "While the word was in the king's mouth, a voice came from heaven, saying, 'King Nebuchadnezzar, to you it is declared: sovereignty has been removed from you.'"

God goes on to say, "You will go insane. You will live with animals, crawl on the ground like an animal, and eat grass like an animal for seven years until you recognize Me as Sovereign of the universe." That prophecy was fulfilled immediately (see v. 33). Nebuchadnezzar went insane, looking and living like a beast. He lost his mind because he forgot who he was.

Seven years later, Nebuchadnezzar came to himself. "But at the end of that period I, Nebuchadnezzar, raised my eyes toward heaven, and my reason returned to me" (v. 34a). When did he start to regain his sanity? When he knew where to look. What did he do? "I blessed the Most High and praised and honored Him who lives forever" (v. 34b).

Nebuchadnezzar said, "Lord, it's Your dominion. It's Your kingdom." Then he confessed:

> And all the inhabitants of the earth [including me] are accounted as nothing, but He does according to His will in the host of heaven and among the inhabitants of earth; and no one can ward off His hand or say to Him, "What hast Thou done?" (v. 35)

Some of us are crazy when it comes to thinking about God, because we think wrong about Him. Until we start thinking right about God, we won't think right about ourselves. Only after Nebuchadnezzar started thinking right about God could he say, "At that time my reason returned to me. And my majesty and splendor were restored to me" (v. 36). Then he caps his experience:

> Now I Nebuchadnezzar praise, exalt, and honor the King of heaven, for all His works are true and His ways just, and He is able to humble those who walk in pride. (v. 37)

Sovereignty and Status

Do you get the point? No matter how high you climb, no matter what name you get, no matter how much money you accumulate, our God is sovereign. That means that while you respect people, no person intimidates you. You give people the honor due them, but you recognize that underneath God, everyone is nothing.

Some years ago, we had a fairly wealthy man coming to our church and giving a fair amount of money. He wanted to know when I was going to make him a leader.

I said, "Excuse me?"

He said, "Well, you know, I give a lot of money and I'm a very noted person."

I replied, "That's nice, but that's not the criteria for being a leader. Your spiritual development has to determine that."

"Do you know how many churches would love to have me as a member?" he came back.

Now he's going down the wrong road with me, so I said, "Well, maybe you should start visiting some of them."

"You mean to tell me that you would stop me from being a leader based on some criteria you come up with or the Bible comes up with when I'm giving all this money?"

I said, "You are absolutely right, because when it comes to your standing before God, what your bank account looks like is irrelevant."

You are not to be intimidated by people because they have more than you have, because they have greater names, greater prestige, or greater power. Before God, all of us stand as sinners in need of a Savior. We all stand on level ground at Calvary, and understanding this is absolutely critical.

That's why you can't be overly proud of your race. You are only black because God made you that way; you are only white because God made you that way. You can't get too proud about how God made you unless you think He endowed you with something that makes you better than the next man.

Black and white people and all colors in between will live both in heaven and in hell, because God is no respecter of persons. You cannot look at your race and find pride in that. Like Paul, you can only say, "I am what I am by the grace of God." That's what you are, and *that* you can be proud of because God has made you in His image.

So, Nebuchadnezzar came to find out that God doesn't play. He raises up people and brings down people. It's time for my church to get rid of me when I say, "Look at this great Oak Cliff Bible Fellowship Church that I have built."

While it's legitimate to be grateful that God uses you, believing He uses you because of who you are is illegitimate. Remember, He gave you even the gifts, skills, and abilities you have. So He should get the glory that you have the ability to pull off what other people give you credit for.

A poem called "Invictus" illustrates the defiance of autonomous man:

Out of the night that covers me
Black as the pit from pole to pole,
I thank whatever gods may be
For this unconquerable soul.

In the full clutch of circumstance,
I have not winced nor cried aloud.
Under the bludgeonings of chance,
My head is bloodied, but unbowed.

Beyond this place of wrath and tears
Looms but the horror of the shade,
And yet the menace of the years
Finds and shall find me unafraid.

It matters not how straight the gate
How charged with punishment the scroll,
I am the master of my fate.
I am the captain of my soul.[1]

That is the attitude of autonomous man who does not want God ruling over him, who wants to be like God, who wants no one to whom he must answer. But make no mistake about it, all of us will answer to God one day. You may be running, but you can't hide. We must answer to God for our autonomy.

GOD'S SOVEREIGNTY AND OUR SIN

One might mention at this point the question of the origin of evil. Since God is sovereign, why did He allow the existence and proliferation of evil, especially in light of the fact that God hates sin (Romans 1:18), is completely holy (Isaiah 6:3), and cannot sin (Psalm 5:4; 1 John 1:5) or tempt others to do so (John 1:13)? Theologians have pondered this question for ages, and I certainly don't claim to

---

1. William Ernest Henley, "Invictus."

possess the final word on that subject. However, I do have some thoughts. First of all, since God does everything for His greatest glory (Ephesians 1:11–12), we must naturally conclude that God will get more glory with the existence of sin than without it. This makes sense because some of God's attributes are most clearly demonstrated against the backdrop of sin. The greatness of His love shows most clearly in contrast to our sinfulness (Romans 5:8). God's holiness and wrath, two indispensable aspects of His nature, could never be fully seen without the reality of sin (Romans 1:18; 9:22–23). Most important, the magnificence of His grace could hardly be measured except against the ugliness of sin (Ephesians 2:1–7). Thus, in allowing sin, the glory of God's attributes and character is most visibly displayed.

Second, in allowing the existence of evil, God is allowing everything that can be attempted to thwart His kingdom so that throughout the ages to come, it will be unquestionably clear that no enemy or scheme can succeed against the Almighty One. When this is over, no one is ever again going to come up with the dumb idea of rebelling against His authority, for history will demonstrate that every attempt has been tried and none has been successful. This comprehensive defeat of evil will be a primary basis for God's people giving Him praise (Revelation 19:1–6).

Finally, God allows evil because of His love. He does not wish to coerce obedience. For God to coerce obedience would invalidate the authentic nature of that obedience, especially since God looks at the heart (Romans 8:27), which remains disobedient. In order for man to function authentically as God's image-bearer, which includes functioning as a moral agent with the power to choose, the possibility of evil must exist. For God to have negated that possibility would be for Him to nullify the very thing He created. Personhood would be reduced to robotics.

We must, therefore, conclude that God neither causes sin, incites it, authorizes it, or approves it. He does, however, permit it by allowing His creatures, whom He has endowed with a moral will, to rebel against His authority. He then sovereignly overrules their evil to accomplish His sovereign predetermined purposes. In the allowance of evil, God demonstrates how great He really is. Or as Joseph so accurately articulated when giving his analysis of the evil done to him by his brothers who sold him into slavery, "You meant evil against me, but God meant it for good in order to bring about this present result, to preserve many people alive" (Genesis 50:20).

GOD'S SOVEREIGNTY AND OUR PERSPECTIVE

The sovereignty of God provides the Christian with the proper perspective in which to view all of life. If you ever get the sovereignty of God straight, your life will begin to take shape.

Strength

Paul says, "I can do all things through Him who strengthens me" (Philippians 4:13). That's the proper kind of positive thinking. As Christ supplies, I can do. But I am totally dependent upon His supply.

Comfort in Circumstances

God's sovereignty also gives comfort in the midst of life's circumstances. Life is bittersweet. One day you can wake up and be on top of the world. The job's going well, the money's flowing, the relationships are intact. You just wake up and say, "What a beautiful morning! The people are great! The kids are great! My mother-in-law is great! Just everything is great!"

But all of that can change in five seconds. Your mother-in-law can come visit you. You can get a headache. But when you have a sovereign God, it means that the negative and the positive do not come by chance. The flat tire that made you miss the interview you were banking on to get that job was part of God's sovereign plan. The situation you thought was going to work out a certain way, the job you were sure was yours which was given to someone else, was all a part of God's sovereign plan.

Confidence

His sovereignty means He allows no chance happenings, no luck, no mistakes, no accidents. You can have confidence, "Lord, You did what I thought You weren't going to do. That's because You want to do something else in my life, and I'm excited to see how You are going to use what You just did to do what You want to do. So go ahead and do Your thing."

Some ingredients of a cake taste good by themselves. Other ingredients taste terrible by themselves: nutmeg, baking soda, etc. But when you mix those things together and get the mixer churning, the good and the bad blend and turn out for the better. When that cake comes out of the oven, the good and the bad have been so mixed, so integrated, that they have produced something well worth the wait.

God is baking a cake in your life. He's taking the bad and the good and mixing them through the Holy Spirit, and when He finishes baking it through the various trials He brings you through, you will come out of the oven smoking. That's what Romans 8:28 means: "God causes all things to work together for good to those who love God, to those who are called according to His purpose."

That's why at the end of Romans 8, Paul says:

> I am convinced that neither death, nor life, nor angels, nor principalities, nor things present, nor things to come, nor powers, nor height, nor depth, nor any other created thing, shall be able to separate us from the love of God, which is in Christ Jesus our Lord. (vv. 38–39)

The Whole Picture

When you walk with God, when you live under His control, when you are in His hands, nothing can stifle you. God has allowed the negative, and He's going to use it to propel you. It's not evident at first because we have limited perspective. We're like the boy who was trying to work a puzzle. He couldn't even get two pieces to come together. His father came, and after a couple of minutes, put the whole puzzle together.

The boy asked, "Dad, how did you do that?"

"Son, you were looking at the pieces. I saw the whole picture."

It all depends on what you see. From our perspective we see one piece at a time because we live one day at time. But God sees the whole picture and He can put the whole thing together. When you understand the sovereignty of God, you believe in the power of prayer because you are convinced of what God can do.

You can't change people. You can't change your mate, but you can get out of the way so God can run over him. That's why I'm amazed at people who want to quit on things they've never fasted and prayed over. If you haven't fasted and prayed, you have not done all that God has called you to do because Jesus says that certain things only come by fasting and prayer.

Certain things you don't get just because you want them and you've done the best you can. Certain things only come because you've prayed about them to the point of giving up the craving of your appetite to get them. Unless you've understood the sovereignty of God, then God appears to be just a nice person who does things every now and then.

Sovereignty and Impossibilities

If I'm excited about one doctrine in my own life and ministry, it is God's sovereignty. I don't believe He can give me a vision to do anything that can't be done as long as it is in His will. Since I have that view, the obstacles seem irrelevant to me. I find the fact that it's never been done before irrelevant. The fact that no one else believes it can be done is irrelevant because the Bible says nothing is impossible with God (Luke 1:37). The vote doesn't mean anything when it comes to deciding if it can be done, because God is not limited.

YOU KNOW WHAT OUGHT TO DRAW US TO CHURCH ON SUNDAY? THE FACT THAT THE SOVEREIGN GOD, WHO HOLDS UP THE UNIVERSE BY THE WORD OF HIS POWER, WANTS TO HAVE A MEETING WITH US.

Have you ever met people you think even God can't save? We are talking about sinful sinners. But Hebrews 7:25 says that God can save to the utmost. That person you think will never become a Christian? Bring him or her to God in prayer and He can melt that heart of stone.

I like the confidence of Paul. He says in 2 Timothy 1:12, "I know whom I have believed and I am convinced that He is able to guard what I have entrusted to Him until that day." When you understand that our sovereign God is in control, you know you can bank on Him.

GOD'S SOVEREIGNTY
AND WORSHIP

The sovereignty of God should lead us to enthusiastic worship of Him. You know what ought to draw us to church on Sunday? The fact that the sovereign God, who holds up the universe by the word of His power, wants to have a meeting with us; that this great God, who gives us the air we breathe every day, who provides us everything we need, wants to meet with us. People who don't understand the sovereignty of God, who think they did this all by themselves, may just as well go to "Bedside Baptist" or "Mattress Methodist."

Giving God Honor

But when you have a sovereign God, you can't wait to meet with Him. When you have a boss who's responsible for your paycheck, you can't wait to get to work even if you hate the job because you know you are not autonomous. If we give our bosses the honor due them for a paycheck, how much more should we give God the honor due Him for the life we have each day? Worship is the proper response to God's sovereignty.

First Chronicles 29 brings this out clearly. David is in a building program, and Israel is getting ready to build God a house. David challenges the people to bring their offerings for the temple they will build for God:

> Then the rulers of the fathers' households, and the princes of the tribes of Israel, and the commanders of thousands and of hundreds, with the overseers over the king's work, offered willingly; and for the service for the house of God they gave 5,000 talents and 10,000 darics of gold, and 10,000 talents of silver, and 18,000 talents of brass, and 100,000 talents of iron. (vv. 6–7)

So the people give very generously to the house of God. And as they do so:

> David blessed the Lord in the sight of all the assembly; and David said, "Blessed art Thou, O Lord God of Israel our father, forever and ever. Thine, O Lord, is the greatness and the power and the glory and the victory and the majesty, indeed everything that is in the heavens and the earth; Thine is the dominion, O Lord, and Thou dost exalt Thyself as head over all. Both riches and honor come from Thee, and Thou dost rule over all, and in Thy hand is power and might; and it lies in Thy hand to make great, and to strengthen everyone. Now therefore, our God, we thank Thee, and praise Thy glorious name." (vv. 10–13)

That's what ought to draw you to church on Sunday—to praise God's glorious name, because what king is like our God? Who else can create moons, stars, planets, and other galaxies? Who can create just the right temperature and keep the earth rotating at just the right speed so that it rotates around the sun at just the right season?

Who can give us just the right animals from which we get just the right clothes and the right food? Who can create just the right wood so we can build just the right houses? Who is like our God? He deserves your worship, your homage. He deserves your bowing before His face, glorifying His name. He deserves your passionate worship.

God Wants Your Worship

If your newspaper boy missed a day a week, you would call him unfaithful and fuss because you don't want to pay for a week when he's missing a day each week. If your refrigerator stops one day a week, you call a repairman; it's undependable. If your water alternates between hot and cold, you get it fixed; that's an uncomfortable way to take a shower. If you miss every other mortgage payment, you will be moved out of your house because that's not how a loan works.

What we expect of ourselves and others, should not our sovereign God expect of us, and even more? He wants our dedicated, committed worship. You say, "But I find it hard to worship God. You don't know what's going on in my life."

You're right. I don't know what's going on in your life, but I know this. It was in the year that King Uzziah died that Isaiah saw the Lord (Isaiah 6:1). Maybe your Uzziah is dying. That is, maybe your circumstances are tough because only in the midst of chaos will you take time out to look to God. A sovereign God can arrange circumstances to accomplish His purposes.

Responding to God's Sovereignty

Some of us need our "Uzziahs" to die so that we will learn to worship God's majesty, exalt His name, and honor His person, for He alone is worthy. Ask God to use the following tools to help you respond properly to His sovereignty:

1. If worship is the proper response to God's sovereignty, then it's time to measure your "Worship Quotient" (WQ). For example, do you see worship as something you do once a week? Or do you see your daily work as an act of worship to God? Can you worship when things are a little rocky, or does everything have to be smooth before you can genuinely offer God worship? Take a reading of your WQ, and make any necessary adjustments.

2. Read today's newspaper or watch this evening's newscast in light of the truth of God's sovereignty. Is anything going on in our world that might scare you out of your socks if you didn't know and believe that God had a firm grip on this place? Thank Him that ABC, CBS, NBC, or CNN can show you nothing that YHWH (the "I AM" God) can't handle.

3. If God is sovereign, that means He's capable of helping you do whatever He's called you to do. Make the affirmation of Philippians 4:13 personal by completing this statement: "I can do ——————————— through Him who strengthens me."

4. Is there a "Nebuchadnezzar" in your family or circle of acquaintances who you know is heading for a collision with our sovereign God? Tell God you're available to be used in that person's life to snap him or her awake and avoid the crash.

6
THE GLORY
OF GOD

L ast October, an otherwise ordinary week was turned upside down and inside out by some discouraging, debilitating, depressing, and disheartening news: Chicago Bulls star Michael Jordan announced his retirement. Michael Jordan, the man who had taken professional basketball to another level, was hanging up his sneakers. I wanted to fast and pray because he's definitely elevated the game.

It was interesting to note the reaction to his retirement. The media would show clips of "Air Jordan" in action, going up high, tongue hanging low, hitting the shot to win the game. They would talk about how it was impossible for anyone to stop him once he decided that the ball was now his, the game was now his, and he would call the shots; how he would raise the play of his teammates to another level, particularly during the playoffs, so that no matter how far the Bulls were in the hole, with Michael Jordan they knew the game wasn't over till it was over.

Then they would show the replay I like: Jordan coming down the court, getting to the top of the key, feet lifting off the floor, moving in mid-air. As he dunked the ball, the commentator would say, "Ladies and gentlemen, you are watching living proof that men can fly."

Regardless of their feelings toward Chicago, everyone wanted to see Michael. Regardless of how poorly the Dallas Mavericks were playing, the Chicago Bulls game was always sold out well in advance, because everyone wanted to see Michael. Do you know why? Because Michael had glory. He had a unique ability to transcend the normal, to rise above that which is admirable and do what many would feel is supernatural: to fly through the air.

That's glory. Glory is the process of manifesting, demonstrating one's attributes; letting everyone in the stands see you strut your stuff; letting people in on who you are and what makes you tick. That's glory.

THE GLORY OF GOD IS BEST DESCRIBED AS THE VISIBLE MANIFESTATION OF HIS ATTRIBUTES, HIS CHARACTER, HIS PERFECTIONS.

But when it comes to true, pure glory, we are talking about someone greater than Michael Jordan or anyone else on earth. Only our God has true glory. Nothing can ever happen to dim or diminish His glory. Now that's interesting because Michael Jordan's attempt to break into major league baseball in the spring of 1994 tarnished his athletic glory somewhat. As he struggled to hit and field, Jordan suddenly looked very ordinary. One major league scout summed it up in his report: "Average speed, very hard worker, no chance." Michael Jordan's glory has dimmed, but that will never happen to God's glory.

GOD'S GLORY
MANIFESTED IN HIS NATURE

The glory of God is best described as the visible manifestation of His attributes, His character, His perfections. The word translated *glory* in the Old Testament is very interesting. It means "to be weighted, to be heavy." We would use the word *awesome*. When we discuss God's glory, we talk about someone with an awesome reputation because He has awesome splendor. God is glorious. He is, to put it quite bluntly, awesome.

In this chapter I want to show you five things about the glory of God. First, the glory of God is the sum total of His intrinsic nature. When I talk about the glory of God, I mean the composite nature, the comprehensive grouping of all that makes Him who He is; the sum of His being. Exodus 33 brings this to light well. As Moses leads the people of Israel toward the Promised Land, he makes three requests of God.

In verse 13, Moses says, "I pray Thee, if I have found favor in Thy sight, let me know Thy ways, that I may know Thee." If you want to know God, you must know His ways. You must say to Him, "Help me to know Your ways so that I might understand You, because You do things differently than I."

Notice how the Lord answered Moses: "My presence shall go with you" (v. 14). In other words, "Don't worry about it, Moses. I will be with you. You will see me do My thing."

Then Moses makes a second request in verse 15: "If Thy presence does not go with us, do not lead us up from here." Moses is saying, "If you don't go before me into the Promised Land, I would rather stay here in the wilderness." Here we see another important principle. It's better to be in an apartment with God than in a house without Him!

God responded to Moses, "I will also do this thing of which you have spoken; for you have found favor in My sight, and I have known you by name" (v. 17).

Then Moses makes his third and final request: "I pray Thee, show me Thy glory!" (v. 18). Moses asks, "Who are You, God? What makes You tick? I've talked to You, I've related to You, but I know there is a lot more to You than what I see. I want to see the whole 'kit and caboodle.' Show me Your glory. Let me in on Your essence. Unveil Yourself to me."

God answered this prayer too:

> "I Myself will make all My goodness pass before you, and will proclaim the name of the Lord before you; and I will be gracious to whom I will be gracious, and will show compassion on whom I will show compassion." But He said, "You cannot see My face, for no man can see Me and live! . . . I will put you in the cleft of the rock and cover you with my hand . . . and you shall see My back." (vv. 19–20, 22–23)

In other words, "Moses, I can't grant your full request because you wouldn't be alive long enough to enjoy it. No man can look at My inner essence and live. However, I will pass My goodness before you." The Hebrew word for goodness was used of jewelry. It means "splendor." God bears intrinsic glory.

To put it another way, our God is glorious by nature. We are only glorious when we are made to feel glorious; that is, we have *ascribed* glory. In fact, many people spend a lot of time trying to make themselves glorious. The Bible says, for example, that a woman's hair is her glory. That's why women spend hours in a beauty shop to take their hair and turn it into that which will manifest or enhance their beauty.

People buy cars of certain makes and models in an attempt to enhance their glory and to give them a greater sense of recognition. People buy some of the clothes they buy not simply because it's the style they like, but so that someone will tell them how nice they look. In other words, they buy based on their need to have someone ascribe glory to them.

But God's glory exists whether or not you ever say something about it or recognize it. God's glory is intrinsic glory. He has glory by virtue of who He is, not by virtue of what you say. That's why the biggest help for self-esteem is "God esteem," because once you know who you are in God, it doesn't matter if everyone else sees it too. God's glory is unique, so distinct that He says He will not share it with anyone (Isaiah 42:8). The psalmist writes, "Not to us, O Lord, not to us, but to Thy name give glory" (Psalm 115:1).

The glory of God, then, has to do with His intrinsic character, who He is at the core of His being. It is not predicated on what He does, but on who He is. God reveals His glory by what He does, as we shall see in a moment. But God is glorious just because He is God. Psalm 29:3 calls Him the "God of glory." That's who He is. His glory is the total of His essence and attributes.

GOD'S GLORY
MANIFESTED IN HISTORY

We also know that God is glorious because He has manifested Himself gloriously in human history. God's internal essence is made known externally by what He does. The Jews had a word for this: *shekinah* glory. The word *shekinah* means "to dwell or reside with," the glory of God residing with men so men can see it.

This is a very important point, and I want to do it justice theologically without overstating the case, so stay with me for a moment. If you could pull out the nucleus of God, so to speak, His internal essence would be a huge, radiating light. If God were to come to us and show us His inner self, we would see a big light. Where do I get that? Listen to Paul describing to Timothy God's inner essence as he discusses the second coming of Jesus Christ . . .

> which He will bring about at the proper time—He who is the blessed and only Sovereign, the King of Kings and Lord of Lords; who alone possesses immortality and dwells in unapproachable light; whom no man has seen or can see. To Him be honor and eternal dominion! Amen. (1 Timothy 6:15–16)

God's inner core is a radiating, unapproachable light. This explains why God created the sun with its "unapproachable light" to rule the day. The earth is 93 million miles from the sun, but you couldn't get within a million miles of the sun without burning to a crisp. The sun is that hot; that much gas comes out of that big ball of fire. That's all the sun is, a big ball of fire with so much power and so much light that it lights the whole world and will burn you to a crisp from a million miles away.

Now you understand what God meant when He said, "No man can see Me and live." You would disintegrate because at His core, God is light (1 John 1:5). That's why whenever God shows up in history, it's always in relation to light.

For example, when Ezekiel saw the glory of God, he said it was like a "surrounding radiance" and the prophet fell on his face (Ezekiel 1:28). When the shepherds were in the field at the birth of Jesus, "the glory of the Lord shone around them" (Luke 2:9). And concerning the New Jerusalem, the Bible says "the city has no need of the sun or of the moon to shine upon it, for the glory of God has illumined it" (Revelation 21:23).

Revealed in Creation

God reveals the light of His glory in a number of ways. Let me cite them for you. The first of these I want to look at is creation. In Psalm 19, the classic passage on this truth, the psalmist says,

> The heavens are telling of the glory of God; and their expanse is declaring the work of His hands. Day to day pours forth speech, and night to night reveals knowledge. . . . Their line has gone

out through all the earth, and their utterances to the end of the world. In them He has placed a tent for the sun, which is as a bridegroom coming out of his chamber; it rejoices as a strong man to run his course. Its rising is from one end of the heavens, and its circuit to the other end of them; and there is nothing hidden from its heat. (vv. 1–2, 4–6)

In the same way that nothing is hidden from the sun, nothing can hide from God's glory. God says, "If you want to see how great I am, go outside. The heavens tell of My glory." We get confused because we talk about Mother Nature, not Father God. God says we can see His glory simply by looking at His creation. You've only got to go outside, and the heavens will tell you a story about the glory of God.

And what a story they tell! For example, on a clear night, if you could look at the whole sky covering the earth at one time, you could see about three thousand stars with the naked eye. But scientists with their telescopes can see to the edge of the Milky Way, and they have calculated that our galaxy alone houses 200 *billion* stars. And those same scientists estimate that the universe contains at least one million other galaxies like the Milky Way.

Now let's go back. With your naked eye, you could see three thousand stars. That means God is pretty sharp. With the telescope, we can "guesstimate" 200 billion stars in our Milky Way. God's getting bigger and bigger. But if a million other galaxies hang in space, we're talking about a God of glory! This God created the universe to display His glory, and it didn't take Him long to do it either. He just said, "Let there be light." That's how glorious our God is.

God's glory can be seen in the vastness of space, and it's also seen in life's particulars. It's seen when snowflakes fall. It's seen in the fact that no two people have the same fingerprints. It's seen in the fact that when the earth spins on its axis, it doesn't spin too fast lest we be thrown off. It doesn't spin too slow lest we feel it and become dizzy to death. It spins just right so we neither fall off nor feel dizzy because it spins at the same rate as our ability to function within the force of gravity. How could that happen? Our God is glorious. That's how it happens. We have a glorious God.

Revealed in the Tabernacle

God's passion is for His glory, that there be a visible recognition that He alone is God. His glory was visible to Israel at the tabernacle. Israel built a tabernacle which wasn't particularly exciting to look at on the outside. But after they built it, the glory of the Lord came in the "glory cloud." Exodus 40 tells us about it:

> Then the cloud covered the tent of meeting, and the glory of the Lord filled the tabernacle. And Moses was not able to enter the tent of meeting because the cloud had settled on it, and the glory of the Lord filled the tabernacle. And throughout all their journeys whenever the cloud was taken up from over the tabernacle, the sons of Israel would set out; but if the cloud was not taken up, then they did not set out until the day when it was taken up. For throughout all their journeys, the cloud of the Lord was on the tabernacle by day, and there was fire in it by night, in the sight of all the house of Israel. (vv. 34–38)

What a great passage. God came down and rested on the tabernacle as the glory cloud filled the Holy of Holies and all of the tabernacle. The reason God had to come in a cloud was because He had to veil His glory. He could not reveal His inner core, His full inner light. But the beauty of the glory cloud was that when the cloud moved, Israel moved. When the glory cloud stopped, Israel stopped. They wouldn't budge until the cloud moved, and when it moved, they got up right away.

Here is a very important principle for Christian living. When you live your life for the glory of God, you don't have to worry about His will. The glory cloud leads you. When you follow the glory of God, when you have a passion for it, God's glory will always pick you up and pull you forward when it's time to move, then set you down and keep you still when it's time to stay. So don't look for God's will; look for His glory, and you will find His will. The tabernacle demonstrated God's glory.

Revealed in the Temple

Later, Israel built a permanent residence for the glory of God called the temple. At the temple's dedication, the glory cloud so filled the place that the priests couldn't do their work (1 Kings 8:10–11). God now had a permanent resting place for His presence among His people.

When God's presence was among His people it meant His attributes were among His people. So they had the power of God, the knowledge of God, the presence of God, the truth of God, the revelation of God, the Spirit of God, the guidance of God, and anything else necessary because to have the glory of God is to have God, to have all His attributes at work for you. Nothing is more important in life than the glory of God.

Conversely, when the people disobeyed God, the Bible says that over Israel was written "Ichabod," which means "The glory has departed from Israel" (1 Samuel 4:21). When the glory cloud leaves you, you are in trouble because you have no presence of God. You can pray, but you won't experience God's power. You can call out, but you won't experience God's presence. God's glory was revealed in the temple.

Revealed in Christ

But neither creation, the tabernacle, nor the temple was the ultimate revelation of God's glory in history, of course. God's visible glory was most fully seen in the person of Jesus Christ. John 1 puts it this way:

> In the beginning was the Word, and the Word was with God, and the Word was God. . . . And the Word became flesh, and dwelt among us, and we beheld His glory, glory as of the only begotten from the Father, full of grace and truth. . . . No man has seen God at any time; the only begotten God [Jesus], who is in the bosom of the Father, He has explained [revealed] Him. (vv. 1, 14, 18)

In His earthly life, Jesus Christ was God's glory in human flesh. That's why He did what only God could do: heal the blind and the sick, raise the dead, read people's minds, know what was happening ahead of time. Jesus was the visible manifestation of God in human flesh. His glory was veiled, though, because no one can look on God and live.

But in Matthew 17 Jesus took Peter, James, and John up to a mountain. There Christ zipped down His humanity, so to speak. He took off the veil of flesh for just a minute, and the Bible says that bursting out of His humanity was a bright light. And the voice from heaven was so awesome they had to hide their faces because the glory of God was on the mountain (vv. 1–8). Jesus Christ is God incarnate, the magnificent revelation of God in terms human beings can understand because He was God become Man.

Revealed in the Church

God has not only manifested His glory in nature, in the tabernacle, in the temple, and in Christ. God's glory is also manifested in the church:

> Now to Him who is able to do exceeding abundantly beyond all that we ask or think, according to the power that works within us, to Him be the glory in the church. (Ephesians 3:20–21)

Not only is there to be glory in the Son of God, there is to be glory through the people of God. We should reflect the attributes of God in our world. The church is designed to be a unique gathering of God's people through whom God mirrors His glory. This world should see our glorious God when they see the functioning of His people.

Only then will the church see that He is "able to do exceeding abundantly beyond all that we ask or think." In fact, that's not only true collectively, it's true individually because Ephesians 1:12 says that God saved you that you might live "to the praise of His glory." That is, He wants your life to glorify Him.

GOD'S GLORY: THE BASIS OF BLESSING AND CURSING

Paul informed us of this truth when he wrote:

> If our gospel is veiled, it is veiled to those who are perishing, in whose case the god of this world has blinded the minds of the unbelieving, that they may not see the light of the gospel of the glory of Christ, who is the image of God. (2 Corinthians 4:3–4)

In other words, unbelievers are judged because they do not perceive or reflect God's glory. What does Romans 3:23 say? "All have sinned and fall short of the glory of God." We are not sinners because we've committed a horrible crime. We are sinners because we are unlike God. Our attributes and God's attributes don't match. Our inner core does not react like His inner core. We've all sinned, we don't measure up to God's glory, and we face judgment because something is wrong with our glory.

But for us as believers, the glory of God which shows us to be sinners has now become the basis of our blessing. Let's go back to 2 Corinthians 4:

> For God, who said, "Light shall shine out of darkness," is the One who has shone in our hearts to give the light of the knowledge of the glory of God in the face of Christ. But we have this treasure [the glory cloud] in earthen vessels, that the surpassing greatness of the power may be of God and not from ourselves. (vv. 6–7)

So where's the blessing? Look at verses 8–9: "We are afflicted in every way, but not crushed; perplexed, but not despairing; persecuted, but not forsaken; struck down, but not destroyed."

Paul is saying that when you have the glory cloud, your problems don't have to crush you. You may get confused, but you don't have to commit suicide in despair. Someone may give you a hard time at work, but that's OK. God will never forsake you. You can go to work with your head up high, because God walks to your desk with you. You may be struck down, but if you have the glory cloud, you won't be destroyed.

THE PROOF OF HOW MUCH WE VALUE GOD'S GLORY IS HOW WE RESPOND TO IT.

That's fantastic! The glory of God brings with it His support, encouragement, blessings, strength, and everything else necessary for Him to take you from where you are to where He wants you to be. And by the way, don't let anyone give you that old line which says that if you claim to have a loving heavenly Father, nothing bad should ever happen to you.

That's a false line of argument. Everyone has problems. The difference is that the Christian knows there is a purpose behind his pain, he is not alone in it, and he has God's promise for strength to go through it (1 Corinthians 10:13). The unbeliever has none of this. He should be the one on the defensive with the tough questions to answer, not the Christian.

GOD'S GLORY
DEMANDS A RESPONSE

Only two groups of beings won't voluntarily glorify God: fallen men and fallen angels. Both will be discarded from His presence because throughout all eternity, God will only fellowship with those who voluntarily bring Him glory.

You see, your claim to esteem God will be validated by how you respond to the God you say you esteem. The proof that you glorify God, that you recognize His intrinsic value, will be the value that you ascribe to His glory.

We parents often have trouble teaching our children how to handle money. We spend a lot of time trying to teach them the value of money because we want them to handle it wisely. Of course, kids will always say, "I got it. I know how to handle money. I've learned how to value it."

But the test is not having your kids tell you they value money. The test is, how do they spend it? How much money do they squander? The proof of how much we value God's glory is how we respond to it.

Sing to Him

How should we respond to God's glory? Psalm 96 gives us some great answers:

> Sing to the Lord a new song; sing to the Lord, all the earth. Sing to the Lord, bless His name; proclaim good tidings of His salvation from day to day. Tell of His glory among the nations. (vv. 1–3)

One of my favorite songs some years ago was by the Wynans. They sang, "Everything you touch is a song. . . ." Many of us don't know that when cows moo, they are giving glory to God. When kittens meow, they give glory to God. Dogs bark to the glory of God. When the rooster wakes up and crows, he's saying, "Cock-a-doodle, God!" We don't understand that when the lion roars, he's giving glory to God.

You say, "Wait a minute! I don't believe those things are giving glory to God." Look at verses 11–13a of this psalm:

> Let the heavens be glad, and let the earth rejoice; let the sea roar, and all it contains. Let the field exult, and all that is in it. Then all the trees of the forest will sing for joy before the Lord, for He is coming.

If everything on earth shouts God's glory, what should we be doing? Go back to verses 7–9a:

> Ascribe to the Lord, O families of the peoples, ascribe to the Lord glory and strength. Ascribe to the Lord the glory of His name; bring an offering and come into His courts. Worship the Lord in holy attire.

Even your clothing ought to be whistling the glory of God. Watch how you dress when you worship. "Tremble before Him, all the earth" (v. 9b). That's what people do who glorify God. They don't come and mumble little words. Even if they can't sing, they break out in song because the ability to make a joyful noise was given by God.

Praise Him

Many people don't even give God what the animals give Him. Because we can't interpret all those sounds, we think they're just a lot of noise. No, the Bible says that all of creation resonates with the glory of God except people. God demands and deserves glory. We can't *give* Him glory, because He already has it. It's intrinsic. We *ascribe* to Him the glory that He's due.

A judge becomes glorious when he puts on his robe. But when he takes off the robe, he's just another man. A policeman is glorious when he has on a badge and a blue uniform, but take off the badge and the uniform and he's just another person. God is always glorious because He never takes off His "uniform." He never takes off His robe of glory. He is the King of the universe. He is glorious.

How much should we do this thing called glorifying God? Psalm 113:3–4 puts it this way: "From the rising of the sun to its setting the name of the Lord is to be praised. The Lord is high above all nations; His glory is above the heavens." In other words, when you open your eyes in the morning, praise Him. When you go into the bathroom and look in the mirror, praise Him. When you go to the breakfast table, praise Him. When you get in your car, praise Him. When He takes you safely to work, praise Him.

For the fact that you have work to go to and He gives you a mind to understand it, praise Him. When the day ends and you are still alive to go back home, praise Him. When you get home and have dinner, praise Him. When you see the rest of your family that He brought safely home, praise Him. When you retire for the night, praise Him. The Bible says the Lord is enthroned on the praises of His people (Psalm 22:3).

Glorify Him

One day Jesus came upon ten lepers who cried out, "Have mercy on us!" (Luke 17:13). The Lord had pity on them and said, "Go and show yourselves to the priests" (v. 14). As they went, their skin became like babies' skin. The leprosy was gone.

Nine of the lepers kept going, but one—a foreigner, a Samaritan—turned around, came back, fell on his knees before Jesus, and glorified Him. Jesus looked at him and said, "Were there not ten cleansed? But the nine—where are they?" (v. 17).

He asked a great question. Where are all the people to whom God has given life, health, and strength? How can we stay in bed on Sunday morning when God has given us strength? How can we be too tired for Him when, if it were not for Him, we wouldn't be here at all? How can we not give Him glory? He deserves glory, not excuses. It's inconceivable to me that a man would stay in bed and send his family to church. What's his problem? God didn't do anything for him that week?

God deserves glory, not only in terms of our worship but by what we do each day. The Bible contains many examples:

1. God is glorified when we "bear much fruit"—show Christlike character (John 15:8).
2. God is glorified when we do good works—apply biblical truths to human situations (Matthew 5:16).
3. God is glorified by our sexual purity (1 Corinthians 6:18–20).
4. God is glorified when we confess our sins (Joshua 7:19).
5. God is glorified when we live by faith and not by sight (Romans 4:19–21).
6. God is glorified when we proclaim His Word (2 Thessalonians 3:1).
7. God is glorified when we appeal to His glory in our suffering (1 Peter 4:14–16).
8. God is glorified when we do His will (John 17:4).
9. God is glorified when we confess His Son (Philippians 2:10).
10. God is glorified when we reflect the character of Christ (Romans 15:6).

I said earlier that unbelievers don't voluntarily glorify God. But God still gets what He wants—glory to Himself—even out of them. Remember what Pharaoh said to Moses in Egypt? "I'm not going to let you and your people go."

However, God told Moses, "Don't worry about Pharaoh. His heart is hard. I'm going to make it harder. I'm going to make him so mad at Me that he will do exactly what I want him to do. I will harden Pharaoh's heart and still get glory from him" (see Exodus 14:17).

So the issue is really not whether we will give God glory. Whether we give it to Him voluntarily or He has to squeeze it out of us against our wills, we are going to give God glory. God will get glory, but given the fact of all that He's done for us, doesn't He deserve it? Shouldn't we be hurrying to give Him glory?

GOD'S GLORY
TRANSFORMS THOSE WHO RESPOND

Second Corinthians 3:18 is another beautiful passage of Scripture. Paul writes:

> But we all, with unveiled face beholding as in a mirror the glory of the Lord, are being transformed into the same image from glory to glory, just as from the Lord, the Spirit.

If you ever catch hold of this principle of the glory of the Lord, you will be transformed. Do you want to transform yourself? Do you have things in your life that need to be changed? Catch hold of the glory of God. Do you want to change your mate? Don't nag him or her. Point the person to the glory of God.

A *Temporary Glow*

To understand what Paul's talking about, we need to go back to verse 13: "Moses . . . used to put a veil over his face that the sons of Israel might not look intently at the end of what was fading away." Paul is referring to an incident in Exodus 34, which continues the text discussed at the opening of this chapter.

On that mountain, Moses saw the glory of God (actually, he saw God's back because that's all he could take). Then as Moses came down the mountain, his face started to shine because he had been in God's presence. But the farther he went, the more the shine started to fade. By the time he got to the people, he had only a little shine left. Moses covered his face so the people wouldn't see his shine fading. When he needed a new fix, he marched right back up to the mountain and got a new shine. But when he came down to the people, his shine began to fade.

We're sort of like that. When we walk out of church on Sunday morning, most of us are shining because we've been in God's presence and have seen His glory. But by the time we get home and sit down around the table for lunch, we have lost our shine.

When my children were younger, I used to take them to amusement parks. Whenever we went, they always had those long green strings that glowed in the dark. Maybe you remember them.

My kids always wanted one, of course, so I'd buy one for each of them and they would wrap those strings around their necks or wrists and watch them glow. When we got in the car to go home, the kids wanted all the lights out so they could watch their strings glow. When we got home, they would go in their rooms and turn off the lights to watch the glow.

But after about an hour at home, the "glory" in those strings began to fade. The glow began to get dim. By the time the kids woke up the next day, the strings did not glow at all. The salesman does not tell you when you pay a small fortune for those strings that they have no light in them at all. They aren't glowing because they have light in themselves. They glow only because of their exposure to light.

IF YOU WANT TO BE TRANSFORMED, SUBMIT TO GOD'S GLORY. STOP TRYING TO SHARE HIS GLORY, LET HIM BE GOD, AND LET THE LIGHT OF THE GLORY OF GOD TRANSFORM YOU.

The moment a person removes that string from the light, it loses its ability to glow because it is no longer exposed to the thing that made it glow in the first place: the light. To make it glow again you need only to wrap it around a light bulb and let the light infiltrate the covering. In other words, simply expose it to that which gives it the ability to glow.

A Permanent Glow

When Jesus Christ saved you, He put a new covering on you so that when you're exposed to the light of the glory of God, it will put a glow in your life. But when you remove yourself from God's glory, your glow begins to diminish. When you find that happening, you need to wrap yourself around the light of God's glory. Then the transforming work of God can begin to glow in you again.

David said that when he made the Lord the priority of his life, he had great gladness and joy (Psalm 16:8–9). The way he got joy was not by looking for it. He exposed himself to the glory of God. If you get exposed to His glory, the light begins to shine; change begins to take place; you have power you didn't have before; you have victory you didn't have before. Why? Not because of you, but because of the glory cloud. It begins to transform you from within.

So what's the bottom line? "Whether, then, you eat or drink or whatever you do, do all to the glory of God" (1 Corinthians 10:31). God says, "If you would just remember to thank Me every time you do anything, you will begin to shine and the glory cloud will transform your life." If you want to be transformed, submit to God's glory. Stop trying to share His glory, let Him be God, and let the light of the glory of God transform you.

Responding to the Glory of God

God's glory is so all-pervasive that it should shape the way we live our lives each day. What a privilege we have—to bring glory to the most glorious Being in all the universe. Use these ideas in your life to help bring Him glory:

1. Take another look at your schedule for the next week or so in light of God's glory. How much of what you hope and plan to do will in some way enhance the glory of God? That doesn't mean everything you do has to be a "spiritual" or church activity. You can bring Him glory mopping the floors. If your schedule doesn't reflect your desire to glorify God as much as you'd like, you may need to make some additions—or cancellations.

2. Is there anyone you're working hard to change these days? Only God can change hearts. Why not begin praying instead that your "project" will be touched and transformed by the glory of God? After all, God will do a lot better job than you will anyway!

3. Feeling a little crushed or beaten down right now? Go to God and ask Him to clear away some of the haze so that you can see the "glory cloud" again. Make a renewed commitment to be faithful to Him regardless of the circumstances.

4. First Corinthians 10:13, God's promise of sufficient strength for any trial, is another of those key verses you need to file in your spiritual inventory. Commit this great verse to memory if you haven't done so already.

7
THE OMNISCIENCE OF GOD

f your grade school was anything like mine, you had a "know-it-all" in your class. He or she seemed to have every answer, and whatever the subject Mister or Miss Know-it-all could expound at length about it. Nothing made you madder than to see that kid who acted like he or she knew everything, because you knew he or she didn't know half of it.

The universe only contains one "know-it-all," and it isn't the kid in your fifth-grade class. The only one who knows everything is the great God whose perfections we have been studying. One of the attributes of our God is His *omniscience,* a word made up of two words: *omni,* which means "all," and *science,* which has to do with knowledge.

So when we talk about the omniscience of God, we are referring to His "all-knowingness," what God knows. Omniscience begins a trilogy of "omnis" we want to consider. In the next two chapters we will look at God's omnipotence, His all-power; and God's omnipresence, the fact that He exists everywhere simultaneously. But here we want to focus on His omniscience. A simple definition is that God's omniscience refers to His perfect knowledge of all things both actual and potential.

Let's put it down straight right up front. The omniscience of God means that there is absolutely nothing He doesn't know; that no informational system or set of data exists anywhere outside of God's knowledge—nothing. He depends on no one outside Himself for any knowledge about anything.

That's so unlike us. We are all dependent on someone else's knowledge. In fact, we sometimes stake our lives on the fact that someone knows something. Every time you fill a prescription at the pharmacy, you bank on the fact that the person behind that counter is not a fool. You trust your life to the assumption that your pharmacist went to school and that he doesn't confuse medicines.

Very few of us ever check on it. We don't open up the pills to make sure they contain the right medicinal ingredients. We wouldn't know them if we saw them anyway. We know only that the doctor wrote the prescription, the pharmacist filled it, and we are going to swallow it. We depend on the knowledge of others.

Every time you get on an airplane, you assume your pilot has done this before. You hope all those switches mean something to him. When you go to school, you depend on the fact that your teacher has been to school, although sometimes you may doubt it. I could multiply the examples, but you get the idea. We depend heavily on the knowledge that other people possess.

I like the story of the very wealthy grandfather who was getting up in age. He was going deaf, but he went to the doctor and was fitted with a unique hearing aid. It not only overcame the old man's deafness, but it allowed him to hear perfectly. When he went back to the doctor for a checkup, the doctor commented, "Well, your family must be extremely happy to know that you can now hear."

The grandfather said, "No, I haven't told them about my hearing aid. I just sit around and listen to the conversations. I've already changed my will twice."

When folks don't think you know, it will greatly affect what they say and do. So we had better understand that God knows everything, because it will affect everything we say and do. In this chapter I want us to see four important truths about the omniscience of God.

GOD'S OMNISCIENCE
IS INTUITIVE

In Isaiah 40:13–14, the prophet gives us this very valuable piece of information about God's perfect knowledge:

Who has directed the Spirit of the Lord, or as His counselor has informed Him? With whom did He consult and who gave Him understanding? And who taught Him in the path of justice and taught Him knowledge, and informed Him of the way of understanding?

To put it in our terms, where did the Lord go to school? Isaiah raises the question to illustrate a fundamental principle, that God does not gain His knowledge by learning. He does not need to study, read, and analyze. He knows what He knows simply because He knows it. He did not learn it.

BECAUSE [GOD] IS ETERNAL, HE DOES NOT HAVE TO LOOK BACK TO THE PAST TO REMEMBER OR LOOK FORWARD TO THE FUTURE TO PROJECT.

In an earlier chapter I referred to the fact that I went from high school to four years of college; from there to four years of seminary for a master's degree; then four more years of seminary for my doctorate. I've read about two books a week ever since that time. But I feel more ignorant today than I did in first grade. All that learning only shows me how much I don't know and how much more there is to learn.

As finite creatures, the more we learn the more we know that we don't know all that we need to know. That's a real dilemma, but God does not have this problem because everything that can be known, everything that has ever been known, and everything that will ever be known, He already knows.

The Bible says, for example, that "the very hairs of your head are all numbered" (Matthew 10:30). I realize for some people, that's an easy count. But the point is that God knows the number of hairs on your head not because He counted them, but because He is God and He knows. God does not have to accumulate information. His knowledge is intuitive.

The closest thing I know to this on earth is the intuitive knowledge which women seem to have. My wife, Lois, will often say to me about something, "Watch out for that."

I will say, "How do you know?"

And she will answer, "Because I know."

I don't question Lois too often at those times, because she speaks out of innate knowledge—and she's usually right. God has innate knowledge of all data at all times. He never forgets, so He doesn't ever have to remember. After God had miraculously intervened in her life to give her a baby, Hannah offered Him a prayer of thanksgiving for little Samuel. In her praise she gave God glory and said, "The Lord is a God of knowledge" (1 Samuel 2:3).

That's who He is. Because God is an eternal being, whatever He knows, He knows immediately and simultaneously. Because He is eternal, He does not have to look back to the past to remember or look forward to the future to project. All knowledge past, present, and future resides in Him in the eternal now. All that is known, has been known, will be known, could be known, or has been forgotten, God knows intuitively and eternally.

This gets very personal. God knows that you are reading this book at this moment. He knows what you are thinking about as you read. When you sit in church, He knows if you'd rather be somewhere else. He knows what you plan to do when you leave church. He is acutely aware of all data at all times that pertains to all people everywhere. His knowledge is intuitive.

All the information in all the libraries of the world; all the data on all the computer chips in the world, including the chips that have not yet been made; all of this data, God knows perfectly and completely right now. Because He is infinite, "His understanding is infinite" (Psalm 147:5).

That is why, in eternity when we will be with God, we will never run out of knowledge because we will never run out of God. With Him dwells the body of knowledge that will go into eternity. God's knowledge is intuitive. It is innate to who He is.

GOD'S OMNISCIENCE IS COMPREHENSIVE

I like the way the author of Hebrews put it when he wrote in Hebrews 4:13: "There is no creature hidden from His sight, but all things are open and laid bare to the eyes of Him with whom we have to do."

No Detail Overlooked

Nothing can be hidden from God. He knows our feelings, our desires, our excuses, and our personalities. He knows everything and anything, and He knows it comprehensively. Nothing sits outside of the body of information He possesses. According to Acts 15:18, He has known everything from the very beginning. Needless to say, it would be quite difficult to give God a surprise party, for 1 John 3:20 also affirms that He knows all things.

God's comprehensive knowledge also includes a moral element. Proverbs 15:3 says that "the eyes of the Lord are in every place, watching the evil and the good." Nothing can escape His all-encompassing knowledge—not the biggest or the most minute detail. We saw this earlier in Matthew 10:30 in reference to the hairs of our heads.

Just one verse earlier Jesus had said, "Not one [sparrow] will fall to the ground apart from your father" (Matthew 10:29). The legendary Baptist preacher, Dr. Robert G. Lee, once said, "God is the only One who attends a sparrow's funeral." According to Psalm 50:11, God knows every beast and every bird of the air. *That's* comprehensive knowledge!

God's omniscience isn't confined to things on earth. The psalmist says every star among the billions of stars that inhabit all of the galaxies has been numbered and named by Him (Psalm 147:4).

God sees what's done in secret and what's done in the light. God is the eternal, cosmic X-ray machine. His eyes penetrate. David says in Psalm 139:12 that the day and the night are alike to God. Moses reminds us that our secret sins are brought to light in His presence (Psalm 90:8). This is powerful information because it means all of our lives are totally known.

That means you never do anything alone. You may be by yourself, but you are not alone. Whether it's good or bad, the all-knowing eye of God sees it. This explains why unregenerate man does not want an omniscient God and why carnal Christians do not want an omniscient God. According to Psalm 73:8–11, because men don't want this kind of God they dismiss Him by telling themselves, "God doesn't know what we're doing."

But God knows. He knows what's done publicly for all to see and what's done privately for none to see. This can be quite intimidating. Before Jeremiah was born, the Scripture says, God knew he would be a prophet (Jeremiah 1:5). In Galatians 1:15–16, Paul says he was appointed to be an apostle to the Gentiles before he was born. God knows.

What Could Have Been

God not only knows what is, He knows what could have been. It's one thing for a person to know actual events, but it's a whole different ballgame for a person to know potential events as well. In Matthew 11, we find Jesus pronouncing this judgment, which reveals His comprehensive knowledge, because Jesus is God:

> Woe to you, Chorazin! Woe to you, Bethsaida! For if the miracles had occurred in Tyre and Sidon which occurred in you, they would have repented long ago in sackcloth and ashes. Nevertheless I say to you, it shall be more tolerable for Tyre and Sidon in the day of judgment, than for you. And you, Capernaum . . . shall descend to Hades; for if the miracles had occurred in Sodom which occurred in you, it would have remained to this day. Nevertheless I say to you that it shall be more tolerable for the land of Sodom in the day of judgment, than for you. (vv. 21–24)

Jesus says if this would have happened, then the people would have done that. That's not what happened, but Jesus said *if* it would have happened, this would have been the certain result. This shows how comprehensive God's omniscience is. He knows the potential as well as the actual events and outcomes of history.

For example, people often speculate that if General Stonewall Jackson had not been killed early in the Civil War, he might have led the Confederacy to victory. Someone else has said that if Adolf Hitler had only listened to the Jewish scientists in Germany, his Nazi regime might have had the atomic bomb first and ruled the world.

We'll never know about these things, but God knows. He also knows your potential history. What if you had been born at another time, in another place, of another race? What if you had married this person instead of that one? God knows what could have been, and because of that you can rest in what is.

Why? Because God could have made your life totally different. But since He allowed you to be as you are, you can have confidence that He didn't change it because He didn't want to change it.

Now don't misread me here. I realize that life often brings us pain and grief: a failed marriage, the loss of a child, a loved one stricken with a deadly illness. When I say that God didn't change your circumstances because He didn't want to, I do *not* mean He is sitting up in heaven letting you suffer needlessly. God permits trials for reasons we don't always understand, but He is able to bring good out of even the worst circumstances. That's what Joseph learned (Genesis 50:20).

Therefore, you're OK right where you are. The omniscience of God can give you confidence because He knows all the possibilities. God has comprehensive knowledge.

Comprehensive Knowledge and Worship

Each Sunday, people all over the world will gather to worship God. Preachers will preach, people will pray, and choirs will sing, all at the same time. God will hear every single vowel of every single syllable of every single word in every single language uttered. He knows every thought of every person. He knows them all right now. He not only knows, He invites us to come to Him with our prayers and praises so He can bask in the enjoyment of them all.

My little granddaughter is talking up a storm right now and coming up with words I'm not even familiar with, which is quite a feat. Inevitably, when we hear them we ask her to say them again, because there is something refreshing about a child coming up with new things. When people come to God on His terms with prayers and praises, God says, "Say it again" because He inhabits the praise of His people. He invites us to worship Him because He's not going to miss one word. He says, "Say it again."

GOD'S OMNISCIENCE IS PERSONAL

The omniscience of God is not only intuitive and comprehensive, but intensely personal. It is vitally related to our day-to-day living. Psalm 139 brings this home in a very graphic way. The psalmist David begins, "O Lord, Thou hast searched *me* and known *me*. Thou dost know when I sit down and when I rise up" (vv. 1–2a, italics added).

God Knows Us

Now, I don't know of a more mundane activity than sitting down and rising up. How many times do you pray before you sit down? How often do you meditate on the fact that it's time to stand up? We don't get into the details of daily life. We just go about them because it's normal to do so. But the Bible says that God is acutely aware of the smallest detail of our lives.

Suppose the next time you sit down, you were to sit on a tack. You would suddenly become acutely aware of this mundane detail. Now suppose the tack was infected, the infection entered your bloodstream and moved throughout your body, and you had to spend a week in the hospital on antibiotics.

Even worse, suppose that by the end of the week the infection had spread so quickly they didn't know whether you were going to live or die. By then you might ask, "Lord, why did you let me sit down on that tack without letting me know it was in the chair?"

*B*UT GOD NOT ONLY KNOWS WHAT YOU DID, HE KNOWS WHY YOU DID IT. EVEN WHEN OTHERS MISREAD YOU, GOD KNOWS THE TRUE STORY.

That isn't likely to happen. But even if you were about to sit on a chair with a bad tack on it, God would see the tack, He would know you were heading toward the chair, and He could protect you. You can praise God for your sitting down and your rising up because He doesn't miss any detail.

David goes on to say, "Thou dost understand my thought from afar" (v. 2b). God is acutely aware of our thinking. Ezekiel 11:5 says that God knows the things that come in our mind. He knows where they came from and how they wound up there. The Bible says that God reads our hearts. He understands every thought and intent of the heart (1 Samuel 16:7).

The psalmist also says, "Thou dost scrutinize my path and my lying down, and art intimately acquainted with all my ways" (Psalm 139:3). In other words, "You scrutinize my direction in life. You look at the way I am traveling." That's why when you are lost, you can pray because God knows the right path to get you back on the right road.

"Even before there is a word on my tongue, behold, O Lord, Thou dost know it all" (v. 4). God knows your thought before it even gets into your mind. Once you have the thought, He knows how it's going to be expressed before it ever reaches your tongue. So by the time the first word gets out of your mouth, God has already waxed eloquent on that information.

No wonder David observes in verse 5: "Thou hast enclosed me behind and before, and laid Thy hand upon me." He's saying, "I'm locked in by Your knowledge." To put it another way, we have nowhere to run, nowhere to hide. God knows all things related to our personal lives. But that's good news, and let me tell you why.

God Understands Us

One day Jesus said, "Sitting under a tree over there is a man named Nathanael, in whom there is no guile" (see John 1:47). Jesus knew Nathanael's motives were pure. Has anyone ever misread your motives? Has anyone ever taken what you intended and turned it totally around? Has your mate ever misunderstood you?

As the old folks used to say, "I've been 'buked and I've been scorned. And I've been talked about sho' as you born." They were saying that people misunderstand us. But God not only knows what you did, He knows *why* you did it. Even when others misread you, God knows the true story.

So if people don't understand you, that's OK. God understands. He knows your true motives. And He not only acts on what you do, He acts on the motives and thoughts *behind* what you do, because He knows why you did it. God is so intimately concerned about the details that He knows everything going on behind the scenes. When Job was going through the fire, he took comfort in this fact: "He knows the way I take" (Job 23:10).

Are you going through a fiery trial although you've done nothing to deserve it? Maybe the doctor has given you a bad health report even though you've done the best you can. You haven't abused your body. Maybe people are walking away on you because you want to do right and they want to go the other way. If you haven't been there yet, just keep living; you will be.

At a time like that Job looked up and said, "I don't understand. I can't figure it all out, but one thing I know is that even when all hell breaks loose, One knows and understands."

Psalm 103:14 says God knows that "we are but dust." He knows we are weak. He knows we can't do all that He commands us to do, even though that ought to be our passion and our goal. He knows we are dust. That's not an excuse, it's reality.

The Bible tells us that God bottles up our tears (see Psalm 56:8). Have you cried recently? Have tears run down your cheeks over a person or situation that caused you pain? God says, "I am saving up your tears. I know every teardrop you shed and I know why you shed it. I'm bottling them up. I care."

No one on earth can give you this. Lady, no man can give you this. He can "rap" it, talking about how he'll always be there and how he'll never leave you alone. He's going to love you forever and a day. He can talk the talk. But just ask him, *Where is your tear bottle?* "God bottles up our tears," the psalmist says. He knows every pain and every heartache.

God Sees Through Us

God also knows when we act as hypocrites, wearing our masks. He knows when we look one way on the outside but are totally different on the inside. The Sadducees and Pharisees of Jesus' day went around fooling the people with their righteous talk, their righteous prayers, and their righteous fasting. But then they ran into Jesus. Being God in the flesh, He looked at them and said, "You are like whitewashed tombs . . . full of dead men's bones" (Matthew 23:27).

Jesus was referring to the Jewish law which said that anyone who touched a grave would be defiled. To avoid defilement, they would whitewash the tombs to mark them clearly so travelers could avoid them. But whitewashing a tomb didn't change the reality that it held dead people's bones.

That grave was still a place of death. It was just a place of death that looked good on the outside. If we're not careful, we can become whitewashed tombs. Some folks are all painted up lovely on the outside, but if we could open their hearts, we'd find rot, treachery, and immorality. You can fool some of the people some of the time, but you can fool God none of the time.

When my mother thought I was doing something wrong, she used to look at me and say, "Son, you can jive the baker because he'll give you a bun, but you can't jive me, because I ain't got none."

She was saying to me, "I'm your mother and I know you."

God says, "I'm your Father and I know you." So it's imperative that we come clean with God because He knows what's on the inside.

GOD'S KNOWLEDGE
IS PURPOSEFUL

God doesn't use His omniscience to win contests. He doesn't play "Jeopardy" or spin the "Wheel of Fortune." Everything God knows is plugged into His eternal purposes.

In Relation to Salvation

Ephesians 1 brings this out in relationship to our salvation. God wants us to know that our salvation was not by luck or chance; that we are not going to heaven because He just happened to look ahead and say, "Oh, you're going to trust Me. Let me hurry up and do something." Instead,

> He chose us in Him before the foundation of the world, that we should be holy and blameless before Him. In love He predestined [predetermined] us to adoption as sons . . . to the praise of the glory of His grace. (vv. 4–6)

God does what He does for reasons. His omniscience is purposeful. The Bible says of Jesus' crucifixion that while unregenerate men killed Him, Jesus was crucified by "the predetermined plan and foreknowledge of God" (Acts 2:23). God was responsible for the death of Jesus even though the means He used was ungodly men. God's purpose in this was that His Son would pay for the sins of the world on the cross.

So God's knowledge is intricately tied to His purposes. This raises the issue of God's wisdom. Very simply, the wisdom of God is the interworking of His attributes to accomplish His will and achieve His purposes. And this, of course, raises the very complex question of the interplay of God's election, predestination, and foreknowledge, particularly as they relate to our salvation.

There are two extremes in my view. The hyper-Calvinistic view says God has already determined everything that will happen, meaning that we have no real choice in anything. We are more like robots carrying out God's predetermined will than agents of moral choice who have legitimate and meaningful decisions to make. But that seems to negate the many clear commands to us in Scripture to do this and avoid that. Those commands also have real consequences attached.

The other extreme is the Arminian view, which postures God as sitting in heaven biting His fingernails, if you will, basing His actions and plans on what He knows we are going to do. Based on what we do, He develops and builds His agenda. But He's not quite sure what we will do. I have overstated the case a little, but the Arminian view waters down God's omniscience. Arminianism separates God's omniscience from His sovereignty and omnipotence.

The tension remains there, no doubt about it. How do we handle the reality that God has determined the events of history and at the same time has made us free moral agents with real choices to make?

Someone might argue the issue like this: "If God knows that I'm going to go to the store tomorrow, do I have any choice but to go to the store tomorrow? Can I choose to go to the store the day *after* tomorrow if God already knows that I am going to the store tomorrow?"

GOD'S KNOWLEDGE AND HIS ETERNAL PURPOSES INTERSECT WITH HUMAN CHOICE IN SUCH A WAY THAT WE HAVE REAL CHOICES TO MAKE, AND YET THOSE CHOICES FULFILL GOD'S PURPOSE TO ACCOMPLISH HIS GOAL.

Yes, you can choose to go the store the day after tomorrow. But that means God knows you are not going to the store tomorrow. He knows you will go to the store the next day. So you do get to choose, but you do not thwart God's foreknowledge by your choice. We've already seen that God has to know everything just by virtue of who He is. If God didn't know even one fact, He would not be the all-knowing God we believe Him to be and the Bible teaches Him to be.

The problem is that many Christians think that because the Bible teaches both God's absolute foreknowledge and our capacity to choose, there has to be some sort of contradiction. Let's look at this in more detail.

The Bible clearly teaches two important facts. First, "[God] desires all men to be saved" (1 Timothy 2:4). This is the burden of His heart. He is not "wishing for any to perish but for all to come to repentance" (2 Peter 3:9).

Second, God did something about His desire. He made provision for everyone to be saved. Jesus tasted death for every person (Hebrews 2:9). "God so loved the world, that He gave His only begotten Son" for the world (John 3:16). Jesus was not only the propitiation for the saints, but for the world (1 John 2:2). Therefore, it is not God's fault that some people are not saved.

Yet on the opposite side, the Bible also clearly teaches that God has elected some to be saved (Ephesians 1:4), meaning that He has passed by others—or as John Calvin taught, He has actively decreed the lost to condemnation.

The tension, therefore, is obvious. How can God elect only some people to be saved while genuinely desiring that all be saved? How can He hold the lost responsible for not getting saved when He didn't elect them in the first place? How could it be fair for God to provide salvation for all, elect only some, and yet judge those who were not elected? How can all of those be true at the same time?

No one has the definitive answer that will settle the issue for all time. All I know is that God's knowledge and His eternal purposes intersect with human choice in such a way that we have real choices to make, and yet those choices fulfill God's purpose to accomplish His goal. An illustration may help us here.

Let's say that three thousand people show up at our church in Dallas next Sunday morning. During the service, I send someone out to buy three thousand cans of Coca-Cola® because I believe everyone needs the refreshment that Coke® can bring, and I want every person to share in the experience of enjoying an ice-cold Coke. So out of the kindness of my heart, I buy Cokes for the entire congregation.

I didn't have to do it, you understand. No one "earned" a Coca-Cola by showing up at church. I could have sent the people away thirsty, but I love them and I want to show them my love. In fact, it costs me everything I have to satisfy the thirst of three thousand people. At the end of the service, I bring in all three thousand ice-cold, refreshing Cokes and say, "Whosoever will may come."

The Cokes have already been paid for. I have one for everybody. Anyone who needs and wants a Coke can take one without charge. No one who comes will be turned away. I wanted the people to have a Coke so badly that I spent every last dime I had to provide them. The only problem is, when the service is dismissed not one person comes up for a Coke.

Some say, "I'm on a diet."

Others say, "It has too much acidity."

Still others say, "I like 7-Up®."

Some even say, "I don't believe I care for a Coke right now. I'm not thirsty."

Absolutely no one accepts my offer of Coke. Everyone walks out, even knowing that I've spent everything I had to provide those cold drinks. But I'm not about to let those drinks go to waste; they were too costly. So I run out to the foyer and call to two hundred people, saying "Come back. I want to talk to you."

All two hundred people come back, so I sit them in the front row of the church and begin wooing them. I remind them that this is not just any beverage, it's the "real thing." I explain how it will refresh and energize them, and how they will love it once they've tasted it. I plead with them not to despise my offer.

The two hundred people I invited back then elect to take a Coke, but only because I elected to call them back. Remember, I wasn't obligated to buy anything for the congregation. I bought those Cokes as an act of pure grace, so I could have let all the people go away and no one could have charged me with any wrong.

I wasn't unfair to the other 2,800 people, because I offered them a real opportunity to satisfy their thirst. And guess what? My Cokes still sit on ice, so if they get thirsty they can come back and get one. And the two hundred can't say they earned their Cokes by their own merit. They only got a Coke because I elected to call them back in. They can only thank me for my grace.

I realize no attempt to explain election and free will can be perfect. But we must accept the clear teaching of the Bible that all men who die separated from God will be held accountable, because Jesus Christ paid for their sins on Calvary. And those of us who are on our way to heaven can never brag, since we will get there only because He came out in the foyer, so to speak, and called us back to Himself.

So God has made provision for all but He's elected some, leaving us with a choice but guaranteeing His plan. If the wisdom of our omnipotent God leaves you shaking your head in wonder and amazement, that's all right. If you or I ever figure God out, we're in trouble!

In Relation to Daily Living

The interplay of God's purposes with our freedom appears not only in salvation, but in our day-to-day Christian life. We find a great example in Luke 22, during the Last Supper. In the middle of the meal Jesus turns to Peter and says: "Simon, Simon, behold, Satan has demanded permission to sift you like wheat; but I have prayed for you, that your faith may not fail; and you, when once you have turned again, strengthen your brothers" (vv. 31–32).

Peter responds immediately. "Lord, with You I am ready to go both to prison and to death!" (v. 33). But in the very next verse, Jesus predicts Peter's failure. He says, "You are going to blow it. You are going to deny Me before all of these people. Satan is going to use your self-confidence to drive you to spiritual defeat. I know this in advance, so I've been praying for you."

Do you know what Jesus is doing in heaven right now? He's praying for you and me (Hebrews 7:25). He's praying for us because in His omniscience He knows that at times we will go down to spiritual defeat, and He wants to deliver us from utter failure. So even though we mess up, we can get up because Jesus is praying for us. Even when He knows in advance that we will not always do what is right, He wants to keep us from doing as much wrong as we could do if He were not praying for us.

Thankfully, the story of Peter doesn't end in Luke 22 but continues in John 21, where Jesus gently restores Peter by asking, "Peter, do you love Me?"

Peter says, "I messed up. I denied You. But I like You."

"Peter, do you love Me?"

"Lord, all I can say is that I like You. I failed You."

Jesus then says, "Peter, if you like Me that's good enough."

But then Peter cries out, "Lord, You know all things. You know that even though I messed up with my mouth, I love You with my heart. And Lord, if You can forgive me even though You knew ahead of time that I would fail, that's all I need to come back home."

That's what the knowledge of God should do for us—bring us back home. Do you know why? Because even though He knew beforehand that we would mess up last week, He still says, "I love you." Paul writes, "But God demonstrates His own love toward us, in that while we were yet sinners, Christ died for us" (Romans 5:8). He knew our mess up, yet He's willing to make up.

RUNNING TO GOD

God loves us in spite of our failure. If we will come back to Him, He will receive us because His love is everlasting. The only thing God chooses to forget is our sin. "I will forgive their iniquity, and their sin I will remember no more" (Jeremiah 31:34).

What will you do with this kind of omnipotent God? You can run from His knowledge like the unregenerate person and act like it doesn't exist. Or you can run to it like Peter. When David looked into God's knowledge of him, he said, "Such knowledge is too wonderful for me" (Psalm 139:6). He went on to say that there is no place a man can hide from God. But that didn't scare him, because he saw that God's thoughts toward him were "precious" (v. 17).

When I first brought my future wife home to meet my parents, I took her to the Gwen Oaks Amusement Park in Baltimore, Maryland. They had a ride called the "Wild Mouse." The Wild Mouse was a little roller coaster that went way out and turned back in, so it almost made you feel like you were falling off before it turned.

Let me tell you why I elected to take Lois on that ride. I knew she would be afraid. I knew she would be in turmoil. I knew she would scream. I knew she would wonder why in the world I took her on this ride.

But my knowledge had a purpose. I knew that when the Wild Mouse went out, she was going to come in. I knew that when we dipped low, she was going to hug high. My knowledge of that led me to take her through that trial so she would run to Papa when tough times hit. God's desire for you to hug Him leads you into that difficult situation, that trial, that hard circumstance. If you are on the roller coaster, grab the Father. He knows. He's the all-knowing, all-wise, all-loving God.

Responding to God's Omniscience

Here are some practical ways you can get the truth we have learned in this chapter off the page and into your life:

1. If sin is a problem for you right now, run to the Father. He already knows about it, so don't try to hide it. Lay it on the table. Confess your sin and claim His forgiveness (1 John 1:9).

2. Thank God that He knows you so thoroughly and loves you so completely. No one will ever know you better or love you more!

3. Give to the Lord that situation in which you were misunderstood, that incident in which someone misread your motives. Forgive the people involved if that's needed, and rest your case with God, realizing that He knows your heart.

4. Read Psalm 139:1–18, then take a look at yourself in the mirror today. Remember that you were created by a God whose knowledge is infinite and who had an infinite number of options to choose from. He knew exactly what He was doing when He chose to create you. Nothing about you is an afterthought!

8
THE OMNIPRESENCE
OF GOD

There is no place in creation where God does not exist—and exist in all His divine fullness. It will take a while to wrap our minds around that thought, but we've got a whole chapter to get used to it.

This is the second of God's "omni" attributes we want to study. The word omnipresence itself is very simple to understand: *Omni* means "all," as we learned in chapter 7. *Presence* is a common word, having to do with locality. The omnipresence of God means that His complete essence is fully present in all places at all times.

These "omni" attributes of God operate in tandem with each other. For instance, God can do anything He wants to do (He's omnipotent) anywhere He wants to do it because He's everywhere (He's omnipresent). God knows everything there is to know (He's omniscient) because all knowledge originates from somewhere, and God is present in every one of those places.

More than that, God can do with that knowledge whatever He chooses because His omnipotence gives Him the power to act on what He knows. And since He is omnipresent, He is always wherever He needs to be to do whatever needs to be done. God's full-orbed character allows Him to function in every sphere of existence.

Most people are not comfortable with an omnipresent God. That's why people like idols: They can see them, touch them, and, most important, control them. Even some people who go to church do not want to worship the God of the Bible. They come to His house of worship, but then they go back to their idols. It could be their money, cars, prestige, power, clothes, or their notoriety, but they want something they can control.

Some have taken this to extremes and created entire theological systems in an attempt to confine, limit, or control God. You are probably familiar with pantheism, which teaches that God is an impersonal force. This idea was popularized in the *Star Wars* movie trilogy, where God was the impersonal "force" and was identified with nature.

Be careful when someone or something emphasizes nature in relation to God, because it usually devalues God. People who identify God with nature want to remove a sovereign Ruler over nature and limit Him to nature.

In pantheism, therefore, everything partakes of God. The trees are a part of God; the mountains are a part of God; and the lakes, streams, and oceans are a part of God. Of course, we are a part of God too, so nobody can sin or be separated from Him or need salvation. God becomes merely the harmless, amoral sum total of all natural elements. That is heresy!

The other extreme is deism. Deism says we have seen God's power, but we don't know much of His presence. God set the universe in motion according to fixed laws, then He turned His attention elsewhere. He is not involved in the daily affairs of this world. He exists way out there, an absentee landlord who has little real involvement with His creation. Again, we don't have the idea that we are morally accountable to God for our sin. Deism is also a heresy.

The omnipresence of God says that our God dwells intimately in history and yet exists totally outside of history. He is both transcendent and immanent at the same time. Let me give you three important truths about the omnipresence of God.

GOD IS FREE OF LIMITATIONS

In 1 Kings 8, Solomon dedicates the magnificent temple he built as a dwelling place for the glory of God so that Israel will know it is God's house. But Solomon did not want the people to get confused and think that God's presence was limited to their building. So he prays in verses 26–27:

> Now therefore, O God of Israel, let Thy word, I pray Thee, be confirmed which Thou has spoken to Thy servant, my father David. But will God indeed dwell on the earth? Behold, heaven and the highest heaven cannot contain Thee, how much less this house which I have built!

No Limitations of Space

God's presence is in the sphere of immensity and infinitude. Infinitude, or infinity, means that which is without limit. Immensity refers to that which cannot be contained. God's presence is so vast that not only is He everywhere in the known universe, but He bursts through the limits of the universe and fills everything we do not even know about.

GOD ENCOMPASSES EVERYTHING EVERYWHERE SO THAT WHATEVER YOU DO, WHEREVER YOU ARE, HE IS RIGHT THERE AND ALL OF HIM IS THERE.

Many of us understand the problem of immensity as we gain weight. We search through the closet and put on clothes, and we begin bursting out of them. When man tries to stuff God into the universe, Solomon says to God, "You burst out of it. It cannot contain You."

God's presence is immense. He cannot be contained. God's presence is also distinct in that all of Him exists everywhere. He is not broken up into parts. Each little piece of the universe has the entire presence of God. We know this because God's being possesses what theologians call simplicity. That is, He cannot be divided. We saw in an earlier chapter that God is spirit; therefore, He exists everywhere at the same time.

You recall that on the night before His crucifixion, Jesus told His disciples, "Let not your heart be troubled" (John 14:1a). They were troubled because after being with them for three years, Jesus was getting ready to leave.

But Jesus continued: "Believe in God, believe also in Me. . . . I go to prepare a place for you" (vv. 1b–2). Then He told them, "I will ask the Father, and He will give you another Helper, that He may be with you forever; that is the Spirit of truth" (vv. 16–17a).

We need to realize that if Jesus Christ were on earth today, we would be miserable, we would be defeated, we would be incomplete. If Jesus Christ were on earth today, we would be abysmal spiritual failures. Why? Because although He was God, Jesus Christ limited His deity to His humanity.

In other words, Jesus could only be in one place at a time. His humanity limited Him to the demands of time and space. Now that would be a problem. When I need Jesus in Dallas, I don't want to hear that He's tied up with you in Fort Worth. Someone in China who needs Jesus doesn't want to hear that He's busy at my church in America. In promising His disciples the Holy Spirit, Jesus was saying, "I'm going to send you someone who can be everywhere with each of you all of the time no matter where you are."

No Limitations of Flesh

God is spirit. He's an uncompounded being. So everything everywhere is encompassed by the presence of God. But He is not like any human leader you've ever met. The president of the United States can be in one place, but people all over the world can see him at the same time by turning on their televisions.

But that's not like God. God encompasses everything everywhere so that whatever you do, wherever you are, He is right there and all of Him is there. You don't have to worry about the fact that I am drawing on His omniscience while someone else is using His omnipotence; that you have His omnipresence while someone else is borrowing His power. God is present everywhere in all the fullness of His deity.

It's like the air and the water. Wherever you have air, you have every component that makes air. You do not divide air. One drop of water has the same components as an ocean. Everything that makes water what it is can be found in that one drop. In the same way (although all attempts to illustrate God break down at some point), to have God with you is to have all of Him with you. And you have as much of God with you as I have with me. Now that's good news.

The problem is, sometimes we don't feel that God is with us. We can't see Him, so we wonder if He's there. But we experience many things we don't see, like a chilly morning or the blowing of the wind. We know the wind is blowing because we see and feel its effects all around us. We have to put on a coat to keep off the chill, or struggle to keep the wind from turning our umbrellas inside out.

This is why the Bible says, "The fool has said in his heart, 'There is no God'" (Psalm 14:1). Only a fool would say to himself, *It's not chilly,* or *It's not windy,* when all the evidence pointed to the contrary and all he had to do to confirm it was go outside and feel the cold.

It's obvious to anyone who goes outside that God's presence is everywhere. Just as light and air fill a room, God fills the universe and more. He is omnipresent. We can trick ourselves into thinking otherwise by becoming spiritual ostriches. Ostriches are said to put their heads in the ground when danger approaches, and they actually think that because they can't see you, you can't see them. That's the way a lot of people live. They put their heads in the spiritual sand and say, "We can't see God, so God can't see us."

GOD IS WITH US

But God is in all the nooks and crannies and crevices of life. Some people say, for example, "I don't think my prayers are getting past the ceiling." They don't have to get even that high. God stands in the room with us. As I said before, we are dealing with a Being unlike anyone we've ever met because He lives in infinity. We are limited to space. We can only be in one place at a time. He has none of these limitations.

It's important to understand that Satan is not omnipresent. He is a created being who can be only one place at a time. But if Satan is limited, how can he seem to be everywhere causing so much trouble all the time? Because he's the ruler of a demonic kingdom (Ephesians 2:2). He has a vast army to whom he issues orders, and Satan is so effective because his followers do what God's followers too often don't. They obey, and in their obedience they wreak havoc.

But Satan is not omnipresent. That's why John can declare, "Greater is He who is in you than he who is in the world" (1 John 4:4). "He who is in you" is everywhere equally all the time. That's the God we have. We have a God who is free from the limitations of space. My enslaved foreparents didn't understand all the technical terminology of God's omnipresence, but they could tell you this:

He's so high, you can't get over Him.
He's so low, you can't get under Him.
He's so wide, you can't get around Him.

GOD IS INTIMATELY
INVOLVED WITH CREATION

David raises a very important question in Psalm 139:7 when he asks, "Where can I go from Thy Spirit? Or where can I flee from Thy presence?" Then he begins to speculate on what he would find if he went to the farthest corners of the universe:

> If I ascend to heaven, Thou art there; if I make my bed in Sheol, behold, Thou art there. If I take the wings of the dawn, if I dwell in the remotest part of the sea, even there Thy hand will lead me, and Thy right hand will lay hold of me. (vv. 8–10)

Too Big to Avoid

This reminds me of the story of the man who was walking in the marketplace of Damascus and came face-to-face with Death. The man noticed an expression of surprise on Death's face. The man himself was terrified, looking Death in the face, knowing that it had come for him. So he took off running and went to a wise friend for advice. "In the marketplace I just saw Death, and he was staring me right in the face. What should I do?"

The wise man said, "What you've got to do is run to the city of Aleppo. Go to that city and get away from Death."

So the man got on his horse and reached Aleppo in record time to get away from Death. When he arrived, he wiped his brow and congratulated himself that he had escaped Death. But just then, Death came up to him and tapped him on the shoulder. "Excuse me, but I have come for you."

The man looked at him and said, "How can this be? I thought I met you in Damascus yesterday."

Death looked at him and said, "Exactly! That's why I looked so surprised when I saw you, because I was scheduled to meet you in Aleppo today."

That's what running from God is like. When you run from Him and you get to where you were going, you bump into Him. There is nowhere to run, nowhere to hide. David says, "No matter where I go, I run into You." But this is good news to the psalmist, because he goes on to say in verses 11–12:

> If I say, "Surely the darkness will overwhelm me, and the light
> around me will be night," even the darkness is not dark to thee,
> and the night is as bright as the day. Darkness and light are alike
> to Thee.

No matter where he went, David knew that he would run into
the sustaining hand and presence of God.

Too Close to Ignore

The good thing about God is He's so big you can't get over
Him, but He's so close you can't get away from Him. That means
He's near you today. I don't know what you are facing, but He's
right beside you—and because He's omniscient, He knows what's
going on. He's not a "do nothing" God.

God is intimately involved and ever-present in your life, and
therefore aware of all you are going through. As the Bible says in
Acts 17:28: "in Him we live and move and exist." In the same way
air surrounds us, we are surrounded by God.

A man in Scripture tried to run from God. Jonah was a prophet,
a man whose job it was to carry the truth of God to people who
needed to hear it. But when God told him to go to the Ninevites,
Israel's cruel enemies, Jonah didn't want to do it. My purpose here
is not to retell the entire story of Jonah, but to note a few key
points.

For example, Jonah 1:3 is a classic. God said go, Jonah said no:

> But Jonah rose up to flee to Tarshish from the presence of the
> Lord. So he went down to Joppa, found a ship which was going
> to Tarshish, paid the fare, and went down into it to go with them
> to Tarshish from the presence of the Lord.

Note that Jonah "paid the fare" himself because he was trying to
run from God. Whenever you run *with* God, He pays the fare. But
when you try to run from God, you always pay.

Jonah thought he had run away from God, but he forgot something. You can't run from God without running through Him and
winding up running toward Him. Jonah got on that ship, but God
took care of the problem by ordering the sea to track Jonah down.
A fierce storm erupted on the sea. The waves rose and pointed a
finger right at Jonah.

Jonah went two thousand miles to Tarshish when he should
have gone just five hundred miles to Nineveh. When you run from

God, the trip is always longer and harder than it would be if you stayed with Him. Whenever you run from God, you wind up being greatly inconvenienced. But when you run to God because you know He is intimately involved with you, you can get to where you want to go without all the hassles in between.

But that was just the beginning. After the sailors tossed Jonah overboard, God sent him a "whale-o-gram," a fish to pick him up out of the water. God brought Jonah back and finally got him to Nineveh. The people repented, but Jonah wasn't happy about it and took off again, going out east of the city to pout over God's sparing of Israel's enemies (Jonah 4:5).

Jonah wasn't running from God in the same way as he was in chapter 1, but God still had to go after him. What a lineup God used. No waves or "whale-o-grams" this time, but a plant, a worm, and a "scorching east wind" (4:8). It's all at His command, and God can tell the waves or the wind what to do with you when you get to where you think you have moved beyond His presence.

Too Caring to Ignore Us

God knows where He wants to take us and how He wants to get us there. God calls on us to understand that He is intimately involved with us. Having a God who is everywhere and associated with everything means we have nothing we can't bring to His attention. He is acutely aware because He's intimately there. He can identify with the hurts, the struggles, and the pain. He can identify with our difficulties because He is intimately associated with each of us.

GOD'S OMNIPRESENCE BRINGS SPECIAL BENEFITS

We need to be clear on this one. Even though God is equally present everywhere in all of His fullness, He is *not* equally related to everyone and everything. In other words, we have an equality of essence, but not of relationship. God relates to things and people differently, even though He exists equally with them all. The Bible says, for example, that people need to call on God "while He is near" (Isaiah 55:6). That statement does not refer to God's essence, but to the way He relates to people.

Again, the prophet says that God's people "remove[d] their hearts far from Me" (Isaiah 29:13). This is a moral and spiritual statement, since no one can get away from an omnipresent God.

God the Father was present when Jesus died on the cross, yet we know that Jesus looked up and said, "My God! My God! Why hast Thou forsaken Me?"

EVEN WHEN THINGS SEEM TO BE GOING WRONG, THEY JUST COULD BE GOING RIGHT BECAUSE WHEN YOU'RE IN GOD'S WILL, THE NEGATIVES ARE PART OF HIS POSITIVE PROGRAM.

The Bible teaches that God adjusts His presence, so to speak, to things and people based on how He is related to them. Isaiah 43:1–7 brings this out very directly:

> But now, thus says the Lord, your Creator, O Jacob, and He who formed you, O Israel, "Do not fear, for I have redeemed you; I have called you by name; you are Mine! When you pass through the waters, I will be with you; and through the rivers, they will not overflow you. When you walk through the fire, you will not be scorched, nor will the flame burn you. For I am the Lord your God, The Holy One of Israel, your Savior; I have given Egypt as your ransom, Cush and Seba in your place. Since you are precious in My sight, since you are honored and I love you, I will give other men in your place and other peoples in exchange for your life. Do not fear, for I am with you; I will bring your offspring from the east, and gather you from the west. I will say to the north, 'Give them up!' And to the south, 'Do not hold them back.' Bring My sons from afar, and My daughters from the ends of the earth, everyone who is called by My name, and whom I have created for My glory, whom I have formed, even whom I have made."

You can't miss the point here. God takes care of His own. He is present with His children in a way that He is not present with those who don't know Him. If you know Jesus Christ today, you have a special relationship with God. He doesn't relate to you in the same way He relates to the unredeemed sinner. God treats you as His child, as part of His family. You enjoy the special, relational presence of God.

Talk about benefits. It's one thing to say that God is everywhere. It's quite another to realize that because you are His child, He's with you everywhere you go.

But if we're going to enjoy all the benefits of God's special presence, we obviously need to know what they are. I want to discuss some of the major areas where we as God's children ought to be enjoying the benefits of His special presence.

Guidance

If you are a child of God, you get what nonbelievers cannot get: His special guidance.

Jacob found that out in a dramatic way in Genesis 28. He was fleeing from Esau after stealing his birthright. On his flight he stopped for the night. With a stone for a pillow, he went to sleep and had his famous dream of the ladder going from earth to heaven and the angels of God ascending and descending on the ladder.

In his dream, Jacob also saw God standing above the ladder. God reaffirmed His covenant promises to Jacob (vv. 13–14), then He declared, "I am with you, and will keep you wherever you go, and will bring you back to this land; for I will not leave you until I have done what I have promised you" (v. 15). What a promise! No wonder Jacob woke up and said, "Surely the Lord is in this place, and I did not know it" (v. 16).

God is there when you feel Him and when you don't feel Him. He's there when you sense Him and when you don't sense Him. He constantly leads you to keep His promise that He's going to do with you what He said He would do, even when it looks like He isn't doing anything with you. Even when things seem to be going wrong, they just could be going right because when you're in God's will, the negatives are part of His positive program.

Victory over Temptation

Another benefit you get as a child of God is victory over temptation. Paul says in 1 Corinthians 10:13 that "no temptation has overtaken you but such as is common to man; and God is faithful, who will . . . provide the way of escape also, that you may be able to endure it."

How does God's presence bear on your temptations? Paul says that "your body is a temple of the Holy Spirit" (1 Corinthians 6:19). Wherever you go, God goes; whatever you do, God does; you can go no place where He is not. That's why He can provide a way of escape. He knows what door you need to run through. He's with you when you are being tempted.

But this is also a call to holiness because it means that God stays with you when you fail, when you sin. In the context of the verse I just quoted, Paul is talking about the sin of sexual immorality. He says that when you engage in a sexual relationship outside of marriage, you have engaged God in the affair. It's not a private matter done in a secret room, in other words. Why? Because "you are not your own" (v. 19).

Now you haven't contaminated God, anymore than the sun can be contaminated by shining on cow dung. But His presence is associated with us when we sin. We've got to understand that when we sin, it's as if we were doing it in God's throne room. He watches us do what we're doing, think what we're thinking, say what we're saying, act like we're acting. He asks us, "How could you do that with Me standing here?"

That's why when we do sin, we must confess it because God is already in on it. He watched the whole act and heard the whole conversation. He was there during your time of temptation. Sometimes when we want to do wrong, we look to the right and left, behind us, ahead of us, underneath everything, and conclude that no one is watching. But He who sits high and looks low is watching. He's in us, around us, over us, under us, and beside us. He is the all-present God.

Provision for Needs

God's special, relational presence is also available to us in our needs. For example, have you ever had bills you can't pay, financial turmoil you can't handle? Hebrews 13:5 has a glorious promise for you, but an important condition is attached to it. The first half of the verse says, "Let your character be free from the love of money, being content with what you have."

That's often the problem, isn't it? We are not content, and so we don't experience God's special presence. We would be further along financially today if we had been more content yesterday. But because we weren't content yesterday, we got into debt yesterday that we can't pay today. Now we don't have enough to get us through, but it's not because God didn't supply. It's because we weren't content with what He gave us.

How can we be content even though the bills keep coming? Glad you asked, because here's the promise in the last half of verse 5:

"For He Himself has said, 'I will never desert you, nor will I ever forsake you.'" It's so good let's keep on reading to verse 6: "So that we confidently say, 'The Lord is my helper, I will not be afraid. What shall man do to me?'"

You can be content with what you have because you have God's forever presence. Therefore, you don't have to be afraid of recession or inflation. You just need to be content in the apartment God has provided for you until He gives you the ability to afford a house.

You may say, "But I don't see where the money will come from to pay my bills." You don't see God either, do you? But you know He's there. You don't have to see Him to know that He's at work. The Lord is an entrepreneur par excellence. He can provide funds in ways you never even thought of. He can change any circumstance, but first He has to get you free from the love of money. Otherwise, it won't do any good to deliver you from financial bondage because you'll soon be right back.

You see, some of us love money so much we don't have time to go to church. We love money so much we can't give any to the Lord because we are paying the bills we ran up satisfying our own pleasure. We don't work to live, we live to work, but we are never content. God can tell us to be content because He has promised us His presence.

Here's another great one. Paul says, "My God shall supply all your needs according to His riches in glory in Christ Jesus" (Philippians 4:19). But the context of this promise discusses liberal giving to God's work.

Freedom from the love of money and contentment are what keep us from trying to turn God's promises of supply into a "health and wealth gospel." You can't command God to make you wealthy. It won't do you any good to run up a bunch of bad bills and then bring them to church in a wheelbarrow for someone to pray over them and demand that God pay them. It doesn't work like that.

I'm not saying don't try to improve or get ahead. I'm saying to be content on the way there. Paul gives us invaluable insight on this in Philippians 4:11–13. He calls what he learned a "secret," and it must be a secret because so few folk seem to know about it. Whether he had nothing or was abundantly supplied, Paul had learned to be content with what God provided because he had learned, "I can do all things through Him who strengthens me" (v. 13).

He is saying that God's presence stays with you even when you are not where you want to be. More than that, God can get you where you need to go if you will do it His way. "Let your character be free from the love of money." Set your spiritual priorities. I think of the single parents in my church who are lonely and struggling to make ends meet. I remind them what God once said to a young servant named Hagar.

Hagar was pregnant with Abraham's child, but Sarah drove her out of the house (Genesis 16:6). Hagar sat out by herself in the desert with no one to care for her. She was in distress, wondering, "How am I going to make it?"

But the angel of the Lord came to Hagar and told her, "Wipe those tears. Everything is going to be all right. Return to Sarah's house. I will take care of you." Then Hagar called the God who spoke to her *El Roi,* "the God who sees" (v. 13). Even in Hagar's loneliness and distress, she wasn't alone. The all-present God saw her and took note of her need. This was important to Hagar because later Sarah sent her packing for good (see Genesis 21:14), and Hagar became a single parent, alone with her son in the scorching desert.

Freedom from Anxiety

God lets you get lonely so you will discover what kind of friend He can really be. The truth is, some of us haven't gotten lonely enough yet. We don't run to God when no one else is around. Instead, we go looking for someone else instead of saying, "Lord, let me snuggle up to You."

No, you can't see God, but you don't have to see Him to know He is there. As I said earlier, you don't have to see the wind for it to affect you. If it's blowing hard enough, it will turn your umbrella inside out, pull your coat off your back, make your car swerve as you drive down the road.

You don't need to see God to know that He's right by your side. He only has to let the wind of His spirit blow by you in that lonely room, or wherever you are. The good news of God's relational presence is that you can talk to Him no matter what you are doing, no matter what the time of day, no matter what your circumstance. The old folk knew that. That's why even when they were doing the work of slaves, they would be singing about God's amazing grace. They understood.

In your lonely time, God is present. When you are afraid, when the crime rate goes up, when you don't know how you are going to make it, God is with you. In Isaiah 41:10, God makes this wonderful promise: "Do not fear, for I am with you; do not anxiously look about you, for I am your God. I will strengthen you, surely I will help you, surely I will uphold you with My righteous right hand."

When life's challenges hit you, when you're facing something you've never faced before, God says, "I'm omniscient. I know what you're facing. I'm omnipresent. I'm with you as you face it. And I'm omnipotent. I can do the job. So are you going to trust yourself or trust Me? Without Me, you can do nothing."

Remember Moses in Exodus 3–4? He told God, "I can't lead this people."

God said, "Yes, you can."

But Moses objected, "I can't talk. I'm not skilled in speech. How am I supposed to do this?"

God said, "I'm going to go with you, that's how."

God not only told this to Moses, He told it to Moses' spiritual son, Joshua. When Joshua took over from Moses, God told him not to be afraid because God's presence would be with him just as it had been with Moses (Joshua 1:5, 9). Joshua just had to be obedient to what God had commanded.

It makes all the difference when you know that God is going to be there. The prophet Elisha was once surrounded by the armies of Syria in Dothan (2 Kings 6:8–14). As Elisha's servant stepped out of the house that morning, he saw a huge Syrian army circling the city. In great distress, he ran in to Elisha and cried, "What shall we do?" (v. 15).

Elijah replied, "Don't worry about it."

This poor servant was saying, "What do you mean, don't worry about it? We're getting ready to die and you're saying, 'Don't worry about it?!'"

Then the Bible says that Elisha bowed his head and said, "O Lord, I pray, open his eyes" (v. 17). The scales dropped from the servant's eyes and he saw the mountain filled with an army of angels. That Syrian army wasn't going anywhere! They weren't going to do anything because God's presence was with His people.

Maybe today you don't need a new neighborhood to live in. Maybe you need to see God's angels surrounding your current neighborhood. The same thing could be said about your job, your financial circumstances, and a whole host of other things. The challenge all of us face is to see God's presence surrounding us, not just to escape the trial. That's why Peter urges us to keep our conscience sensitive toward God, so that when we suffer we can know that our suffering has a purpose (1 Peter 2:19).

Let me state it once again. God is with you if you are with God. He's with you regardless in His essence, but I'm talking about His relational presence. Those of us who are married know what it means to have a mate who is there, but not there. Sometimes, my wife looks at me and knows I'm not listening to her, even though I can repeat everything she said. My mind is a million miles away. It's possible for humans to be there and yet not be there. God is present everywhere, but only His children who are committed and following Him experience the special "there" of His comforting, strengthening, reassuring presence.

So what's the bottom line? Philippians 4:6–7 tells us:

> Be anxious for nothing, but in everything by prayer and supplication with thanksgiving let your requests be made known to God. And the peace of God, which surpasses all comprehension, shall guard your hearts and your minds in Christ Jesus.

When you thought you were going to go under and lose your house, do you know why you are still living there? God carried you. When you thought that losing your job was going to be the end of the world, God carried you. In fact, you are still eating today because God carries you. And He will continue to carry you until one day He carries you home.

Responding to God's Omnipresence

I sn't it good to know that God is there? Since that's true, we need to do what little children do when their world comes caving in. Even though they may be crying, they know who to run to, who to hug. God has His arms open for you. Here are some ways you can make the truth of God's omnipresence real in your life this week:

1. Make sure that if God wanted to speak to you today, He wouldn't have to battle other distractions—or, like with Jonah, send His "waves" after you just to get your attention. Turn off the TV or lay aside the newspaper a little earlier than usual for the next few days, and spend those extra minutes enjoying His presence.

2. Perhaps you're angry at God right now because it seems He has forgotten or abandoned you. If so, don't let another day go by without dealing with your hurt. Be honest before Him; He can handle the truth. If it would help, discuss your problem with your pastor or a trusted friend, and ask for prayer support.

3. The reality of God's presence should renew your confidence in prayer. Look at your prayer list today and pick out your toughest circumstance, greatest need, or biggest fear. Thank God that He is present in this situation, and ask Him for the grace to continue praying about it and awaiting His answer.

4. Be sure you are taking full advantage of God's presence and promise of victory in spiritual warfare. Read over the Christian's list of armor in Ephesians 6 and "polish up" any piece of your armor that may have become a little rusty.

9
THE OMNIPOTENCE OF GOD

We have seen that there is nothing God does not know; that's His omniscience. There is no place He does not exist; that's His omnipresence. But in addition to those, there is nothing God cannot do; that's His *omnipotence*.

As we look at the omnipotence of God, we once again enter a realm far beyond anything we have ever experienced before. All of us are concerned at one level or another with the issue of power. People want political power. Our generation has seen the power of atomic energy unleashed. In the past few years we have seen the power of nature in unforgettable ways as water, wind, fire, and earthquakes have wreaked havoc on this country.

But we will see that none of these can even begin to compare to the power, the omnipotence of God. We already know that *omni* means "all." Therefore, God is all-powerful. But His omnipotence involves more than just raw power. God's omnipotence includes the exercise of His choice to use His unlimited power to reflect His divine glory and accomplish His sovereign will.

Like His other attributes, God's omnipotence has a moral base. He does not just do things to impress people. He uses His power to magnify His glory and accomplish His perfect will. One of the false gospels written in the early days tells a story about Jesus when He was a boy. It seems He and some friends made birds out of clay, but because Jesus was God, He turned His bird into a real one and it flew away.

That's not the omnipotent God of the Bible. He's not strutting His stuff—but make no mistake, God is powerful. The sum total of all the power in all the universe would be like a toenail on the person of God. I want you to see four things that will help us understand our great God and His omnipotent power.

GOD'S POWER IS UNLIMITED

God's power knows no limits. Because He is infinite, He is infinitely powerful. Since His being is unlimited, so is His power. Isaiah asks, "Do you not know? Have you not heard? The Everlasting God, the Lord, the Creator of the ends of the earth does not become weary or tired. His understanding is inscrutable" (Isaiah 40:28).

The psalmists agree. David declares, "Power belongs to God" (Psalm 62:11). "Great is our Lord, and abundant in strength," the writer says in Psalm 147:5. That's why the Bible says that a person has to degenerate into a fool to deny that God exists and that He is extremely powerful. No one is born an atheist; people have to go to college to conclude that God does not exist.

Creative Power

All that has ever been made or that will ever be made was created by the power of God. According to Psalm 89:11, "The heavens are Thine, the earth also is Thine; the world and all it contains, Thou hast founded them." God can create a universe because He has no limitations. He has made things we haven't even discovered yet. And when we add to this the fact that God is infinitely greater than all of His creation, we are talking about Someone who is unbelievable in power.

One Sunday a little boy was standing in the church foyer waiting for his family. The pastor saw him, and knowing that the boy had just come from Sunday school, decided to ask him a few questions. "Young man, if you can tell me something God can do, I will give you a shiny new apple."

The boy looked up at the pastor thoughtfully and said, "Sir, if you can tell me something God can't do, I will give you a whole box of apples!" The challenge is not finding something God can do, but trying to find something He can't do because He is absolutely unlimited in power.

Now autonomous man has turned away in rebellion from this fact and taken refuge in science. In science classes at every level of education, especially in college and postgraduate work, you find that puny, independent, insignificant, rebellious, on-his-way-to-the-grave man has dismissed God from the discussion and decided to take His place. Mankind does not want to give credit to anyone or anything greater than himself.

But do you know what true science is? It is the process of observing the consistency of God. Scientists look for consistent patterns. When they see that a pattern does not change, they call it a law. But then they give nature the credit for this law when they have really only discovered that God is consistent. He never meant for us to take credit for His work or to give the credit to some ambiguous entity called nature.

God's power is difficult for us to grasp because of our limitations. Maybe this illustration will help. Did you know that I can lift a ton? You may not believe it, but I can. So now you're going to say, "Show me." All right, just let me hitch a ride on the next space probe that lands on the moon. Then turn on your television and watch me lift a ton.

How can I do that? Because the law of gravity is vastly different on the moon than it is on earth. What would be impossible for me on earth is easy on the moon because I'm in a different sphere and I have different power. On the moon I am less limited by the law that says, "What goes up must come down."

In other words, if you change my environment, I can do things I can't do now. We have problems with the power of God because we keep Him in our environment. We try to limit Him to what we know on earth, so we just know that He can't do this or that. But God lives in a realm far beyond us, and His power operates according to vastly different rules.

"Out of Nothing" Power

God is not only unlimited in what He can do. He is unlimited in how He gets it done. God's power is so limitless that He can create ex nihilo, meaning "out of nothing." He did not need raw material to put together His creation. None of us has ever seen anything created ex nihilo.

Neither has science, which shows the foolishness of evolution. Evolutionists want to bring everything from nothing, but the process has never been observed in any laboratory. Yet the Bible declares that God "calls into being that which does not exist" (Romans 4:17). That's power! It's one thing to have the power to form something; but to make something with nothing requires real power.

Effortless Power

You need to know about God's unlimited power that it is effortless. He does not exert energy to do what He wants to get done. He doesn't strain, grunt, or groan. He doesn't get sweaty because something is too hard to lift or too difficult to make. We just read in Isaiah 40:28 that God does not get weary.

Self-generating Power

This is because God's power is self-generating. It can be compared to a generator that always runs and never needs fueling or fixing. God never needs anything outside of Himself to generate or sustain His power. His omnipotence is such that by His speaking the word, "the heavens were made" (Psalm 33:6). "He spoke, and it was done" (v. 9), because God generates His power within Himself.

IT TAKES NO MORE EFFORT FOR GOD TO CREATE A UNIVERSE THAN IT DOES FOR HIM TO CREATE AN ANT.

One of the best examples of God's power is the angel Gabriel's visit to Mary in Luke 1. Let me paraphrase the conversation. The angel said, "Mary, you are going to have a baby. And what's more, He will be the Son of God!"

Mary pondered this and said, "How can this be? I'm not even married."

The angel continued (and now I'm quoting), "The power of the Most High will overshadow you" (v. 35). Then he added, "Not only are you going to have a baby as a virgin, but your cousin Elizabeth is going to have a son in her old age, even though her womb is barren."

How could all of this happen? The angel had the answer: "Nothing will be impossible with God" (v. 37). The virgin birth could happen because it was God's virgin birth. If you take Him out of the picture, it's impossible. But once you include God, it's a whole new situation.

The disciples had a hard time grasping the power of God. They once watched a rich young man approach Jesus and then go away sorrowful (Mark 10:17–22). Then they heard Jesus say, "It is easier for a camel to go through the eye of a needle than for a rich man to enter the kingdom of God" (v. 25).

That was too much, so they asked, "Then who can be saved?" (v. 26).

Jesus answered, "With men it is impossible, but not with God; for all things are possible with God" (v. 27).

People often say that God has to show them His power before they'll believe. But He *has* shown us His power. The evidence of it surrounds us. God asked Job a very interesting question: "Where were you when I laid the foundation of the earth!" (Job 38:4). God was saying, "I didn't have to get advice or help from you to pull any of this off."

Think about this. It takes no more effort for God to create a universe than it does for Him to create an ant. All He has to do is say, "Ant be," and you've got an ant. He says, "Universe be," and You've got a universe. No effort is involved here.

Some time ago, I came out to my kitchen late at night and found a roach on my counter. But this was unlike any other roach I had ever seen. This was a "jump bad in your face, get down" roach. I walked up to the roach, but this brother didn't run away. He just stood there as if to say, "Look, this is my house."

I couldn't believe it. It was amazing to look at this thing. I would move my hand in front of it, and it did not move. Obviously, he did not know who I was, because I squashed that boy flat!

That's what autonomous man does. He gets "roachy" on God. He pops back like he is someone, like he has a little power. He's got a little degree behind his name. He's got some machines that can take him into outer space, and he thinks he's got some power. But it's suicide to "jump bad" against God. He has unlimited power.

GOD'S OMNIPOTENCE
IS BROAD IN SCOPE

The prophet Jeremiah says, "Ah Lord God! Behold, Thou hast made the heavens and the earth by Thy great power and by Thine outstretched arm! Nothing is too difficult for Thee" (Jeremiah 32:17).

Once you know God can make the universe, nothing else is hard. If He can pull that off, He can do anything because the universe includes everything. God's power is broad in its scope and its sweep. He has power over nature. That's why you cannot equate the power of God with nature.

Power over Nature

If you don't believe God has power over nature, ask Pharaoh. Ask the children of Israel, who went through the Red Sea and saw God hold back nature and then collapse it on the Egyptians. Ask the people of Sodom and Gomorrah after the brimstone fell from heaven to destroy those two cities. Ask Noah's family after it rained for forty days and forty nights. Ask the disciples who were in the boat with Jesus when He said, "Peace, be still!"

Not only does God have power over nature, but His power is so broad that it sustains as well as creates things. The author of Hebrews puts it this way: "He [Jesus] is the radiance of His [the Father's] glory and the exact representation of His nature, and upholds all things by the word of His power" (Hebrews 1:3).

The word *upholds* means "to sustain." As I said in an earlier chapter, we don't fly off the earth because God sustains the law of gravity. The earth doesn't spin out of its orbit because He keeps it intact. We don't burn or freeze to death because God keeps the sun at just the right distance from us.

You aren't holding this book right now because you jogged and kept yourself healthy. It's because the power of God sustains you. God upholds things by the word of His power. He keeps them on track. He keeps them going. He holds the universe together. He can keep your life together and sustain your marriage because He is the great Sustainer.

Power to Give Life

We keep coming back to Psalm 139 as we talk about these "omni" attributes of God. That's because the psalm talks about all three: God's omniscience, His omnipresence, and His omnipotence. David is meditating on the greatness of God, and he says in verses 13–14: "Thou didst form my inward parts; Thou didst weave me in my mother's womb. I will give thanks to Thee, for I am fearfully and wonderfully made."

Any doctor will tell you that the two cells which come together in a mother's womb already carry the DNA code to determine the baby's race, height, and every other trait down to the shape of its nose. God has to know what He's doing to pull that off! He has to be powerful.

Suppose both of your ears were located on the same side of your face. Suppose you had one eye in the middle of your forehead. Suppose your legs came up out of your shoulders, and your arms out of your hips. You wouldn't be a person, you'd be a monster. But God knows where everything goes. Science can't explain it, but a little child can tell you, "God made me."

Here's the problem with abortion, by the way. Abortion destroys that which has been woven by God. That's the issue, not the freedom a woman has over her body, not even the "rights" of a mother or of her baby. David says, "I was a person even in my mother's womb. I was a person because You knit me together very skillfully."

Power over the Enemy

God's power is seen in His ability to create life. It's also seen in His ability to handle the other side of life—the demons. In Matthew 8:28–34, Jesus came upon two demon-possessed men. They had lost their minds and turned violent as a result of this demonic oppression. The demons saw Jesus and cried out, knowing what His power could do to them. So the demons asked Jesus for permission to leave the men and go into a herd of pigs nearby. Jesus dismissed the demons, who entered the herd of pigs and destroyed them.

The devil wants to destroy you, but one Person has more power than the devil and his entire realm, and that is God. He is the only One who can dismiss those things that will drive you crazy and tear you apart.

Power over Illness

God also has power over illness. Luke 9:11 says the people brought their sick ones to Jesus, and He healed them. I could multiply examples here, but it would take the rest of the chapter.

Power over Circumstances

God has power over circumstances. This is another of the wonderful lessons that Jeremiah learned. God told the prophet, "I'm going to judge Israel by bringing the Babylonians in to destroy the nation and carry you off." But with the city of Jerusalem under siege by the Babylonians, God told Jeremiah to buy himself a plot of land (Jeremiah 32:6–9).

Jeremiah obeyed and bought the land, although as he thought about it later, it seemed to make about as much sense as arranging deck chairs on the *Titanic*. In verse 25, he expressed his misgivings to God. After all, wasn't Israel about to be carried off into captivity? What good would a piece of land do Jeremiah?

ONLY GOD HAS POWER OVER LIFE AND DEATH AND EVERYTHING IN BETWEEN. HIS OMNIPOTENCE IS BROAD IN SCOPE.

The prophet was distressed. His circumstances were bad, but God had another word for him. First, though, the Lord needed to establish some ground rules. So He asked Jeremiah, "Behold, I am the Lord, the God of all flesh; is anything too difficult for Me?" (v. 27). This was not a multiple-choice question, so Jeremiah knew the answer had to be no.

Why did God make this declaration of His omnipotence? Because He was about to tell Jeremiah that when the captivity of Israel was finished, He would bring the nation back to its land and the people would enjoy prosperity again (vv. 36–44). Then Jeremiah's deed would mean something. The negative was not the last word because God has power over circumstances.

Power over Death

God is even more powerful than death. By His power every man, woman, boy, and girl who has ever lived will be raised from the dead.

I will never forget preaching a funeral in Philadelphia for two friends of mine, a young man and his wife who had been viciously murdered. My associate at Oak Cliff, Pastor Martin Hawkins, was with me. It was a huge funeral because of how this couple died. They were lying side by side in a two-person casket.

At the graveyard, as the casket was being lowered into the ground, a man broke through the crowd, stood over the grave, and commanded the couple to rise from the dead. I looked at Pastor Hawkins, he looked at me, and we were trying to decide who was going to run to the car first.

Nothing happened that day. But let me tell you, whenever Jesus said to a dead person, "Get up!" that person got up. He called Lazarus from the grave, and Lazarus came out bound in graveclothes even though he had been dead for three days. Jesus had to tell someone to unwind Lazarus and let him go.

Now that's good news, because when the doctor says to your family, "He's gone," if you know Jesus He is going to say at the same time, "Get up! Come on out of there and come home."

Because only God has power over death, no one else can offer you that hope. Many people believe in reincarnation today. But I want to know, who oversees the reincarnating? Who's in charge here? Who has the power to bring you back from a past life to this life to a future life? No one can do that, because only God has power over life and death and everything in between. His omnipotence is broad in scope.

GOD'S OMNIPOTENCE
IS PURPOSEFUL

Let's look at what God says about a man who up to this point was known as Abram:

> Now when Abram was ninety-nine years old, the Lord appeared to Abram and said to him, "I am God Almighty; walk before Me, and be blameless. And I will establish My covenant between Me and you, and I will multiply you exceedingly." And Abram fell on his face, and God talked with him, saying, "As for Me, behold, My covenant is with you, and you shall be the father of a multitude of nations. No longer shall your name be called Abram, but your name shall be Abraham; for I will make you the father of a multitude of nations." (Genesis 17:1–5)

Now if you know anything about the story, you know we've got a problem here. God promises a ninety-nine-year-old man that "a multitude of nations" will come from him and his eighty-nine-year-old wife, who has never been able to have kids anyway. Ask any nursing home worker, and he or she will tell you that you have a problem on your hands when you make that kind of promise.

But that's exactly what God did. In Genesis 18, the Lord told Abraham,

> "I will surely return to you at this time next year; and behold, Sarah your wife shall have a son." And Sarah was listening at the tent door, which was behind him. Now Abraham and Sarah were old, advanced in age; Sarah was past childbearing. And Sarah laughed to herself, saying, "After I have become old, shall I have pleasure, my Lord being old also?" (vv. 10–12)

The idea of getting pregnant at her age, especially when she looked at old Abraham, struck Sarah as so improbable that she laughed at God. But Sarah did give birth to Isaac, and Abraham did father a nation called Israel. God said that this nation would never, ever be destroyed. And when everyone said this nation was gone, they raised their flag May 1948 and became a nation again because the omnipotence of God is purposeful.

Now if you are eighty-nine years old and pray, "Lord, I want to get pregnant," you may have a problem. It's not that God can't do with you what He did with Sarah, but in His purposes it is not necessary. He had a specific purpose in Sarah's pregnancy. Her child was the fulfillment of God's covenant promise. He was building a great nation through which He would show the world His mighty power and grace, and starting that nation through a miraculous birth showed His ability to keep the other promises related to the nation of Israel.

But God just doesn't go around showing you how strong He is. He does what He does for a reason. He has purposes tied to His power. That's why you don't get everything you want—not because He can't, but because it's not best. It is not His will. It doesn't magnify His glory.

You can never detach God's omnipotence from His sovereignty. Revelation 19:6 puts it this way, "Hallelujah! For the Lord our God, the Almighty, reigns." That is, His omnipotence is tied to His rule, and His rule is tied to His will. So to get His power, you must be tied to His will. If you are not in the will of God, you won't experience the power of God because God always exercises His power with a purpose.

Jesus understood this. According to Hebrews 5:7, Jesus cried out to His Father, knowing that the Father had the power to deliver Him from death. Jesus did not want to die on that cross, but in the Garden of Gethsemane we find Him praying, "Yet not what I will, but what Thou wilt" (Mark 14:36). With God, it's never a question of power. The issue is matching His power with His will. We need to ask God, "What does Your ruling power wish to do?"

Every parent understands this. We choose not to do some things for our children, even though we have the ability, because it's not in their best interests. But they misinterpret us and say, "You don't love me. How come you won't?" We could do what they request, but we don't because we choose not to exercise our will in the use of that power. But it has nothing to do with power.

IF YOU EVER FORGET THE WORD OMNIPOTENT, IF THE WORD POWER DOESN'T DO ANYTHING FOR YOU, JUST DO WHAT THE WRITERS OF THE BIBLE DID. THEY REACHED BACK TO AN OLD PHRASE AND SIMPLY SAID, "HE'S ABLE."

God may not have come through for you yet either because you are not in His will or because you haven't learned what He wants you to do before He exercises His power. But it's not a question of His omnipotence. He can change that job. He can change those finances. He can give you a mate. Remember, He doesn't even need raw material to do what He's going to do. He could just do it ex nihilo, out of nothing.

So the question is always, what is God's will? That should be our major concern, finding and getting in line with the will of God. God's desires are never more extensive than His powers. He says in Isaiah 46:10, "My purpose will be established, and I will accomplish all My good pleasure." God uses His power to accomplish His will.

GOD'S OMNIPOTENCE
IS PERSONAL

Here's the best part. The ones who really get to see God's power are His people. I like Ephesians 3:19–20. Paul prays that we might comprehend the love of Christ and "be filled up to all the fulness of God." Then in verse 20 Paul says, "Now to Him *who is able* to do exceeding abundantly beyond all that we ask or think, according to the power that works within us" (italics added).

If you ever forget the word *omnipotent,* if the word *power* doesn't do anything for you, just do what the writers of the Bible did. They reached back to an old phrase and simply said, "He's able." If you lose all the theology of it, if you don't know how to match omnipotence with sovereignty, just remember this phrase: "He's able."

In his magnificent benediction in Ephesians 3:20, Paul is simply saying, "He's able." That's all I'm saying. God is able. Despite your circumstances, God's power is very personal to you. He's able, and if you can think it or ask it, He can do it because He's able.

He's Able to Save

What is God able to do? The Bible says, first of all, that He is able to save you forever (Hebrews 7:25). Not only that, but "[God] is able to guard what I have entrusted to Him until that day" (2 Timothy 1:12). That's why you can't lose your salvation. You can't lose your salvation once you are truly saved, not because you are holding on to God, but because He's able to hold on to you.

If we had to maintain our own salvation, we'd be saved one day, lost the next day; saved one minute, lost the next minute. I'm grateful that God is able because if He weren't, I would be living in fear of committing a sin and being lost forever. But now that I know He's able, I realize my salvation does not depend on me. It's not me holding God's hand, it's God holding my hand.

When I took my kids to the fair, if they were simply holding my hand, they were in trouble. But if I was holding their hands they were OK even when they let go, because I was able. God says He's able to save from the "guttermost" to the uttermost and to maintain us all the way.

He's Able to Meet Needs

Not only is God able to save you, but He's able to meet all of your needs. In 2 Corinthians 9:8 Paul writes, "God is able to make all grace abound to you, that always having all sufficiency in everything, you may have an abundance for every good deed." Now you need to understand that he is speaking to Christians who have honored God and not robbed Him in giving, who have not given God the leftovers and then come to Him later for a blessing.

God is able, Paul says, to take care of those bills. He's able to pay off those credit cards. He's able to handle that mortgage note. He's able to deal with the finances of those who are following Him, who are His people.

He's Able to Heal

God is also able to heal. In Matthew 9:27–29, two blind men followed Jesus crying out, "Have mercy on us, Son of David!"

Jesus looked at them and had just one question: "Do you believe that I am able to do this?"

They said, "Yes, Lord."

That's all it took. Jesus said, "Be it done to you according to your faith," and He healed them.

He's Able to Deliver

The Bible says God is able to deliver us. In an earlier chapter, we looked at the story of Shadrach, Meshach, and Abednego (Daniel 3). King Nebuchadnezzar threatened to throw them in the fiery furnace. They replied, "Our God whom we serve is able to deliver us from the furnace of blazing fire" (v. 17).

Then in chapter 6, Daniel himself was thrown into the lions' den. The king came down the next day, removed the stone, peered in, and asked Daniel, "Has your God, whom you constantly serve, been able to deliver you from the lions?" (v. 20).

Daniel's answer (paraphrased), "He's able. He delivered me."

He's Able to Keep You

God is also able to keep you from falling. Listen to the opening of a great benediction: "Now to Him who is able to keep you from stumbling, and to make you stand in the presence of His glory blameless with great joy" (Jude 24).

God may let you trip, but He won't let you fall because He's able. He may allow you to have some difficulty, but He will hold your hand. If your marriage is falling apart, God can put it back together because He's able.

Now don't misunderstand me. I am fully aware that marriage takes the commitment of two people. If you are committed to your marriage but your mate insists on acting faithlessly, I am not saying that God will just "zap" your mate and bring him or her into line. Unfortunately, human sin and rebellion still operate. Some marriages fail even though one partner prays fervently and remains faithful. But God's ability to restore a marriage is never in question.

If you've got a habit of any sort that you can't handle, bring it to God because He's able to help you beat it.

In light of all this, we need to do what Paul advised the Ephesians to do: "Be strong in the Lord, and in the strength of His might" (Ephesians 6:10). How can Paul say that? Because God is able to make us strong. Remember, God's ability to do "exceeding abundantly beyond all that we ask or think" is "according to the power that works within us."

If you don't have any power at work in you, then you won't see any power at work through you. The biggest problem with seeing God's power is that Christians aren't committed. They aren't submissive to His will, so they don't believe God has all this power. But if He can create the universe, He can handle your problems. If He can create the trees that make the paper on which the money you need is printed, He can handle your bills.

The problem isn't power. The problem is "according to the power that works within us." You can't be a half-hearted Christian and expect to have glorious power. You can't be a "shucking and jiving" saint and expect to see glorious power.

FOUR THINGS TO KNOW

Let me show you four final things you need to know about God's omnipotence:

1. *God must have your fully committed heart.* He doesn't want you to be divided. He doesn't want you committed to Him on Sunday and to the world on Monday. He doesn't want you to be two-timing Him. "The eyes of the Lord move to and fro throughout the earth that He may strongly support those whose heart is completely His" (2 Chronicles 16:9). Think about it. God is trying to find someone to show His power through.

2. *You must also have faith.* But you say, "My faith is weak." Well, in Mark 9 Jesus was met by a father who wanted his son healed. He made a pretty weak statement of his faith to Jesus: "If you can do anything, take pity on us and help us" (v. 22).

Jesus immediately challenged that, and the man cried out, "I do believe; help my unbelief" (v. 24). This man was saying, "I kind of believe. I want to believe. I need to believe, but my belief system is not working right today."

Jesus healed the boy anyway, because the father was willing to bring his unbelief to Christ and let Him turn it into belief. So even if your faith isn't working right, if you bring your weak faith to a mighty God that's all the faith you need, because He's able. He doesn't *need* your faith in order to work; He merely needs you to stop trusting yourself and be willing to trust Him.

3. *The Bible also says you need to be humble (1 Peter 5:5–6).* We know that God has always been opposed to the proud, but He gives victory to the humble. So if you are going to experience His omnipotent power and discover for yourself that He's able, you must be humble and willing to submit to Him.

4. *You must be ready to wait on the Lord.* The prophet Isaiah says:

> Do you not know? Have you not heard? The Everlasting God, the Lord, the Creator of the ends of the earth does not become weary or tired. His understanding is inscrutable. He gives strength to the weary, and to him who lacks might He increases power. Though youths grow weary and tired, and vigorous young men stumble badly, yet those who wait for the Lord will gain new strength; they will mount up with wings like eagles, they will run and not get tired, they will walk and not become weary. (Isaiah 40:28–31)

Does "wait on the Lord" mean sit and do nothing? No. It means don't rely on human schemes. "Wait on the Lord" means do it God's way, not your way. Many of us have not seen God's power because we are too busy trying to create our own power. We haven't seen God's power because we are too busy concocting our own schemes.

We haven't seen God pay the bills, for example, because we believe the only one that can help us is MasterCard, American Express, or Visa. We keep using our power, so we never get around to seeing God's power. And God will not share power with anyone.

Our churches ought to be filled every week with believers ready to testify about the power of God: how He made them love someone they didn't think they could love; how He gave them the ability to meet a need they didn't think they could meet; how He turned things around. We ought to be willing to go before the Lord, even if it means fasting and praying, and say, "I can't, Lord, but You can. You're able."

We're often like the little boy whose father told him to pick up a heavy rock that was in their way. The boy tried, grunted, and said, "Daddy, I can't lift it."

His daddy said, "Yes, you can."

The boy tried again. "Ughhhh. Daddy, I can't lift it."

"Yes, you can."

The boy went back again. Same result. "Daddy, I can't lift it!"

"Yes, you can. You're not using all your strength."

This went on two or three more times, the boy insisting that he was using all his strength. Finally, the father put his arm around the boy and said, "Son, you don't understand. You did not use all your strength. You did not ask me."

God can pick up the rocks in your life, but you've got to ask Him. He can move the heavy rocks in your marriage, your job, or your family, but you've got to ask Him. He doesn't want you grunting and groaning in your own strength because He already knows, "Without Me, you can do nothing."

God is able. He is omnipotently able!

Responding to God's Omnipotence

Along with the suggestions above, here are some more ways you can apply what you've learned to your life and experience the mighty power of God on a day-to-day basis:

1. In light of what we have learned, are you in a situation where you have been pushing too hard, trying to arrange things or make something happen on your own? If so, you could be blocking God from exercising His power. Step back from your efforts for a while, and ask God to show you His power.

2. Take some time to recall recent occasions when God revealed Himself to you in a mighty way. Try to be specific; it doesn't have to be a major event. Discuss your findings with your spouse, your family, or a friend. If your list is blank, maybe it's time for some time alone with God on your knees.

3. What about that person, situation, or need you've given up on as impossible? If God can create a universe, He can do the impossible in your universe. Take that "impossible dream" and put it at the top of your prayer list. Do so exercising faith in God's power and in His sovereignty. If you need to, do like that distraught father and pray, "I do believe; help my unbelief." Remember, a powerful God can act even on weak faith.

4. Turn to a great passage like Isaiah 40:28–31, or one of the psalms we have looked at, and read God's Word back to Him. He loves to hear it. Make the verses *your* prayer, saying, for example, "Lord, I need new strength. I need to mount up wings like an eagle, I need the stamina to run and not get weary." God delights to hear and answer the prayers of His people.

10
THE WISDOM
OF GOD

Maybe by now in this study of our great God you feel as I do, like a kid playing in the sand at the edge of a mighty ocean. Our subject is so vast, because God is so infinite, that we can only scratch around in the sand. But He gave us a pail and a shovel and invited us to dig in, so let's talk about His infinite wisdom.

The wisdom of God is His unique ability to so interrelate His attributes that He accomplishes His predetermined purpose by the best means possible. This definition contains a lot of parts, so let's break it down a little.

God's ability to use His attributes in perfect wisdom is unique because He is the only one who can do it. His attributes, as we've seen before, are His qualities, His perfections, the outworkings of His perfect character. And we know from our study of God's sovereignty (chapter 4) that He has a predetermined plan and purpose He is bringing about for His glory. His power and perfections guarantee that He will always accomplish His plan by the best means possible.

When we talk about wisdom, we refer to more than just knowledge. Wisdom is more than having information. All of us know people who are well educated but just plain dumb when it comes to day-to-day living. They have a lot of book sense, but no common sense. So simply accumulating data is not having wisdom. Wisdom has to do with the use of the information we have rather than just its possession.

A good example of this use of wisdom appears in Exodus 31:1–5. Israel was building the tabernacle, and one of the skilled artisans doing the work was a man named Bezalel. The Lord told Moses that He had filled Bezalel with "the Spirit of God in wisdom" for all kinds of craftsmanship. In other words, Bezalel knew how to use his skills in the best way possible to make the most of his work and help achieve God's plan for the tabernacle.

When we talk about wisdom, we must consider a specific goal, the best means to reach that goal, and the materials necessary to get there. All three components are embodied in the idea of wisdom. Wisdom is the ability to work with information in such a way that you accomplish the right purpose with that data in the right way. With this in mind, I want to show you five things about the wisdom of God.

GOD'S WISDOM
AND ETERNAL PURPOSE

I alluded to this briefly above, but let me say it again: God's wisdom does not operate outside of His purpose. Paul makes this clear in Ephesians 1:7–11:

> In Him we have redemption through His blood, the forgiveness of our trespasses, according to the riches of His grace, which He lavished upon us. In all wisdom and insight He made known to us the mystery of His will, according to His kind intention which He purposed in Him with a view to an administration suitable to the fulness of the times, that is, the summing up of all things in Christ, things in the heavens and things upon the earth. In Him also we have obtained an inheritance, having been predestined according to His purpose who works all things after the counsel of His will.

God's wisdom is tied to His purpose. And Paul states His eternal purpose to be "the summing up all things in Christ" for His glory. Everything God does in wisdom propels creation toward that one purpose, which is the same in history as it is throughout eternity: His own glory.

No One Wiser

Now that upsets a lot of people. They say, "Who does God think He is, constructing all events for all times just so that He might be glorified and Christ might be exalted? It's all Him, Him, Him; His will, His glory, and His Son. It's all Him!"

The best explanation I can offer is that God exists for Himself. The reason is simple: There is nothing or no one greater than Him for whom He could exist. God exists for Himself because He is the highest possible goal or end that could ever be reached. You may have to think about that one for a minute.

You see, you and I exist for someone else because there is someone greater than us we can reach out to. But who is greater than our awesome God? Nobody! In fact, if some unknown something out there were greater and wiser than God, we would be lost in the dark, groping for its identity and our identity.

But since no one is greater than God, and since He has set His own glory as His highest goal, it shouldn't surprise us that He has designed everything to achieve that goal. No one expressed it any better than Paul in Romans 11:33–36:

> Oh, the depth of the riches both of the wisdom and knowledge of God! How unsearchable are His judgments and unfathomable His ways! For who has known the mind of the Lord, or who became His counselor? Or who has first given to Him that it might be paid back to Him again? For from Him and through Him and to Him are all things. To Him be the glory forever. Amen.

Everything that God constructs, He constructs with that goal in mind. Now remember the ingredients of wisdom. Wisdom is arranging things so they meet a goal in the best way possible. God's wisdom so constructs circumstances and people that they all wind up achieving His goal because there is no higher goal to which they could ever go. God is unique in this.

No wonder He is called "the only wise God" (Romans 16:27)! No one else could take all the events of history and so arrange them that they achieve one solitary, all-encompassing purpose. Throughout history, various demagogues, dictators, and madmen have tried to bend history to their will and purpose.

But they always fail for at least three reasons. First, they aren't God, even though some of them think they are. Second, because they aren't God, they aren't smart enough to pull off their twisted and grandiose plans for very long. And third, they all die someday. God alone is all-wise.

No One Greater

You don't have to embrace God's goal. You don't even have to like it—but God will reach it anyway. You could only stop God from reaching His goal by being greater than He is, by having more attributes than He has. Since most of us know better than to try and checkmate God, we'd be much better off to cooperate with Him in achieving the goal His wisdom has set. When you do this, life begins to come into focus.

THERE ARE NO ATHEISTS IN HELL. EVEN IN HELL [GOD] WILL ALWAYS ACHIEVE HIS PURPOSE OF BRINGING GLORY TO HIMSELF.

My youngest son recently started playing football. When he first went out to practice he did not wear his glasses, so things were fuzzy. That meant he was getting up off the ground quite regularly because he was not properly focused on the target.

We bought him some athletic glasses, and that brought things in focus. He's not getting hit any less often. The glasses don't prevent bumps and bruises, but now he can see what's coming and know where he's going. That's what wisdom does. Wisdom doesn't mean you don't have problems, it means you can see better. It puts life in a proper focus.

So like it or not, here comes God. His glory is His purpose, for He could attain no higher purpose. Therefore, in wisdom He moves all events, all people, and all circumstances toward it. Whether you resist it or cooperate with it, He's still going to achieve His purpose.

Did you know that God will ultimately achieve His purpose even in hell? The people in hell will help achieve the purpose of God, for they will glorify God throughout all eternity. As I said earlier, there are no atheists in hell. Even in hell He will always achieve His purpose of bringing glory to Himself.

GOD'S WISDOM
IS UNIQUE

We touched on this at the opening of the chapter. God has an awesome array of attributes. We've studied a few of them, and we have a few to go. God's wisdom is His unique ability to use those attributes in perfect harmony and balance: to blend them together, to take two attributes out over here and add two more over there, to so correlate them that they achieve exactly what He desires.

A Revealing Wisdom

Daniel 2 shows us this interworking in an interesting way. Daniel has just been given the interpretation of the king's dream, and he praises God for it. Notice that Daniel uses the term *wisdom* coupled with another of God's attributes to show how they operate together: "Then the mystery was revealed to Daniel in a night vision. Then Daniel blessed the God of heaven; Daniel answered and said, 'Let the name of God be blessed forever and ever, for wisdom and power belong to Him'" (vv. 19–20).

God's infinite wisdom worked in tandem with His unlimited power to reveal this secret to Daniel and achieve God's purpose in that situation. But Daniel continues his portrait of our all-wise God:

> It is He who changes the times and the epochs; He removes kings and establishes kings; He gives wisdom to wise men, and knowledge to men of understanding. It is He who reveals the profound and hidden things; He knows what is in the darkness, and the light dwells with Him. To Thee, O God of my fathers, I give thanks and praise, for Thou hast given me wisdom and power; even now Thou hast made known to me what we requested of Thee, for Thou has made known to us the king's matter. (vv. 21–23)

An Ordering Wisdom

In His wisdom, God rearranges people, nations, and situations. Daniel also relates God's wisdom to His omniscience. Because God knows all things, He knows the best choices to make in the outworking of His plan. It takes infinite wisdom to pull that off. More than that, it takes infinite wisdom guiding perfect attributes. I'm not up to that, and neither are you. Only God can do it.

Acts 15:18 puts it this way: "Known unto God are all his works from the beginning of the world" (KJV). Knowing everything in advance puts one in a privileged position. God can't lose because He knows how the smallest detail will or will not work. He has the whole equation in front of Him, and He can arrange even the smallest details to make everything work.

A Detailed Wisdom

I'm glad we've got a wise God putting it all together instead of leaving it up to us, because most people don't care about the details. When we see a machine with a lot of little parts in it, most of us are not concerned with the parts, but simply with whether the machine works.

Your watch is a perfect example. When you want to know the time, you don't open your watch and examine all of its intricacies. You just look at it. But that watch only tells you the right time because intricate parts move together to make the watch work. When was the last time you asked someone to explain to you how a watch works? You only care about the goal: the time.

But the watchmaker is very concerned about the details. He knows that unless the details work together right, the goal won't be achieved. Any manufacturer pays attention to details. God, the manufacturer of the universe, pulls together the details to guarantee that the watch of history achieves its goal: His glory.

In other areas we are concerned about details. When we fly, we may notice the little things more because a lot more is at stake. That doesn't mean we examine the details. We don't climb all over the cockpit of the airplane and grill the pilot on his experience. But we sure want to know that he knows what he's doing. We hope this isn't his first flight, and we hope the maintenance people did their job and the air traffic controllers aren't asleep in the tower.

God knows the details of all of His works so well that we can have confidence He's going to reach His goal and get there by the best means possible. His wisdom is unique because it allows Him to interrelate His attributes. He can use His characteristics as He needs to do so.

GOD'S WISDOM
IS EVIDENT

Let me cite four activities in history through which we see the wisdom of God.

In Creation

Psalm 104:24 says that "in wisdom" God made all of His works. God's wisdom is clearly seen by creation. In the same way as we can see the wisdom of the watchmaker in the watch, we can see the wisdom of the Earthmaker in the earth. When we see the wonders of this planet, we see a wise God who gave us a home to live in that is perfectly suited to sustain the life that God created. David declares, "The heavens are telling of the glory of God" (Psalm 19:1).

In Salvation

God's wisdom manifests itself in a glorious way in the plan He devised for our salvation in Jesus Christ. In fact, in 1 Corinthians 1 Paul throws some jabs at folks who think they are smart:

> It is written, "I will destroy the wisdom of the wise, and the cleverness of the clever I will set aside." Where is the wise man? Where is the scribe? Where is the debater of this age? Has not God made foolish the wisdom of the world? (vv. 19–20)

None of us would have ever come up with the plan of salvation that God did. In our "wisdom" we would have made it much more confusing, complex, and inequitable. Earn your way to heaven. We would have devised a "lay-away" salvation plan. But God designed a salvation free for all, available to all, by sending His Son to die for our sins.

Our wisdom wouldn't have gotten the job done. God had a superior plan, even though the cross looks foolish to a dying world that prefers to depend on its own wisdom:

> For since in the wisdom of God the world through its wisdom did not come to know God, God was well-pleased through the foolishness of the message preached to save those who believe. . . . Because the foolishness of God is wiser than men, and the weakness of God is stronger than men. . . . But God has chosen the foolish things of the world to shame the wise, and God has chosen the weak things of the world to shame the things which are strong, and the base things of the world and the despised, God has chosen . . . that no man should boast before God. (vv. 21, 25, 27–29)

In other words, God doesn't want to share His glory, so He chooses nothingness. He chooses the thing that you would least think of to get the job done. That's why so many things in the Bible don't make sense. You and I wouldn't do it that way. Why does God do it that way? So that He gets the greatest glory. That's why when we believers look among ourselves, we don't see too many of the world's wise and mighty among us.

God didn't look just for the rich and the powerful folks. In fact, Jesus told us it was easier for a camel to go through the eye of a needle than for a rich man to get to heaven. Why? Because God will never let a rich man flash money in His face at the gates of heaven and expect the gates to fly open. He won't let a power broker flash his power in His face.

Does God call *any* wise or mighty to Himself? Of course He does. A noblewoman once approached the great British preacher John Wesley and told him she was saved by an *m*. Naturally, Wesley wanted to know what she meant. "God says that not many noble can be saved. He did not say not *any*," she replied.

In Jesus Christ

Jesus Christ is the wisdom of God in the flesh. The Bible says that in Him "are hidden all the treasures of wisdom and knowledge" (Colossians 2:3). In the passage we just considered above, Paul says that Christ "became to us wisdom from God" (1 Corinthians 1:30).

You get smart when you know Christ. Atheists are some of the most brilliant, dumbest people you ever want to meet. Their brilliance can explain the world, but their ignorance lets them explain the world in a way that explains God away.

In the Church

Here is another way in which God demonstrates His infinite wisdom:

> To me . . . this grace was given, to preach among the Gentiles the unfathomable riches of Christ, and to bring to light what is the administration of the mystery which for ages has been hidden in God, who created all things; in order that the manifold wisdom of God might now be made known through the church to the rulers and the authorities in the heavenly places. This was in accordance with the eternal purpose which He carried out in Christ Jesus our Lord. (Ephesians 3:8–11)

Paul says that God's wisdom, which is tied to His purpose, is *manifold,* the Greek word that means "multi-colored," or "variegated," or many-sided.

As the wisdom of God shines through the church, the church becomes a prism that reveals all the colors and textures of His wisdom. Open the doors of any church, and you will see a collection of people who despite all their faults and failures are the living body of Christ. As a pastor, I can verify that only the wisdom of God could pull that off! God does this to show through the church how brilliant and wise He really is.

In the Ordering of Life

In another way God shows His wisdom: by the way He orders our lives. The Bible uses a lot of illustrations of this. Joseph was sold into slavery and wound up being second in command in Egypt. How did he explain it? Was it luck? A good education? Having a lot of money? No, it was none of these.

Then how did a Jewish slave boy rise to the office of prime minister in Egypt? How did he explain going from the prison house to the White House? Joseph told his brothers, "You meant evil against me, but God meant it for good" (Genesis 50:20).

YOU ARE NOT WHERE YOU ARE BY LUCK OR CHANCE. THE INFINITELY WISE GOD HAS BEEN ORDERING YOUR LIFE.

When God gets in the mix and begins to order your life, He can even take people who messed you over and use them as a means to accomplish His eternal plan. He's able to take enemies and make them footstools.

Some of the people who thirty years ago would have been abusive to a man like Dr. John Perkins, founder of the Voice of Calvary ministries in Mendenhall, Mississippi, author, speaker, and widely recognized Christian leader, now come to sit at his feet and say, "Show us how to deal with the economic and community issues we face."

I like the Book of Esther. The name of God does not appear anywhere in the book, but His thumbprint shows all over it as He ordered Esther's life to achieve His purpose. For example, He made her beautiful so that when King Ahasuerus went looking for a wife, he would choose her.

That way, when Haman plotted to destroy the Jews, Esther would have access to King Ahasuerus's presence as his queen. Her access would then lead to the saving of the Jews and the death of the very man who was out to destroy God's people. Esther's cousin Mordecai got it right when he told her, "Who knows whether you have not attained royalty for such a time as this?" (Esther 4:14). In other words, God ordered all of it. He had a plan to accomplish His glory.

In 2 Corinthians 1:4–5, Paul says that God gave him his trials so that he could comfort others. In 2 Corinthians 12:7–9, Paul describes his "thorn in the flesh" that God sent in order to humble him. God was going to use Paul so greatly that He had to keep him dependent, so God gave him a thorn he couldn't get rid of. God ordered Paul's life for a definite purpose.

I am in Dallas, Texas, by the wisdom of God. Dallas Theological Seminary was not on my agenda. But God moved in this and that circumstance, brought this person and that influence into my life, and I wound up in Dallas. We had no thought of an Oak Cliff Bible Fellowship Church, but while I was going through seminary, God brought men like Dr. Ruben Connor and Dr. Gene Getz into my life, and the vision for OCBF was conceived.

All of this happened not by my planning, but in the wisdom of God. The same is true for you, no matter what your present circumstance. You are not where you are by luck or chance. The infinitely wise God has been ordering your life. You were in His mind before the creation of the earth. So if you are inclined to say, "I was lucky," bite your tongue.

GOD'S WISDOM IS GENEROUSLY AVAILABLE

You may already know James 1 well. But it's so important that I want to look at it again:

> Consider it all joy, my brethren, when you encounter various trials, knowing that the testing of your faith produces endurance. And let endurance have its perfect result, that you may be perfect and complete, lacking in nothing. But if any of you lacks wisdom, let him ask of God, who gives to all men generously and without reproach, and it will be given to him. But let him ask in faith without any doubting, for the one who doubts is like the surf of the sea driven and tossed by the wind. (vv. 2–6)

Can you see what James is saying? When God sends you a trial, He sends it for a reason. Therefore, you can "count it all joy." That doesn't mean to be happy that you have a problem. It means be happy that your problem has a purpose. James is talking about those trials that God allows in your life, not the mess you get yourself in through sin.

In Trials

When God brings a trial into your life, His eternal purpose is that through this test you might bring Him glory. But you bring Him glory by passing the test, not by ducking it or just coasting through. Life operates on this principle too. You don't get a good career until you pass all the tests. You pass the test in first grade, then in fifth grade, and again in seventh grade. You pass the test to get out of high school, then you must pass the test again and again in college.

All those tests, or trials in our context, are designed to produce in you the knowledge and ability necessary to function in your chosen career. Without the tests, there would be no way to verify your knowledge—and without the knowledge, you couldn't perform the task. God wants you to perform the task of bringing glory to His name, but without the test you will never know if you have what it takes spiritually to accomplish the task.

But God knows that this creates a problem for us. How do we handle the trials He sends? That's why the promise of James 1:5 is so important. God offers us His wisdom, and He offers it generously!

Notice, however, that God does not offer you His wisdom so you can figure out how to beat the system and avoid problems. Wisdom has to do with the response you need to make for His glory in the midst of problems. Many people pray the wrong prayer: "Lord, get me out of this trial!"

That's like going to your teacher during final exams and pleading, "Get me out of this room!" But the teacher's job is not to dismiss you from the test, but to help you successfully complete the test and move on. And the teacher knows that he or she has to keep you in that room despite your protests, or you're going to be a severely handicapped person farther down the road.

That's why James cautions, "Let endurance have its perfect result" (v. 4). God will keep you in His classroom until you finish His test. Now if you have taken tests like the ones I've taken, you sit in the room and try to outwait the teacher. But in this case, that can't happen. You will not outwait God. God is going to stay until you finish the test and you pass. If you fail, you get to retake the test. So you might as well study the first time so you can finish the test and move on.

Let God finish doing what He's doing, because He will give you the wisdom you need to pass the test. When you face business decisions, marital challenges, financial setbacks, or emotional trials, God will give you the wisdom to make the response that will bring Him glory. That's why Ephesians 5:17 says, "Do not be foolish, but understand what the will of the Lord is." God will show you how to bring Him the most glory by showing you what His will is for you in your time of testing.

In Our Constant Need

Now let me explain a few things about the wisdom God gives. First, we need it constantly. How do I handle this rebellious child? I don't want to be too strict, yet I don't want to be too lenient. How do I relate to that difficult co-worker? God doesn't want me to run off and get another job. Every day we face issues like this, so every day we need to be praying for wisdom. God says, "I will grant you My wisdom for handling trials if you will pray for it and be committed to it."

When We Ask

Second, we need to ask in faith (James 1:6). A double-minded person is by definition uncommitted because he is trying to go in two directions at once. He's not sure if he's going to do what God wants done when God reveals it, and God's not going to waste His revelation on people who want to debate Him about it.

God doesn't want you to say, "Lord, show me what You want me to do so I can decide if I'm going to do it." It's got to be, "Lord, show me what You want me to do because I'm determined to do Your will. If You show me, I will do it."

Many of us don't get our prayers for wisdom answered because we are double-minded. We have not decided ahead of time that we will do what God asks us to do.

One Dose at a Time

A third thing you need to know about God's wisdom is that He gives it one need or trial at a time. To pray "Lord, give me wisdom for this year" or "Help me to live my life wisely" doesn't really get you anywhere. If anything is clear in James 1 it's that God offers wisdom related to the specific trial that He has allowed.

When We Want Answers

Fourth and finally, getting God's wisdom does not guarantee that you will figure out why He allowed the trial. I always come back to Job, who never knew why his world fell in on him. He just knew that God was putting him through a heavy trial.

Yet Job acknowledged the Lord's great wisdom and strength (Job 9:4; 12:13). He said to God, "I'm going to trust You even if You take my life. I'm not going to be double-minded. I don't know why You are doing this to me, but I want You to show me how to walk through it."

That's what God guarantees us, the wisdom to steer our lives over the twisting and sometimes treacherous roads of life. If you have ever driven the famous Highway 1 along the California coast, you know what a treacherous piece of road that is. You ride near the edge of the cliff with no guard rails, and it goes a mile straight down. It's called a "scenic highway." I call it "Suicide Road."

IF IT'S THE NORMAL WAY UNSAVED PEOPLE THINK, THEN IT'S BORN IN HELL. YOU'D EXPECT A CHILD OF THE DEVIL TO THINK LIKE HIS DADDY. THAT'S WHY YOU CAN'T BE MANIPULATED BY WHAT EVERYONE THINKS.

In fact, when my family and I were driving Highway 1, my kids told me, "Get off this thing at the next exit!" They were basically saying, "Dad, we have a fundamental problem with your driving skills on regular highways, so we certainly don't want to be at your mercy on Highway 1."

You know what's interesting about driving on roads like that? When you come to a treacherous curve, you don't get into a discussion of why they built this highway like this, why they put this curve here. You don't ask that. Your only concern is to negotiate the curve properly. Getting God's wisdom doesn't mean you get all the answers. But it will help you negotiate the curve that God has put in your path.

So God may not answer the question, "Why have I been single so long?" But He will give you the wisdom to negotiate the road of your singleness for as long as He wants you to travel it.

He may not answer, "Lord, why did You give me this person to marry? Why didn't You show me all this stuff up front?" But He will give you wisdom to negotiate through the turns in your marriage for His glory.

In other words, God's wisdom reveals what His will is for us while we are going through our trial. That often means that He has to spend a lot of time resisting our will. It's like taking your dog for a walk. If you come to a pole and don't pull the dog over, he will keep going around the pole and get hung up. Then when you pull the dog back, instead of coming straight back he will wrap around and come back on your side.

The dog's intentions are good, but now he's got himself all tangled up. You want him to go forward and the dog wants to go forward, but he's all wrapped up. So what do you have to do to untangle the dog? You have to resist what seems to him the right way to go, pushing him back in the opposite direction to get him headed the right way.

Many of us respond like this to God. We move out in our own direction, then we get ourselves wrapped around the pole of life and wonder why we can't move forward. God has to resist us even though we are trying to go the right way, so we wind up praying, "Lord, I'm trying. How come You're resisting me?"

He's resisting us so He can get us unwrapped from ourselves and we can get on with our walk. We have trials because we tend to walk on the wrong side of the pole. Only God in His wisdom can move us forward so that we can achieve His glory.

GOD'S WISDOM
AND THE WORLD'S WISDOM

For my final point I want to turn to James 3, another great passage of Scripture that lays down a fundamental truth: You cannot mix human wisdom and divine wisdom. God's wisdom is visibly different from the wisdom of this world. That is, you can see what each kind of wisdom produces. Listen to James: "Who among you is wise and understanding? Let him show by his good behavior his deeds in the gentleness of wisdom" (3:13).

Visibly Different

To be wise biblically doesn't necessarily mean to be educated and be able to crank out a lot of knowledge. That's why if you need advice, you shouldn't necessarily go to the most educated person you know. You may get only sophisticated-sounding ignorance. The most educated person is not always the wisest person. God's wisdom is *walk,* not *talk.*

Beginning in verse 14, James distinguishes between God's wisdom and the world's wisdom:

> But if you have bitter jealousy and selfish ambition in your heart, do not be arrogant and so lie against the truth. This wisdom is not that which comes down from above, but is earthly, natural, demonic. For where jealousy and selfish ambition exist, there is disorder and every evil thing. (vv. 14–16)

Just as there is heavenly wisdom, there is hellish wisdom. James says, "It's the way everyone thinks, but it's straight from hell." Notice how he couples the words *natural* and *demonic.* So if it's the normal way unsaved people think, then it's born in hell. You'd expect a child of the devil to think like his daddy. That's why you can't be manipulated by what everyone thinks.

This wisdom has visible results. It produces jealousy and selfish ambition. It promotes itself, pushing others down so it can climb up. It's prideful and deceitful. It produces divisiveness instead of unity. The result of worldly wisdom is "disorder and every evil thing."

Experientially Different

Do you know why our homes have disorder? Because too many of our marriages and families operate out of envy and ambition. Instead of everyone upholding the central goal of the home, every family member wants his or her agenda. What else can you have but discord? That's earthly wisdom.

A true story tells of an infidel who bequeathed all of his property to the devil. The court didn't know what to do with the man's will, so the judge said, "The only way to carry out such a will is to order that this farm be left untouched by human hands throughout its history." So they did that, and in a few years brush and weeds had grown up. The buildings became dilapidated, and the farm was a scene of disorder and ugliness.

This happens to anyone whose life has been willed over to the devil's way of thinking. The weeds begin to grow, and his life becomes dilapidated. He can't hold his relationships together. He can't keep weeds from sprouting in his mind. He can't hold his passions together. He can't hold *anything* together.

But James offers us another kind of wisdom, the "wisdom from above" (v. 17) which he says is first of all "pure." That means it's authentic, transparent, clean, like God's Word. Psalm 19:8 says, "The commandment of the Lord is pure."

God's wisdom is also "peaceable," promoting unity and not strife; "gentle," meaning considerate; "reasonable," willing to take instruction, ready to listen to people who make sense; "full of mercy and good fruits," giving practical help to others; "unwavering," taking a stand on principles instead of flowing one way today and another way tomorrow; and "without hypocrisy," not wearing a mask. That's what a wise person looks like.

Our wise God wants to order your life, and that includes your trials. You will travel your own Highway 1 in life. God will not take you off the road until He has finished with you, but He will teach you how to negotiate the turns.

Every summer, our family jumps into our mini-van and goes north to see the grandparents. One summer, we were going through the hills of Virginia and noticed a number of signs inviting us to visit one of Virginia's caverns. So we decided to do something different and see a cavern. An elevator took us down into a dark, cold cavern. Our guide told us how the cavern developed and showed us the different rock formations.

Now that cavern had a lot of little tunnels you could go off into, but the guide warned, "Stick with me. If you wander down one of these little side tunnels on your own, you can get lost. But if you stick with me, you won't get lost."

That's what God says. Follow Him and you can't get lost because He knows where the different trails lead. He knows where to take you even if you are in a dark relational, financial, spiritual, or emotional cavern.

Psalm 90:10–12 says that you can expect to live seventy years—and if you are really strong, you may make it to eighty. Moses prayed, "Teach us to number our days, that we may present to Thee a heart of wisdom."

You would be wise to number your days. I did that in 1993 and figured out that I had fewer than nine thousand days left if I live a normal life span. Do you know what would be a good exercise? Take as many sheets of paper as you have days left, and each day ball up a piece and throw it away because that day is gone and you will never live it again. There's not a lot of time to waste.

And if you've taken a wrong turn in life, go to God and say, "I've been unwise." Then get off at the next exit, cross over the highway, and start back down the other way. You can't change yesterday, but you can do a number on tomorrow. Our God is wise, and He wants to lead us in His wisdom.

Responding to the Wisdom of God

Do you want God's wisdom? I do. Let me give you four things you can do to get wisdom from our all-wise God who has made His wisdom available to us:

1. Admit that you need it. Proverbs 11:2 says that wisdom is only given to the humble. You've got to admit that you don't know what you thought you knew. Make this your prayer: "Lord, I need You. I don't know how to negotiate the turns in the road of my life today."

2. Fear the Lord. The Bible declares again and again that "the fear of the Lord is the beginning of wisdom" (Psalm 111:10). That doesn't mean to be petrified of God, but to stand in awe of Him, believing that He knows what He's talking about. It means to reverence God, to hold Him in high esteem. God doesn't want to give you His wisdom if it's going to be treated like leftover information. Come to God recognizing who He is.

3. Study the Word. Read Psalm 119:97–100 and you'll see that David's study of God's Word gave him wisdom and made him wiser than his enemies and even wiser than his elders and his teachers. Only God can make you wiser than all of those folks. How are you doing in your personal Bible study? No number of books can replace that.

4. Pray for wisdom. Go back to James 1:5 where we're told to ask God for His wisdom. If you don't ask for it, He's not going to give it to you because if you don't ask for it, you don't want it bad enough.

11
THE WORD
OF GOD

One day a pastor visited some of his parishioners. He came to the home of one woman to pay his respects, and this sister wanted to impress him. So she said to her daughter, "Honey, would you go into the den and get the good book? You know, the book that we all love so much in this family and spend so much time reading." The little girl hurried to obey, but much to her mother's chagrin, she came back with the Sears catalog.

Unfortunately, for too many of us the Bible comes in a distant second to the catalog, or another book, when it comes to what we really value. We live in a world that has lost the glory of God's Word. The Bible has begun to play second fiddle to so many other things that have no lasting value attached to them.

But the problem belongs to us, not to God. It's almost impossible to overstate the importance of His revelation. It is the inerrant (errorless) means by which He communicates and accomplishes His will in history. So important was the Word of God to Job that he said "I have treasured the words of [God's] mouth more than my necessary food" (Job 23:12).

In other words, what God had to say was more important to Job than his fried chicken, greens, and cornbread. It was more important to him than three meals a day. It was the fuel by which Job lived his life, and by which he was sustained during his severe trial. We live in a time of trial as a people today. Our need for the Word of God is critical, because we are watching a generation "perish for the lack of knowledge."

We live in a world of theory. Everyone has an idea and will get mad at you if you think you have the ultimate idea. It's hard today to stand up and say, "This is truth," without getting an argument. Someone will retort, "Who do you think you are?" People no longer believe there is a final word—even from God.

One recent Sunday, a brother in my church stopped me in the hallway and said, "I almost got in a fight this week."

I asked, "What happened?"

"I was on my job talking to this guy and he said, 'Your church and your pastor are a cult!'"

"So I asked him why he said we were a cult. He replied, 'Because you folks tell people how they are supposed to live.'"

*W*HEN THE BIBLE CALLS ITSELF "INSPIRED," IT MEANS THAT YOU HAVE ON ITS PAGES THE VERY BREATH, THE VERY WORD, OF GOD.

People get offended by the idea of an authority which sits in judgment over their lives, even if that authority is God. Now don't get me wrong. There *are* cults and other groups that misuse the Bible, but the definition of a cult is *not* a group that teaches the authority of God's Word. God is not into suggestions. He's big on commandments.

In this world of theory, we need a sure word. People live by their reason, their emotions, and their experiences, but God has come on the scene with a sure word. We'll see in this chapter that the Bible and only the Bible is the absolute, definitive, errorless, authoritative, comprehensive, and eternal Word of God. God does not have two or three words, nor did He write four or five books. One definitive, written revelation has been sent by God for mankind, and that is the Bible.

GOD'S WORD
IS DIVINE IN ORIGIN

The Bible is unique because it came directly from God. Paul writes these words to Timothy, his son in the ministry:

> All Scripture is inspired by God and profitable for teaching, for reproof, for correction, for training in righteousness; that the man of God may be adequate, equipped for every good work. (2 Timothy 3:16–17)

It's Inspired

The word *inspired* comes from the Greek word *theopneustos,* which means God-breathed. So when Paul says the Bible is inspired by God, he's not using the word the way we normally use it. When we say, "The choir's music was inspired this morning," we simply mean that the choir lifted our spirits or moved us. Or a sister sang and triggered an emotional response. Or the speaker gave us a lift. He was "inspirational." That's how we use the word.

But the Bible means much more than that. When the Bible calls itself "inspired," it means that you have on its pages the very breath, the very word, of God. It's the Word of God when you read it; it's the Word of God when it sits on the shelf; it's the Word of God when you like it; it's the Word of God when you don't like it; it's the Word of God when you want it; it's the Word of God when you don't want it. The Bible is the "breathing out" of the very words of God.

Because the Bible is the objective statement of God, it is not just another book. It's not like a novel, or one of the great books on the all-time bestsellers' list. When you open the Bible, you find the very breath of God recorded on a page. That makes the Bible unlike any other book.

It's Consistent

The Bible is also unique because it was compiled over some 1,600 years by more than forty human authors, coming from all different backgrounds: fishermen, tax collectors, prophets, politicians, even a medical doctor. They wrote the sixty-six individual books that make up this one great book. The amazing thing is that all those authors over all those years *delivered a single, consistent message.*

Only one thing can explain how that could happen: Those forty-plus authors had to be getting their data from the same source—the very mind of God. The Bible claims exactly that for itself (2 Peter 1:21).

It's Alive

The Bible also gives this testimony concerning itself in Hebrews 4:12–13:

> The word of God is living and active and sharper than any two-edged sword, and piercing as far as the division of soul and spirit, of both joints and marrow, and able to judge the thoughts and intentions of the heart. And there is no creature hidden from His sight, but all things are open and laid bare to the eyes of Him with whom we have to do.

The Word of God is alive! That's why reading the Bible can convict you of sin and change your life. The Bible can lead you on the right way because it's alive, it's active. God's Word can penetrate below the skin and get to the soul and spirit, right into the "joints and marrow" of your inner person. It can unveil the hidden motives of the heart.

This is a unique book. Near the end of Peter's life, he pointed to the uniqueness of God's Word to validate his ministry:

> We did not follow cleverly devised tales when we made known to you the power and coming of our Lord Jesus Christ, but we were eyewitnesses of His majesty. For when He received honor and glory from God the Father, such an utterance as this was made to Him by the Majestic Glory, "This is My beloved Son with whom I am well-pleased"—and we ourselves heard this utterance made from heaven when we were with Him on the holy mountain. And so we have the prophetic word made more sure, to which you do well to pay attention as to a lamp shining in a dark place, until the day dawns and the morning star rises in your hearts. (2 Peter 1:16–19)

Peter says, "We were with Jesus on the Mount of Transfiguration when He zipped down His humanity and exposed His deity. We saw the Shekinah glory of God burst through His humanity so powerfully we couldn't even look at it. What an experience that was!"

But Peter goes on to say, "As great as that was, though, we have a more sure word. We have something that can beat being on the mountain, and that is the Word of God." Peter is writing to a group of people who didn't get to make the trip to the mountain with him. Their sentiment would be, "Oh, if we could have been there with Peter."

Peter assures them, "You have something better than being there with me. You have a more sure word that can do for you what the mountain did for me." Peter says if they pay attention to the written word, "the morning star [will rise] in your hearts" (v. 19). The morning star, of course, is the star that comes up in the morning, the sun.

Peter says, "We saw the Son as bright as the sun, but even though you can't go to the mountain, you can have the Son break forth in your hearts like the sun if you pay strict attention to this sure word, because it is as alive as the living Word was on that mountaintop."

It Comes from God

Now, someone will say, "The Bible was written by men." The person may even admit that it's a good book and it has a lot of nice stuff in it, but he or she will insist that it's a purely human product.

The next line is always, "Men aren't perfect. So if men put their pens to paper to write this book, it must have error in it because it was crafted by the hands of imperfect people."

Knowing that this complaint would come, Peter continues in the same chapter:

> But know this first of all, that no prophecy of Scripture is a matter of one's own interpretation, for no prophecy was ever made by an act of human will, but men moved by the Holy Spirit spoke from God. (vv. 20–21)

Peter claims here that men wrote Scripture, but they wrote it under the hypnotic influence of the Holy Spirit. In other words, while human authors held the quills, the Holy Spirit so consumed their minds that what went through their minds to their fingers and got recorded on the parchment were the very thoughts from the mind of God.

The process Peter describes is like a stained-glass window. When the sun shines through a blue piece of stained glass, the light looks blue. When the sun shines through a red piece of stained glass, the light looks red. When the sun shines through a yellow piece of stained glass, the light looks yellow. The light is the same in each case, but it will take on the color of the vehicle through which it passes.

Paul had a certain writing style, John had a different style, while James had yet another style. Peter was different too, for that matter. But Peter's point is that no matter who was writing, they were all recording the mind of God. The Bible is the very thought of God, and as such it is self-validating as the Word of God.

That's why we don't need to spend a lot of time arguing that the Bible is the Word of God. Martin Luther said: "The Bible is like a lion. You don't have to defend it, just let it loose. It will take care of itself." You and I have the responsibility to know it so that we can use it, and then let it take care of itself.

The Word of God is intricately tied to the person of God. When God wanted to record something in the Bible, He allowed the vehicle to simply transmit it. He even used a donkey on one occasion when He couldn't get the attention of the prophet Balaam (Numbers 22:28–30).

*I*F GOD CAN'T BE TRUSTED TOTALLY, THEN I CAN'T RISK TRUSTING HIM AT ALL. I HAVE TOO MANY OTHER PEOPLE I TRUST PARTIALLY.

Even animals know what to say when God tells them to speak. When it comes to His revelation, He controls what's recorded in the Bible through normal, and sometimes through supernatural, processes.

GOD'S WORD
IS ABSOLUTE TRUTH

The Word of God reflects the character of its divine Author, so it couldn't be anything but absolute truth.

How important is that? If one thing in this book is wrong, then we have no basis for trusting anything that's in it. If I can't believe God in Genesis 3:3, how do I know I can believe Him in Revelation 3:3? If He makes a mistake early on, how do I know I can trust Him later? If He makes a scientific mistake, for example, how do I know

I can trust Him with my eternal destiny? I don't want to go into eternity and find out God blew it!

So it's an all-or-nothing ballgame when it comes to the truth of God's Word. People want to take apart the Scriptures. They want to say, "Well, I believe that. That sounds like something God would do. But I don't like this other over here, because that doesn't sound like what I think God would do."

The Whole Truth

But if God can't be trusted totally, then I can't risk trusting Him at all. I have too many other people I trust partially. I don't need a God I trust partially too. Make no mistake about it; the issue on the floor is whether God is totally trustworthy when He transmits His Word. Let's look at John 17:

> These things Jesus spoke; and lifting up His eyes to heaven, He said, "Father, the hour has come; glorify Thy Son, that the Son may glorify Thee, even as Thou gavest Him authority over all mankind, that to all whom Thou has given Him, He may give eternal life. And this is eternal life, that they may know Thee, the only true God, and Jesus Christ whom Thou hast sent. I glorified Thee on the earth, having accomplished the work which Thou hast given Me to do. And now, glorify Thou Me together with Thyself, Father, with the glory which I had with Thee before the world was. I manifested Thy name to the men whom Thou gavest Me out of the world; Thine they were, and Thou gavest them to Me, and they have kept Thy word. Now they have come to know that everything Thou hast given Me is from Thee." (vv. 1–7)

Notice how the truth passes down. Jesus says, "What I have, Father, You gave to Me; what I have, I gave to them." God gave the truth to His Son, and Jesus entrusted the truth to His disciples. Jesus went on to say in verse 8: "The words which Thou gavest Me I have given to them; and they received them, and truly understood that I came forth from Thee, and they believed that Thou didst send Me."

In other words, God gave the truth to Jesus, Jesus passed the truth on to His disciples, and they wrote down the truth for us. How do we know that when they wrote, they didn't mess up what Jesus gave them? Because Jesus promised to give them "the Spirit of truth" (John 14:17) who would guide them "into all the truth" (John 16:13).

The God of Truth

So this whole process has been overseen by the perfect hand of the only true God. Jesus caps all of this by praying: "Sanctify them in the truth; Thy word is truth" (John 17:17). To have any mistakes in the Bible, there would have to be a mistake with God. And if there were to be a mistake with God, He would no longer be God.

But the Bible declares that God is comprehensive truth. Psalm 108:4 says that His truth "reaches to the skies." Titus 1:2 and Hebrews 6:18 both assert that it is impossible for God to lie. Exodus 34:6 says God is abundant when it comes to dispensing the truth.

In other words, the Bible is clear that God functions in the realm of absolute and total truth all the time. When we deny that and say there is error in the Bible, we do not only indict His Word. It's like staring into the face of God and saying, "God, You are a liar!"

If you are a football fan, you know that in 1993 the NFL did away with the use of instant replay by officials up in the booth to decide questionable calls. It took so much time to make a call that it delayed the game, so they got rid of the instant replay rule and decided they would live with human error. Of course, the TV networks still use instant replay, so you still know it when the official blows a call.

Most people would say, "It's OK to blow a call in a football game, but I don't want anyone 'blowing the call' with my life. I don't want someone giving me wrong information about my eternal destiny. I want someone who doesn't need a replay, who can make the right call first time, every time."

The Word of Truth

The beauty of the Word of God is that God calls it right the first time, every time. He calls it like it is. Now let me explain an argument that is often used by people who claim to have found contradictions in the Bible.

They will take you to a passage like 1 Corinthians 10:8, where Paul says that 23,000 Israelites died in judgment for their idolatry. But the actual story in Numbers 25:9 says that 24,000 people died in this judgment.

"See, that's a contradiction," these people will say. "You can't have one author claiming 23,000 people were killed and another author saying it was 24,000. Someone is either lying or making a mistake. That proves the Bible contradicts itself."

Actually, that doesn't prove anything, and I'll show you why. In this case the difference is easily accounted for, because Paul adds the qualifying phrase "in one day." It's possible that another 1,000 people died on other days.

But beyond that, this kind of reasoning ignores the fact that it's perfectly acceptable for one writer to use an approximate number, while another counts every head. The Bible is literature, and God did not suspend the normal rules of human communication when He inspired the Bible. Here's an example. Suppose after church next Sunday someone were to say to me, "How many people were at church today, pastor?"

I might say, "We had 2,500 people in church today."

Now suppose this same person turns around and asks an usher, "How many people were in church today?"

The usher looks at his records and says, "Let's see, we had 2,615 people."

Those are two different numbers. They don't match. Does that mean one of us lied? Of course not. I was simply giving a round number. But the usher had counted every single person because that's his job. Both of us told the truth; we just explained it in different ways.

This happens all the time in the newspaper, and no one gets worked up about it. The paper will report that 100,000 people attended a big march. The reporter didn't count every person. Officials know about how much space one person occupies, so they measure the amount of territory people filled and come up with a rough estimate of crowd size. No one is called a liar, and no one demands a head count. We allow people to round off numbers.

Because the Bible is literature, God allows people to round off numbers too. And if someone does take a head count, he can report that as well. Both means of counting are legitimate as long as you understand what each person is doing.

Let me give you another example, a famous so-called contradiction. The Bible says that when Joshua was in the middle of a battle, he needed more sunlight to fight. So the Bible records that "the sun stood still" (Joshua 10:13).

Scientists and others jump on this and say, "You see, the Bible was written a long time ago by people who didn't know that the sun does not move. Joshua was in error. His statement contradicts the known scientific fact that the sun does not move. The Bible is antiquated and out of date."

No, the Bible is *literature,* and it uses normal vehicles of communication like figures of speech. If you watch the weather report tonight, the weatherman will tell you what time sunrise will be tomorrow morning. We all know the sun does not rise, but we understand what he means. He *should* say that the earth's rotation on its axis will turn us toward the sun tomorrow morning. But he only has five minutes to do the weather, so he says, "Sunrise will be at 6:53 in the morning."

*W*E HAVE CHAOS IN OUR WORLD BECAUSE WHAT PEOPLE ACCEPT WITH MATH, THEY WON'T ACCEPT WITH MORALITY OR ETERNAL ISSUES. THEY DON'T WANT AN ABSOLUTE, FINAL STANDARD.

The Bible has no contradictions in it, but it does recognize human methods of communication. When you understand that, what may appear as contradictions are in fact not contradictions at all.

It is absolutely critical that we take seriously this authentic, authoritative word. The Bible is truth—absolute truth. It is truth in all of its parts, and unless you know the Bible and are willing to obey the Bible you will not benefit from the truth. But you won't stop the Bible from being true.

One day, some men were reading the story of Moses when they noticed one little statement that said Moses' mother made a basket for Moses with tar and pitch. Those men said, "Tar and pitch?" They knew that wherever there is tar, there is oil. That began a process of going to the Middle East with machinery to discover that the greatest oil deposits are located in the Middle East—because two men read the Bible and saw a reference to tar and pitch.

The Bible is absolutely true. It's not a science book, but whenever it speaks scientifically, it speaks perfectly. It's not just a history book, but whenever it speaks historically, it speaks perfectly. That's why you must know the Word of God, because it is absolute truth.

Otherwise, you can be tricked and fooled by what people say about the Bible. Don't believe something just because someone says it. You'd better make sure that what you hear or read is the Word of God. Many of us have been believing things for years that do not appear in the Bible: "You take one step, He'll take two." Try to find that in your Bible. Your grandmother may have thought it was in there, but the Bible doesn't teach that. Your Bible was not designed to decorate your coffee table or sit on your den shelf. It is the word of life, the Word of God that is true in all of its parts.

An Enduring Standard

It's important to realize that something cannot be true unless it rests on a foundation of truth. The question is not what's true, but what is *truth?* To determine that, you must have a standard that will sit in judgment on anything and everything.

For example, one plus one equals two. It has always equaled two, and it will forever equal two. What's more, one plus one equals two in Africa, in Asia, in South America, or wherever you go. Why? Because when it comes to numbers, we all operate on the same standard. That's why we can all agree about one plus one being two.

But if our standard changed, our analysis of truth would change. One plus one might equal two to me, but it may be five or even ten to you because you have created your own standard. Suppose someone jumped up and said, "One and one is three."

You would say, "One and one is not three!"

"It's three to me."

You respond, "Yeah, but it's not three."

"Who are you to tell me it's not three? If I want it to be three, then it's three. You can't tell me when I can make one and one equal three and when I can't! You want to fight?"

What stops people from doing that? A universally accepted standard. We have chaos in our world because what people accept with math, they won't accept with morality or eternal issues. They don't want an absolute, final standard. So what do they do? They create their own gods who will let them make one and one equal three in the realm of morality; gods who will let them do what they want to do and legitimize their rebellion.

People make their own standards and then make you feel guilty for having an absolute standard. They call you a fanatic because you have a standard. They call you crazy and tell you that you are a cult member because you have a standard. But you should not be intimidated by that because the whole world works by standards. God is the standard, and He is the only true God.

GOD'S WORD
ACCOMPLISHES HIS SOVEREIGN WILL

In Isaiah 55, the prophet makes a profound and important statement about the Word of God:

> For as the rain and the snow come down from heaven, and do not return there without watering the earth, and making it bear and sprout, and furnishing seed to the sower and bread to the eater; so shall My word be which goes forth from My mouth; it shall not return to Me empty, without accomplishing what I desire, and without succeeding in the matter for which I sent it. (vv. 10–11)

In other words, when God talks, He doesn't blow smoke. When He speaks, something happens. God's Word is always accompanied by His power.

God's Will

In the beginning, the Bible says, God commanded, "Let there be light" (Genesis 1:3). No meeting was held after that, no committee vote. When God called for light, "there was light." Period. That's it. Because when God speaks, something happens. The Bible says that when God speaks, He creates. When God commands, He brings things into existence.

*[S*ATAN] LOVES TO HEAR US RAPPING AND TALKING, BUT HE DOESN'T WANT TO HEAR, "SATAN, LET'S DO A LITTLE BIBLE STUDY."*

In fact, according to Psalm 147:15–18, God controls the weather by His word. I know meteorologists account for the rain by explaining how this front mixes with that front and by showing the movement of air and all of that. But they are only investigating the speech of God. God says that when it rains, it does so because He says so. The elements come under His control.

Jeremiah 1:10 indicates that the nations are controlled by the Word of God. When God speaks, He can raise up and tear down nations. He splits Berlin Walls, dismantles Soviet Unions—and if we don't watch out, He can take down America. God works His will among the nations simply by the word of His power.

God's Word is also the only thing that can deal with the demonic realm. Many of the negative things we experience are the result of activity by the demonic world opposing and attacking us. This world is the realm of Satan's influence (Ephesians 2:2). But the Bible shows us again and again that the demons have to obey God when He merely utters the word. Mark 5:1–20 is a great example.

God's Sword

That's why the Bible calls itself "the sword of the Spirit" (Ephesians 6:17). It is the only thing that can cut through and deal with the spiritual causes of many of our physical problems. You see, if your physical problem has a spiritual cause, then going to a doctor can't help you. The doctor can only give you something to cover it up. You need something that can deal with the spirit realm, and only the Word of God can do that.

Do you remember those old Dracula movies? Dracula would come out at full moon, his teeth getting long, and start biting the necks of helpless victims. He was too strong to be resisted or fought off. But someone finally realized the only thing that could stop Dracula was the cross. Hold up the cross, and Dracula shriveled and ran away because he couldn't handle the cross.

That's how the Word of God is. Satan loves to hear you talk about how strong you are and what you are going to do because he says, "I've got him now." Did you know that Satan loves to hear you make your New Year's resolutions? He knows you are no match for him on your own. But he can't stand against God's Word.

That's why Jesus answered Satan, "It is written." Satan can't handle the Word. He shrinks back. He flees.

Satan wants to hear you and me say, "Well, I think . . ." or, "My mama always said. . . ." He loves to hear us rapping and talking, but he doesn't want to hear, "Satan, let's do a little Bible study." He doesn't want to hear the Word of God because it is sure.

This reminds me of the story in Acts 19:11–16. Paul was casting out demons and performing other miracles by the word of God's power. These seven Jewish exorcists, who happened to be brothers, watched Paul cast out demons and decided they could do it too. They went to a man who was being tormented by a demon and tried to imitate Paul: "Demon, come out of him!"

But the demon said, "I recognize Jesus, and I know about Paul, but who are you?" (v. 15). Then the demon proceeded to whip those seven guys so bad they ran out of the house "naked and wounded" (v. 16).

That's what happens when you don't have the right solution. Many of us don't know about the spiritual realm, so we don't seek spiritual solutions. Or we don't know how the spiritual realm works, so we don't know how to use the sword of the Spirit and our other spiritual weapons and we wind up defeated.

When God wields the sword of His Spirit, it accomplishes His purpose because God's Word is authoritative. Like the hot sun, God's Word will either melt ice or harden clay. It will always do something; it will never come down from heaven and go back without having done what it was sent to do.

GOD'S WORD:
SUFFICIENT FOR EVERY SPIRITUAL NEED

God's Word addresses all of life. That shouldn't surprise us, because life is complex and we need something stable, solid, and dependable to deal with it.

Everything We Need

Psalm 19 gives us at least six examples of what the Word of God can do for us. Look at verse 7a: "The law of the Lord is perfect, restoring the soul." That simply means God's Word is so comprehensive that it can transform the whole person. It can totally turn your life around.

David continues, "The testimony of the Lord is sure, making wise the simple" (v. 7b). That is, the Word imparts wisdom. It teaches you how to live skillfully; that's biblical wisdom.

Then in verse 8 the psalmist says, "The precepts of the Lord are right, rejoicing the heart; the commandment of the Lord is pure, enlightening the eyes." That is, the Word of God shows you the true path to follow as you wind through the maze of life. And it is so clean and so clear that it is not puzzling. It enables you to see things as they really are. In fact, you'll never see life as it really is until you see it through the lens of God's Word.

It just keeps getting better. Look at verse 9: "The fear of the Lord is clean, enduring forever; the judgments of the Lord are true; they are righteous altogether." The Word contains no impurities, no errors that will lead you into a ditch. God's Word is also relevant in every age for every situation. It is, as we saw earlier, an enduring standard against which everything is to be judged.

Better than Gold

Sounds great, doesn't it? So what should you do in response to the good things in God's Word? David answers that in verse 10: "They are more desirable than gold, yes, than much fine gold; sweeter also than honey and the drippings of the honeycomb."

Let's stop and take a test. Do you want to know how much you value the Word? Answer this question: What's more important to you, your Bible or your money? David was called a man after God's own heart because he valued God's Word more than his paycheck. He knew that his paycheck couldn't give him life—and neither can yours or mine.

If you don't have the Lord, your money can only allow you to buy toys that make you forget how miserable you really are. But when you fall in love with God—and therefore, with His Word— then you come to see and value its sufficiency, its authority, and its beauty.

Purifying Agent

But the Bible does something more for us. It will keep you from sin because it will help you discern your hidden faults. David says elsewhere, "Thy Word I have treasured in my heart, that I may not sin against Thee" (Psalm 119:11). In verse 13 of Psalm 19 he writes, "Keep back Thy servant from presumptuous sins; let them not rule over me." Sins that rule over a person are called addictions. Did you know that the Word of God can keep you from addictions?

When God's Word purifies us, it does a comprehensive job. That's why David can say, "Then I shall be blameless, and I shall be acquitted of great transgression. Let the words of my mouth and the meditation of my heart be acceptable in Thy sight, O Lord, my rock and my Redeemer" (Psalm 19:13b–14).

David is telling us that many of our problems result from the fact that we don't take the Word of God seriously enough, either in learning it or obeying it, or both. When you let God's Word permeate all of your being, when you meditate and reflect on it, when you let it purify and discipline you, it transforms you.

It's like the mother who knew her daughter had disobeyed and stolen cookies she wasn't supposed to take. So the mother asked, "Did you take the cookies?"

The girl said, "No."

"I said, did you take the cookies?"

The girl replied, "No, Mommy, I did not take the cookies."

The mother knew different. "I'm asking you again, did you take the cookies?"

"No, Mommy, I didn't take the cookies."

This went on about four more times, until finally the mother said, "This is your mother speaking: Did you take the cookies?"

"Well, the cookies were right there."

"Did you take them?"

The girl said, "Yes, Mommy, I took the cookies."

That's how the Word of God acts in our lives. If you let it search and convict your heart long enough, you will come clean sooner or later. As long as you aren't being confronted with the Word, you can hide from the truth, excuse your sin, and run from the issue. But when the Word of God keeps banging on the door of your heart and mind, you will get right after a while.

SUCCESS IS GETTING TO THE END OF YOUR LIFE HAVING DONE WHAT GOD WANTED YOU TO DO.

"How can a young man keep his way pure?" David asks in Psalm 119:9. "By keeping it according to Thy word." When the Word of God keeps searching and probing your soul, it brings out the junk that's in there and washes it out. It flushes out the spiritual impurities so that you can be clean.

GOD'S WORD
IS BENEFICIAL TO THOSE WHO OBEY

God's Word only benefits those who know it and obey it. It's the fuel of life for those who make it the focus of their lives. Joshua 1 brings this home well. God said to Joshua as he was getting ready to go into the Promised Land:

> No man will be able to stand before you all the days of your life. Just as I have been with Moses, I will be with you; I will not fail you or forsake you. Be strong and courageous, for you shall give this people possession of the land which I swore to their fathers to give them. Only be strong and very courageous; be careful to do according to all the law which Moses My servant commanded you; do not turn from it to the right or to the left, so that you may have success wherever you go. This book of the law shall not depart from your mouth, but you shall meditate on it day and night, so that you may be careful to do according to all that is written in it; for then you will make your way prosperous, and then you will have success. (vv. 5–8)

Success

What a formula for success. The world scratches around trying to find the secret to success, and here it is. God says, "If you want success, don't turn to the right or to the left away from My Word. If you want success, know it, meditate on it, and do it."

To meditate on God's Word means to have it rolling around in your mind as a way of life. It doesn't mean sitting down all day practicing yoga, but having the Word so filter your thought processes that God can ride the wings of His Word into your heart. There, He can give direction for your life, leading you in the path of everlasting life and in the way you ought to go.

Everyone wants to be successful. The Bible says that success comes from completely obeying the Word of God. That's the definition of true success: coming to the end of your life having fulfilled the will of God. Success is getting to the end of your life having done what God wanted you to do.

That's why when it was time for Paul to die, he said, "I have fought the good fight, I have finished the course, I have kept the faith" (2 Timothy 4:7). He was ready to die because he had completed the will of God for his life.

If you get ready to die and you haven't done God's will, you have lived a failed life. It doesn't matter how much money you have accumulated in the bank, how big the house is, or what the make of the car happens to be. A successful life is fulfilling the will of God, and you only get to know and experience God's will as you live under the authority and direction of His Word.

Freedom

The Bible says that God's Word brings freedom (John 8:31–32). Do you want to be free from things that are binding you? Freedom is not doing what you want to do; freedom is doing what you ought to do. What would tennis be without a baseline? What would football be without a sideline? What would baseball be without a foul line? If you don't have any lines, you have chaos. In order to have freedom, you've got to have guidelines that govern the field of play. The Bible gives us those guidelines.

Spiritual Vitality

The Bible does so many other good things for us that I can only list a few of them:

1. God's Word gives us life (Philippians 2:16).
2. God's Word can make us righteous (1 Corinthians 15:1–2).
3. God's Word can produce growth (1 Peter 2:2).
4. God's Word sanctifies us (John 17:17).
5. God's Word gives us wisdom (Psalm 119:98).

It's like taking vitamins. You may not feel them, but if you keep taking them regularly enough you will know they are working because you stay healthy. You know God's Word is working because He's keeping you on track spiritually. The Word is building you up.

Because God does all of this, my job as a preacher is to preach His Word—not sociology, politics, or economics. Now, I can talk sociologically from the Bible. I can talk politically from the Bible. I can talk economically from the Bible. But those subjects aren't my subject. Paul told Timothy, "Preach the word; be ready in season and out of season" (2 Timothy 4:2). In other words, preach it when people want it and when they don't want it.

That's what people need today. They need the authoritative, definitive, perfect, consistent, and errorless Word of God.

Responding to the Word of God

C harles Spurgeon said it best. "Bibles that are falling apart usually belong to people who aren't." If you want a life that's held together, you need to wear your Bible out. Here are some ways you can put the Word to work in your daily walk:

1. Memorize Isaiah 55:11. This is one of the best verses I know of to remind you and encourage you that God will not fail to use His Word in your life to make you more like Christ.

2. Here's another tool for your "witnessing kit." The next time someone hauls out the old objection that the Bible is full of contradictions, ask the person to show you one. Be courteous about it and give the other person a chance to find one, but you don't have a lot to worry about. Almost without fail, the objector will not know a single one. Ask gently if you can lay that issue aside and get to the real issue: his or her soul.

3. I said that the test of what you think of God's Word is how you value it and obey what it teaches. Try this experiment to help you see how much value you are putting on living by the Word. Down one side of a piece of paper list your top three or four personal spiritual goals. Next to each goal list the specific things you are doing consistently to reach that goal. If your paper is pretty empty, you may need to make some revisions in your priorities.

4. Are you hiding a secret sin in your life that's eating you up with guilt and stealing your joy and power? Since God already knows about it, why not write it down as a symbolic act of confession and surrender to the Lord, then offer it to Him in a time of sincere prayer, asking Him to help you remove it from your life. Now tear up the paper—and begin trusting God to answer your prayer.

12
THE GOODNESS
OF GOD

ost of us grew up singing a little chorus that proclaims, "God is so good." That song actually contains some profound theology, because as we will see in this chapter, the goodness of God is one of the infinite attributes of His character.

In fact, God's goodness can be defined as the collective perfections of His nature and the benevolence of His acts. To put it in the words of Psalm 119:68, "Thou art good and doest good." That says it very simply. God is good by nature and good in what He does.

We live in a time when people question the goodness of God. This is not a new problem, however. It really goes back all the way to the Garden of Eden, when Satan informed Eve that the only reason God didn't want her to eat from the tree in the middle of the garden was that God was selfish. He wasn't good, in other words (Genesis 3:1–7).

Once Satan got Eve to focus on the one tree she couldn't eat from rather than the hundreds she could enjoy, she lost sight of God's goodness and plunged herself, her family, and the rest of the world into sin.

Something like this happens in many homes with young children at Christmas. Maybe it happened this way in your home. The kids give you their Christmas lists, and let's say they have listed ten things. You buy nine of them. On Christmas morning, the kids begin to unwrap their presents and show excitement about this and that until they discover that item number ten was not under the tree.

It's amazing how quickly the other nine gifts are forgotten and the discussion centers on why you didn't buy toy number ten. Suddenly, the kids call your goodness as a parent into question over the one gift they didn't receive rather than the nine they did.

If we are honest with ourselves, we have to admit that we act like that with our heavenly Father. We spend our time complaining about the few gizmos we do not have rather than rejoicing in the bountiful benefit of the goodness of God that never fails.

To help remedy our problem, I want to discuss five important truths about the goodness of God.

GOD'S GOODNESS
IS THE STANDARD

The goodness of God is the standard by which anything called good must be judged. Mark 10 makes this remarkably clear because in this chapter, we are confronted with the foundation of goodness. The rich young ruler had it all: wealth, youth, and power, all the things that most people fight to get. But he knew he had a hole inside of him. Something was missing. So one day he ran up to Jesus and asked the famous question, "Good Teacher, what shall I do to inherit eternal life?" (v. 17).

Either No Good—or God

Jesus' answer in verse 18 is instructive: "Why do you call Me good? No one is good except God alone." The young man was using the term good without realizing the full implications of what he was saying or who he was talking to. He needed a quick theology lesson, so Jesus challenged him, "How do you know I'm good? By what standard are you using this term? You need to understand that no one is really good except God."

Jesus' point to this young man was simply this: "Either I'm no good, or I'm God." Jesus was bringing the young man in through the "back door" to realize His deity. Aside from this ruler's particular need, Jesus makes the broader point that anything called good must find its source in God.

If it—that is, anything you can name—does not emanate from God, does not agree with His nature, it cannot be good because only that which agrees with who and what God is that can be called good. It must line up with His perfections and coincide with His activity, or else it's not good. It doesn't matter how good something looks or how good it makes you feel, if it's not from God, it's not good.

Let me give some obvious examples. Drugs have a way of making a person feel good temporarily, but drugs are not good. Some people want to define goodness based on their emotions. They live by the tired creed "If it feels good, do it."

In other words, if something makes them feel good for the moment, it must be good. You find this philosophy in many places. A country song asks the question, "How can it be bad when it feels so good?" You hear people argue, "If God didn't want me to have it, it wouldn't be here." Such people mistake the mere existence of something for its moral quality. If it's available to them, it has to be good.

GOD ONLY PRODUCES THAT WHICH IS GOOD. SO IF SOMETHING IS NOT GOOD, IT DID NOT COME FROM GOD.

But Jesus says to the rich young ruler and to us, "The only thing that can be called good is that which has its source in God, for nothing is good but God." He is the standard for what is good, not our feelings or experience.

Good for You

When we go home to my parents' house every year, my mother cooks a big meal. Inevitably she will cook what I call some unholy vegetable, squash or its cousin okra. You know, something that seems to have no purpose in creation. Anyway, when that vegetable bowl comes around I just pass it right on. But my mother will say, "Boy, what do you think you're doing?"

I say, "Mama, I don't want any squash. I'm forty-four years old. I don't want any squash."

She says, "Yeah, you are forty-four years old in my house. Ain't no hotel sign outside that front door." So she will take the bowl and start putting the food on my plate for me, like we were back to Gerbersville or something. And she always puts more squash on my plate than I would have taken if I had just gone ahead and done it. Then she says, "And you'd better eat it all."

My kids have seen her do this more than once, and they always look at me with looks that say, "Ha, ha, ha!"

Then Mom will cap it all off with this line: "It's good for you." You know, she's right. Medical science will tell you that squash is good for you. Now I'd rather have German chocolate cake à la mode. I can get excited about that. But it's not good for me. Everything that's good does not necessarily taste good, look good, produce nice feelings, or give you a pleasant emotional experience, although sometimes good things do. The issue of goodness is its source, not its experience.

All Good from God

The Bible declares in James 1:17, "Every good thing bestowed and every perfect gift is from above, coming down from the Father of lights." Anything authentically good has its source in the Father of lights in whom there is no "shifting shadow." God only produces that which is good. So if something is not good, it did not come from God.

One day I ran into a man who rejected the concept of a good God. His argument was a familiar one: "How can there be a good God when He allowed six million Jews to be slaughtered in the Nazi Holocaust? I can't believe in a God who would allow six million people to be killed."

I said to him, "OK, let's suppose your conclusion is right. Let's suppose God does not exist. Now tell me, who killed those six million Jews? You see, getting rid of God doesn't solve your problem. You've still got six million people dead."

You address these issues by understanding that if it is not good, it didn't have its source in God. Yes, God is sovereign and He allows things for reasons we don't always understand, but the Bible makes clear that God does not participate in sin in any way. There is no defect in Him.

God cannot be improved upon. He is good. He does not have to work on His personality, improve His character, smooth out flaws. He is impeccably perfect in every detail, because God is good. What's more, He finds great joy in His own goodness. He is so good that He can brag about it and be absolutely correct.

GOD'S GOODNESS
EXPRESSED IN HIS ATTRIBUTES

The goodness of God is expressed in and through His various characteristics. In other words, you know God is good by simply looking at who He is. Let me show you what I mean. We studied Exodus 33 earlier, but let's go back there for a minute. Remember that Moses asked to see God's glory (v. 18), and in response the Lord says, "I Myself will make all My goodness pass before you" (v. 19).

Now compare that with Exodus 34:5–7:

> And the Lord descended in the cloud and stood there with him as he called upon the name of the Lord. Then the Lord passed by in front of him and proclaimed, "The Lord, the Lord God, compassionate and gracious, slow to anger, and abounding in lovingkindness and truth; who keeps lovingkindness for thousands, who forgives iniquity, transgression and sin; yet He will by no means leave the guilty unpunished, visiting the iniquity of fathers on the children and on the grandchildren to the third and fourth generations."

God tells Moses, "I will let My goodness pass by before you," and then when it happens God says, in essence, "Look at My character."

Goodness and Patience

God expresses His goodness to us by attaching one of His characteristics to the circumstances of our lives. Because God is good, for example, He is patient. In the Bible, patience means not avenging wrong done to you even though you have the power and the right to do so.

You say, "I've got it bad, so God can't be good." No, if God were not good, you wouldn't have anything at all. Because if God were not good, He would not execute patience toward you. And if God did not execute patience, the moment you even thought about a sin, you would drop dead because God is so holy that He has to punish every sin.

You are here to hold this book and I was able to write it only because God is patient with us. He's been waiting for years for some of us to come through on our promises to Him. The only reason we're still hanging around and He's still listening to those promises is that He's patient. We would give up on other people a lot sooner than God does.

Goodness and Grace

God's goodness is seen in His love by which He identified with sinful humanity. He gave Himself for us so He could have a love relationship with us. God is so good, He died for you and me. He's full of grace. Grace means giving your absolute best to someone who deserves your absolute worst. That's pure goodness, and only God has it.

He's also merciful, which means removing your misery. He's truthful. He's the only One who will give you the straight story all the time. He forgives you of things that other people will hold against you until they go to their graves. That's goodness!

The goodness of God also shows in the fact that He will apply the appropriate part of His character to your situation. Some people like to point out that God once destroyed the whole world with a flood, and they ask, "How could God do that if He's good?"

But they ignore the rest of the story. For 120 years, God warned those people through Noah, "It's going to rain." Noah builds the ark on dry land, a huge ship almost as big as two football fields. He goes into town every day, preaching the same four-word sermon: "It's going to rain." He prints tracts and hands them out on the corner. They are not hard to read. They only have one line: "It's going to rain." Over and over, year after year, Noah faithfully delivered God's warning.

But our objector might say, "Wait a minute. I can see people going for 120 years and not believing a preacher. Besides, it had never rained before. How were those people supposed to know that Noah was telling the truth and it was going to rain?"

Well, even if I didn't believe Noah, when I saw the animals lining up two by two to get on that ark, I would figure something was getting ready to happen. When Mr. & Mrs. Giraffe and Mr. & Mrs. Anteater start saying by their actions, "It's going to rain," I think I would check out what Noah was saying a little closer. All the signs were present, *for 120 years!* God is good. People want to look at the negative and say, "God can't be good."

He hung in there 120 years waiting for people to repent, and that's not goodness?! Someone else will ask, "Will a good and merciful God really send me to hell?" Answer: absolutely. How can He? Because He's begged, pleaded, convicted, even sent His Son to die for you, and you still ignore Him. You see, the issue is not that God isn't good. The issue is that people don't want His goodness because they want to make it on their own, to rely on their own goodness. Bad choice.

GOD'S GOODNESS
DEMONSTRATED IN HIS PROVISION

Let me show you something very interesting in Genesis 1:

> And God created man in His own image, in the image of God He created him; male and female He created them. And God blessed them; and God said to them, "Be fruitful and multiply, and fill the earth, and subdue it; and rule over the fish of the sea and over the birds of the sky, and over every living thing that moves on the earth." Then God said, "Behold, I have given you every plant yielding seed that is on the surface of all the earth, and every tree which has fruit yielding seed; it shall be food for you; and to every beast of the earth and to every bird of the sky and to every thing that moves on the earth which has life, I have given every green plant for food"; and it was so. And God saw all that He had made, and behold, it was very good. And there was evening and there was morning, the sixth day. (vv. 27–31)

GOD'S GOODNESS IS NOT EQUAL. GOD IS GOOD TO ALL IN SOME WAYS, BUT HE'S GOOD TO SOME IN ALL WAYS.

Earthly Provisions

In His goodness, God not only created you, but He also created everything for you. In other words, God didn't create the plants, animals, or fish just to have them around. He created them for the benefit of mankind. The earth was created to give us a home to enjoy. Every day when you get up and see the sun shine and say, "What a beautiful day!", God sits back and says, "How do you think that happened? Today didn't just jump up here by itself. It's a beautiful day because I'm a good God."

You eat that fried catfish and you say, "Umm, that sure was good."

God says, "Hold it. If you read Genesis 1, you will find that I created the water and the dry land. I separated the dry land from the water. I created every fish in every body of water. So whenever you eat catfish, don't just say, 'It was good.' Say, 'God is good.'"

Every time I pick up a piece of fried chicken, I am reminded that God is good. Every time you see a rose, God says, "I don't want you just talking about how pretty those roses are, or you miss the point. The point is I know what I'm doing when I make flowers because I am a good God."

When it rains and you say, "It's a bad day," God says, "Hold it! Hold it!" Why? Because Acts 14:17 says He gives the rain and makes the seasons change to bring satisfaction to the human race. No rain, no vegetation; no vegetation, no vegetables or fruit. So the next time you enjoy a vegetable or a piece of fruit, you ought to pause and have a time of prayer and thanksgiving because our good God causes it to rain.

Goodness to All

God's goodness is not equal. God is good to all in some ways, but He's good to some in all ways. You may need to think about that for a minute.

Matthew 5:45 gives an example of how God is good to all: "He causes His sun to rise on the evil and the good, and sends rain on the righteous and the unrighteous." You don't have to be a Christian to get God's rain. It doesn't just rain on Christians' yards. It rains on all because God has ordained that certain aspects of His goodness be available to atheists as well as to the most committed Christians.

Goodness to His People

On the other hand, God has provided Christians with the ability to enjoy His goodness in ways that the world can never appreciate. He's given us His revelation, His Holy Spirit to guide us, and a divine perspective on life that opens our eyes to see and enjoy His goodness.

If you are a Christian, you can participate in and benefit from the goodness of God like no unregenerate person can. Romans 8:32 says, "He who did not spare His own Son, but delivered Him up for us all, how will He not also with Him freely give us all things?"

Now I realize that to talk about enjoying things makes some Christians nervous. So I want to get something straight about the enjoyment of God's goodness, and I want to get it straight from God's standpoint. Read the verses below carefully:

> But the Spirit explicitly says that in later times some will fall away from the faith, paying attention to deceitful spirits and doctrines of demons, by means of the hypocrisy of liars seared in their own conscience as with a branding iron, men who forbid marriage and advocate abstaining from foods, which God has created to be gratefully shared in by those who believe and know the truth. For everything created by God is good, and nothing is to be rejected, if it is received with gratitude; for it is sanctified by means of the word of God and prayer. (1 Timothy 4:1–5)

Did you get Paul's point? It's a sin *not* to enjoy the goodness of God! If I were preaching to my people right now, I would say, "Let me say that again." So let me say it again here, because this is probably a revolutionary thought to some of God's children. It is a sin not to enjoy God's goodness. It is a sin to deny and pervert His goodness, as these people were doing.

Where does it say sinners get to have the most fun? Many of us were raised to think that when you become a Christian, you enter into a boring existence while sinners enjoy all the good stuff. That is a doctrine from hell. It's a demonic doctrine that says to be a Christian is to live an empty, boring, purposeless, and dull life of denial. It's false because God says, "Everything that I created is good and meant to be enjoyed by those who know the truth."

Believers should be enjoying nature more than nonbelievers because we know who the Maker is. We should be enjoying relationships more than anyone. We should be enjoying a good meal more than anyone. We should be enjoying the flowers more than anyone. We should be enjoying creation more than anyone because we know the Creator. So don't believe this lie that as a Christian you can't enjoy things.

An Attitude of Gratitude

You see, the issue is not whether we should enjoy the good things our good God gives us. The issue is *how* we enjoy them. The unbeliever takes and takes from God and doesn't stop to say thanks or even to think about the Giver. But Christians acknowledge that all good things come from God by thanking Him for them.

Anything you can't thank God for is not good. Why? Because anything you can't thank Him for didn't come from Him, no matter how good it makes you feel. You've got to be able to say, "God, I know this came from You."

Notice in verse 5 of the text above that Paul says the good things we receive from God must be received "with gratitude." When we do that, these things are "sanctified [set apart] by means of the word of God and prayer."

IT HAS OCCURRED TO ME THAT ONE OF THE FUNDAMENTAL REASONS WE ARE NOT "PUMPED" CHRISTIANS IS THAT WE ARE NOT GRATEFUL CHRISTIANS.

In other words, once you apply God's Word to something as the standard for determining that it is good, and then pray over it as a way of giving it back to God, you have sanctified it. That means God can now get the glory from it because you have set it apart for Him.

Mealtime grace is a good example. Grace has become so dull for many of us because we hurriedly mutter, "Lord, thank You for this food I'm about to receive. In Jesus' name, amen," and dig in. But hold it a minute. That meal comes as a gift from a good God. Our prayer should be a way of sanctifying or setting it apart to His glory.

Does that mean we have to give a theology lesson every night at dinner and pray in pious tones while the gravy gets cold? Of course not. But neither should we just go through our day as though all of this is automatic. Sinners do that. God's heart is hurt by the ingratitude of His people.

It has occurred to me that one of the fundamental reasons we are not "pumped" Christians is that we are not grateful Christians. We go around all day as though this stuff ought to be the way it is. Do you know any ungrateful kids? They get used to things being a certain way. Then they start to demand things and act as though you have done them a great disservice if you interrupt their cozy routine. Fortunately, most kids grow out of that stage. Some Christians never do.

You know what? My dog has never told me thanks once. I go and buy this mutt's food every two weeks. I fill his water dish every day. I've got to pay to get him groomed. He doesn't pay for any of this. He doesn't have to scavenge through trash cans looking for food. He may choose to do so, but he doesn't have to because every day that bowl is filled with food. He has a master who has decided to take care of him.

Now my dog does not understand that if I simply withhold my hand, that brother's on his own. He thinks it's all automatic. He can bank on the fact that he is going to have food. When it rains, he's got a doghouse. Sometimes, we even let him into the big house, and he's never ever told me thanks.

I'll let you draw the analogy. God feeds us every day, gives us a roof over our heads. We have clothes on our backs every day. They may not be designer clothes, and the closet may not be as full as we want. But it's like the guy who said, "I complained that I had no shoes until I met a man who had no feet."

Too often we just say, "It's supposed to be there." As soon as something goes wrong, though, we run to God with the audacity to say, "How could You let this happen to me?"

But God answers, "How can you live day in and day out as though I do not exist, ignoring My goodness?"

That's why so many Christians are tight when it comes to giving either of their service or their financial resources. They give God what's left over. They tip Him a little bit of their time and a little bit of their money. Why? Because they are not grateful. Poor giving reflects ingratitude.

Remember the ungrateful kids we talked about? Any kid who refuses to clean his room or wash the dishes is ungrateful. That's the problem you are dealing with, not just laziness. When a child says, "Mama, cook for me, clean for me, buy me these shoes and those jeans, make sure I'm up on all the new stuff coming out—but don't ask me to do any dishes," that's ingratitude.

The only cure for that is to get a firm grip on the goodness of God. The psalmists knew where their blessings came from. "How great is Thy goodness, which Thou hast stored up for those who fear Thee" (Psalm 31:19). "No good thing does He withhold from those who walk uprightly" (Psalm 84:11).

God is good because He's provided us with stuff and more stuff. Yet we keep saying "Give me more" when we haven't even gotten around to thanking Him for what He gives us every day because His mercies are new "every morning" (Lamentations 3:22–23).

I call these "Rubbermaid" Christians. Have you seen the TV commercial for those plastic storage products? This family looks around at all the things they've got and says, "We've got too much stuff." So they go out and buy things to store their belongings in, but now the house looks so bare they say, "We've got to get more stuff!"

That's not it. We should look around us and say, "We've got so much, we need to have another Thanksgiving Day just to tell God thanks for all of this." Every day should be Thanksgiving for Christians. What a tragedy that Thanksgiving is just a holiday!

GOD'S GOODNESS
TRANSCENDS THE NEGATIVE

Everyone loves to quote and claim Romans 8:28. We've been in Romans 8 before, but I want to look at this beloved verse one more time in its context:

> And we know that God causes all things to work together for good to those who love God, to those who are called according His purpose. For whom He foreknew, He also predestined to become conformed to the image of His Son, that He might be the firstborn among many brethren. . . . What then shall we say to these things? If God is for us, who is against us? He who did not spare His own Son, but delivered Him up for us all, how will He not also with Him freely give us all things? (vv. 28–29, 31–32)

All of this being true, Paul then proceeds to raise a very important question:

> Who shall separate us from the love of Christ? Shall tribulation, or distress, or persecution, or famine, or nakedness, or peril, or sword? Just as it is written, "For thy sake we are being put to death all day long; we were considered as sheep to be slaughtered." But in all these things we overwhelmingly conquer through Him who loved us. (vv. 35–37)

A Contaminated World

Now let me point out something. You and I live in a contaminated world, and it rubs off. We have to shower every day because we get dirty, and what is true in the physical realm is true in the spiritual realm. We get dirty. The effects of a sinful world rub off on us. That's what makes heaven so great. Heaven will be heaven because no sin will be there.

CREATION WAS COMPLETELY GOOD WHEN IT CAME FROM GOD'S HAND, BUT IT HAS BEEN CONTAMINATED BY SIN. THEREFORE, WE LIVE IN A WORLD WHERE MANY BAD THINGS HAPPEN.

But because of sin, we live in a very painful world of cancer, AIDS, personality conflicts, attitude battles, and racial strife. We live in a world where if a sinner decides to pick up a gun, a Christian could be in trouble. Much in our world is not good, but it's not because God is not good. It's because man is not good.

Some people will always try to pin the blame on God for the bad things. No, the blame goes to the people who are doing those bad things. We have to understand that even though God is good, it does not mean bad things do not happen. Creation was completely good when it came from God's hand, but it has been contaminated by sin. Therefore, we live in a world where many bad things happen.

Have you ever had your house all clean and then had people come in and mess it up? It's still a good house, but it looks like a mess because of the guests who've invaded it. God created a good world, but it appears to be a mess because the people He has put here to occupy it have been the worst kind of "guests" possible.

How do you feel when you have guests like that? You may whisper to your mate, "I sure will be glad when they leave." I imagine God feels like saying, "I sure will be glad when they leave because they are messing up My house. They throw their clothing of sin all over the place and the mess rubs off on everyone."

Turning Bad into Good

How then can God be good when negative circumstances make up so much a part of life in this world? "[He] causes all things to work together for good to those who love [Him]" (v. 28). God's goodness does not show only when He doesn't allow problems to happen. His goodness appears in the fact that even when they do happen, a good God will transcend those negative things and ultimately work out that which will be for His glory and our benefit.

I know this is hard to come to grips with sometimes. Just after those two American fighter jets accidentally downed two of their own helicopters in northern Iraq in April 1994, killing fifteen Americans and eleven other people, talk show host Larry King asked Dr. Billy Graham why those kinds of things happen.

Dr. Graham wisely replied that he didn't have the answer. But he affirmed that God has His purposes even in tragedies, although those purposes are often hidden to us.

I think Dr. Graham didn't quote Romans 8:28 because he did not know the people involved. This verse speaks to those who are called according to God's purposes. It is not meant to answer all the whys. It means that your negative circumstances never have the last word. But I can't tell a non-Christian that, because his negative circumstances *will* have the last word.

That's why being a committed Christian is the most important thing you can be. Even if your world starts falling apart, the story is not over because God will steer this and shape that to your ultimate good from His perfect perspective. Our problem is that we really don't know what's good for us.

Children will eat ice cream all day if we let them. To them, many of the things we do as parents do not seem good. A spanking doesn't seem good, but it might be the best thing in the world at the moment. Making your kids turn off the TV and study does not seem good, but they need an education. If we just let God finish what He started, He can turn the negatives to good.

When my oldest son, Anthony, was very small, he had an asthma attack. We took him to the doctor and laid him on the table. The doctor needed to give him a shot, and the needle he brought out was long and intimidating. Anthony saw the doctor beginning to fill the syringe and did a Superman leap off that table and reached out to me. I tried to tell him, "Son, you're sick and the doctor needs to do this."

Then he began crying, "Daddy, no, no!"

The doctor looked at me and said, "You are going to have to hold him down."

I tried to talk to Anthony a little while longer, but he didn't understand. So I had to hold him down, and I will never forget the look on his face, which said, "How can you do this to me? How can you join forces with the enemy? How can you help the doctor hurt me?"

DON'T LET ANYONE TELL YOU THAT GOD'S GOODNESS HAS TO MEAN BAD THINGS SHOULDN'T HAPPEN. GOD IS GOOD BECAUSE HE TAKES THE BAD THINGS THAT HAPPEN TO US AND BRINGS ETERNAL GOOD OUT OF THEM.

I did it because it was good. Painful, yes—but good. Could Anthony understand it? Absolutely not; he was too young, too inexperienced. Could I understand it? Absolutely. I'd been that route before. I'd had those asthma needles when I was growing up. I understood that Anthony's temporary pain was necessary to produce long-term health.

Becoming Conquerors

So even when "tribulation, or distress, or persecution, or famine, or nakedness, or peril, or sword" comes along, God so constructs the trial that when it finishes, good results. And through it we become overwhelming conquerors.

Nothing is more exciting than to see a dying Christian who is an overwhelming conqueror. I don't know when I'm going to die, but I sure want to die as a conqueror. I want to go like a friend of mine who knew he was dying and knew there was no medical hope. He looked up and said, "This is my crowning day. Come quickly, Lord Jesus!"

But those who loved him and were looking on wanted to know, "Why did God let him die?"

Don't let anyone tell you that God's goodness has to mean bad things shouldn't happen. God is good because He takes the bad things that happen to us and brings eternal good out of them.

GOD'S GOODNESS
SHOULD MOTIVATE WORSHIP

My final point is that the goodness of God should motivate His people to worship Him. Listen to Psalm 107:1–2a: "Oh give thanks to the Lord, for He is good; for His lovingkindness is everlasting. Let the redeemed of the Lord say so."

Talk about It

We talk about everything else, don't we? When the big game plays, people aren't afraid to let their voices be heard when their team scores. They burst out with praise. Later, they gather together to celebrate their team's victory.

Then God tells us to talk up His goodness and His redemption and we say, "He already knows I'm grateful." But God doesn't just want to read your mind or heart. He wants to hear your lips praise and thank Him.

You've heard about the husband whose wife asked him, "Honey, do you love me?"

He says, "Woman, when we got married thirty-two years ago I told you I love you. If I change my mind, I'll let you know."

That's not what the lady wants. She wants to hear his love expressed. She wants him to tell her how beautiful she is, that life would not be worth living without her, that she's like the morning sunshine to him, that just seeing her still puts a smile on his face and a gleam in his eyes. I tell the husbands in my church, "If you don't know how to talk to your wife like that, see me after the service." Let the redeemed of the Lord say so.

Celebrate

We are also to come together and celebrate God's goodness. According to Psalm 107:2b–3, the people who were to tell of God's goodness were those He had "redeemed from the hand of the adversary, and gathered from the lands, from the east and from the west, from the north and from the south." Come together and tell of My redemption, God says. That's worship.

Someone will always answer, "I don't have to go to church to be a Christian." You sure don't. Going to church doesn't make you a Christian. But if you are a *grateful* Christian, you will go there to celebrate God's goodness. You won't mind singing to His glory.

You will shout it out. Why? Because He's been good to you. How can you not sing His praises?

Verse 7 of this psalm says that God also leads His people. Therefore, the psalmist's advice is, "Give thanks to the Lord" (v. 8). In verse 9 the writer declares that God gives food to the hungry and water to the thirsty.

Then he says if you are in sin, repent because God has been good:

> Then they cried out to the Lord in their trouble; He saved them out of their distresses. He brought them out of darkness and the shadow of death, and broke their bands apart. (vv. 13–14)

Say "Thank You"

God wants to be praised. You've probably taught your children to say "Thank you." But do you just teach them to say it once a week or once a year? Or do you want them to learn to say "Thank you" as a way of life, so that it's the exception when they don't express thanks? We say to our kids when they receive something, "I didn't hear you say thank you. What do you say?"

God says to us, "What do you say? I can't hear you. I don't hear the thanksgiving."

One day, a Puritan was sitting down to a meal of bread and water. Most of us would say, "God, I only have bread and water."

But this Puritan looked down at his plate and said, "Bread and water and Jesus Christ too! What more can a man ask?"

Praise is not complete until it has been expressed. The goodness of God gives us ample opportunities to be thankful. Psalm 34:8 invites us, "O taste and see that the Lord is good." "Delight yourself in the Lord" says Psalm 37:4.

The familiar song puts it this way:

> Count your blessings,
> Name them one by one;
> Count your blessings,
> See what God hath done;
> Count your blessings,
> Name them one by one;
> Count your many blessings,
> See what God hath done.[1]

1. Words by Johnson Oatman, Jr., 1897, tune by Edwin O. Excell, 1897.

Responding to the Goodness of God

God is so good to us that it will take all eternity to count the ways He has blessed and benefited us. The best thing we can do until then is to live a life of grateful devotion, obedience, and praise to Him in response to His abundant goodness. I hope these ideas will help you appropriate the goodness of God in a new way:

1. If you are allowing or practicing something in your life that may not be good by God's definition of goodness, apply this simple test to it. See if you can pray, "God I know this is a gift from You, and You want me to have it because it is good," without experiencing any conviction. If so, you may be on the right track. But if you can't thank God for it with a clear heart and conscience, it's best to dump it!

2. Maybe you've got a negative circumstance knocking the props out of your life right now. Write it down on a card or piece of paper. Now under it write Romans 8:28—not as a way of just pretending it isn't bad, but as a promise from your good God. Put that card where you'll see it every day. When you do, thank God that He can bring good out of bad. Do that for a while, and see if that circumstance doesn't begin to look a lot different.

3. What have you received—or avoided!—in the last month or so that was purely a gift of grace from a good God? Reflect on it, and thank Him again for it. Can't think of anything? Better check your spiritual batteries to see if you're still running.

4. If you have a church where you gather regularly with God's people to worship and thank Him, keep up the good work. But if you're trying to fly solo right now in your Christian life, make it a priority to find a good church before you crash-land somewhere. Ask a trusted Christian friend for the name of a church where God is worshiped and His Word is taught.

13
THE WRATH
OF GOD

What would you say about a father who failed to warn his children of impending danger? You would have to conclude that he was not being a good parent.

What would you say about a friend who saw you going down a dangerous road and knew disaster awaited you at the other end, yet offered you no counsel and made no attempt to stop you? That person would be a useless friend.

How about a doctor who knew you had a life-threatening illness, but simply told you, "Take two aspirin, go home, and rest"? His compassion for you as your doctor would be in serious question.

Suppose a police officer saw smoke rising from your roof, or witnessed burglars breaking into your home, but never tried to intervene or alert anyone? He could be fired for failing to do his job.

I could go on, but let me ask you just one more question. What would you say about a pastor who told you about God's love and forgiveness and patience, but never warned you of His wrath? I'd like to answer that one myself. That pastor would be doing you a great disservice.

God's wrath is not an easy subject to talk about. But it's as integral to His nature as His other perfections, whether His love or holiness or mercy. If I failed to teach about it, I would be doing my church and others exposed to my ministry a great disservice. And if I tried to ignore it in a book like this, I would be doing my readers a similar disservice.

To be sure, you can go plenty of places today if you don't want to hear about the wrath of God. Many churches run from the subject. They skip it, bypass it, jump over it, ignore it because it's hard to talk about.

But any discussion of God's character that does not include His characteristic called wrath is an incomplete study. Worse yet, it may even be an errant study of God, because one of the very real, inescapable truths about our great God is that *He is a God of wrath*.

The issue is not whether we like it, want it, or agree with it. The Bible has more to say about God's wrath than it does about His love. Of course God is good, kind, loving, and forgiving. But if you put a period there, you haven't got the complete story. God's wrath must be taken seriously. So let's begin by defining our subject. The wrath of God is His necessary, just, and righteous retribution against sin.

God's wrath against sin arises by necessity out of His nature. Because of the justice of His law and the righteousness of His character, God must judge sin. He takes no pleasure in punishing the unrighteous (Ezekiel 33:11), but He will, because He is a God of wrath.

Psalm 18:8 puts it this way: "Smoke went up out of [God's] nostrils" as He huffed with anger at the presence of sin. Moses writes in Exodus 34:7 that God will not let the guilty go unpunished. In Deuteronomy 32:41, Moses records God's declaration that "I will render vengeance on My adversaries." Peter reminds us that God is impartial and will judge all men according to their deeds (1 Peter 1:17).

We can find no way around it, nowhere to run from it. God is a God of wrath. I want to give you the straight scoop because it's better to have a headache now than a "hell ache" later. The Greek words for *wrath* indicate God's intense displeasure at sin and His judgment against it. God does not throw temper tantrums. He doesn't pitch fits, but He has intense anger against sin.

In fact, God takes torrid displeasure at sin: big sin, little sin, medium-sized sin. He does not make a distinction between white and black lies, between felonies and misdemeanors. Because He is a holy God, all sin is repulsive to Him.

GOD'S WRATH
IS ONE OF HIS PERFECTIONS

I mentioned this above, but let's look at it in more detail. Romans 11:22 helps us here:

> Behold then the kindness and severity of God; to those who fell, severity, but to you, God's kindness, if you continue in His kindness; otherwise you also will be cut off.

God's Severity

The word *severity* is the Greek word that means "to be cut off." Paul points us to God's goodness (the part we like to talk about) and His "cutting off" or severity.

GOD'S GOODNESS CONTAINS NOT ONLY THE POSITIVE THINGS HE DOES, BUT HIS NEGATIVE REACTION TO EVIL.

This is a description of His wrath. When His patience against sin expires, God cuts people off from His kindness. He no longer makes available to them His love, His patience, and His support. We need to take a good look at this because God's kindness is perfectly balanced with His severity. Both are part of who He is.

The prophet Nahum describes God this way in verses 2–6 of the opening chapter of his prophecy:

> A jealous and avenging God is the Lord; the Lord is avenging and wrathful. The Lord takes vengeance on His adversaries, and He reserves wrath for His enemies. The Lord is slow to anger and great in power, and the Lord will by no means leave the guilty unpunished. In whirlwind and storm is His way, and clouds are the dust beneath His feet. He rebukes the sea and makes it dry; He dries up all the rivers. Bashan and Carmel wither; the blossoms of Lebanon wither. Mountains quake because of Him, and the hills dissolve; indeed the earth is upheaved by His presence, the world and all the inhabitants in it. Who can stand before His indignation? Who can endure the burning of His anger? His wrath is poured out like fire, and the rocks are broken up by Him.

God's Goodness

But after painting a picture like this, Nahum begins verse 7 by saying, "The Lord is good." God is good, as we've already seen. But don't mistake His goodness for weakness or indifference toward sin. God is so good He cannot let evil go unaddressed.

How could God be good if He looked the other way when faced with evil? How can a police officer be good if he sees a crime and does nothing? How can a firefighter be good if he sees a fire and doesn't try to put it out? How can citizens be good if they see harm being done and do not do anything?

We understand goodness not only to be positive acts, but also to be resistance to wrong. God's goodness contains not only the positive things He does, but His negative reaction to evil. Let me tell you how good God is with regard to His wrath. He is so good that He's going to separate sinners from saints forever. You may ask, "How is that good?"

It's good because if sinners in hell could visit saints in heaven, their mere presence would contaminate heaven. Instead of being a perfect place, therefore, heaven would become a living hell for the saints. God is so good that in heaven, He will keep His children separated from sin forever. We will never have to worry about being contaminated again.

God's Righteous Wrath

But in order to do this, God's wrath must be manifested. Now God's wrath is not at all like ours. Probably one reason people run from the subject of God's anger is that they think God gets mad the way people get mad. We get ticked off when someone does us wrong—or if we *think* someone has done us wrong. We get hot when people get on our nerves, when they do something we don't like. And, too often, we unload on them with both barrels.

That's not how God responds. For example, people get upset if you take something that belongs to them. Well, you can't take anything that belongs to God because He can take it back. He's all-powerful. You can't infringe on Him like that. He knows everything in advance, so you can't trick Him or fool Him. God's other characteristics keep His wrath in perfect balance.

The wrath of God is His response to that which in its essence is against His nature. God's wrath is not cruel, but just. Prison isn't a fun place, but we lock up people who have committed crimes to keep them from committing those crimes again because we want justice and order in society. That's a reflection—although a very poor and imperfect one—of God's righteous anger.

God wants justice and order in His universe, which means He must respond to the crime called sin. The only way you can get God not to respond to you is not to be a sinner. But if you say you are not a sinner, you prove you are because you just lied (see 1 John 1:8). God must respond to sin, and He responds by cutting the sinner off from His goodness. The Bible says these two sides of God must be always held in tension. "Thou hast loved righteousness, and hated wickedness" (Psalm 45:7).

People who only talk about the wrath of God don't have the whole picture. People who only talk about His love don't have the whole picture either. Those who want to emphasize only God's love often throw out this challenge to those who believe in His wrath: "How could a God of love do that?"

Simple answer. He's also a God of wrath. You cannot skip this side to God except at your eternal peril.

GOD'S WRATH
DISPLAYS HIS JUSTICE

This is very important. The wrath of God is the ongoing display of His justice in history. Romans 1:18 contains the most concise statement of God's wrath in the Bible, and we do well to pay close attention to it: "For the wrath of God is revealed from heaven against all ungodliness."

Notice that God does not hide His wrath. He does not put it under a bushel. His wrath is *revealed* so that we can know this is part of His nature. That's why I can't skip preaching about it. Some people act as though God is apologetic about His anger toward sin and doesn't want us to know about it.

No, the Bible says God actively reveals His wrath. He tells us in advance that this is part of who He is.

Someone will always say, "I don't like that part of God."

I say, "Well, adjust."

We have to adjust. Do you know why? Because God says "I, the Lord, do not change" (Malachi 3:6). Have you ever had to tell your children that if they want to live in your house, they have to adjust to your methods? This is God's universe. It's His house, and we need to adjust to His rules.

Romans 1:18 means there is no time when God is not reacting to sin. The problem is that people "suppress [hold down] the truth in unrighteousness." People don't want to deal with the truth. But we've got to tell the truth, pointing out that God's holy indignation reacts against sin every time and everywhere it shows up. The verb in verse 18 is a present tense, meaning God's wrath "keeps on being revealed" against sin.

Tracing God's Wrath

We can go all the way back to the beginning of biblical history and see this principle in action. When Adam and Eve disobeyed God, they got booted out of the Garden. Then the whole world resisted God in the days of Noah, and God destroyed the world with a flood. People got together again in Genesis 11 to build a monument to man at Babel. The Bible says God's wrath was kindled, and He came down and destroyed their program.

The cities of Sodom and Gomorrah are nowhere to be found today because they were blown off the map by the fierce wrath of God.

Pharaoh told Moses he was not going to let the children of Israel go. Ten times God demonstrated His wrath to the Egyptians. But Pharaoh still didn't get the message, so he and his army drowned in the sea.

Korah rebelled against Moses, and Moses said, "Everyone on God's side stand over here. Everyone on Korah's side stand over there." After the people decided whose side they were on, the Bible says that the earth opened up. God in his wrath commanded the earth to swallow Korah and all his followers.

Even Jesus couldn't bypass the wrath of God when our sins were placed on Him at the cross. There, God unleashed the fury of eternal wrath on His eternal Son as He bore the sins of the world. If not even God's sinless Son escaped His wrath, we'd better take this seriously. Don't mess with this. "God is angry with the wicked every day" (Psalm 7:11 KJV). Every time we think an evil thought or do an evil deed, God's anger is kindled because He is so perfect He must react to unrighteousness.

God's Character Distorted

Let's go back to Romans 1, where Paul explains why God reveals His wrath against the unrighteousness of men:

> Because that which is known about God is evident within them;
> for God made it evident to them. For since the creation of the
> world His invisible attributes, His eternal power and divine na-
> ture, have been clearly seen, being understood through what
> has been made, so that they are without excuse. (vv. 19–20)

So while we can't see God's essence, we can see God's effect,
just like we see the wind's effect. Between the truth God put within
us and what is evident all around us, we are left without excuse,
whether we live in Timbuktu or downtown Dallas. God has made
His reality crystal clear. That's why no matter where you go in the
world, you will find people worshiping something.

Our problem is not evolution, it's *de*volution. Evolution says
that man started small and grew great. But the truth is that man has
devolved. That is, man started great but has been growing smaller
spiritually and morally ever since. Why? Because even though people knew God, "they did not honor Him as God, or give thanks; but
they became futile in their speculations, and their foolish heart was
darkened" (v. 21).

Paul says we didn't treat God like He was God. If Paul were to
visit our churches today, he would ask, "How in the world can you
come here on a Sunday morning and claim to worship God as God
and then ignore Him all week long? That's backwards. The human
race has been contaminated by this thing called sin and therefore
deserves God's wrath."

The problem gets worse in verse 23: "[They] exchanged the
glory of the incorruptible God for an image in the form of corrupt-
ible man and of birds and four-footed animals and crawling creatures"—and of cars and of houses and of money and of clothes and
on and on. God has been exchanged. We've taken Him back like a
Christmas present that doesn't fit and we've said, "We want our
money back." Rather than glorifying God as the great God He is,
people have elevated everything but God to His place.

God's "Giving Up"

So what does God do with people like that? It's stated three
times in the remaining verses of Romans 1 (vv. 24, 26, 28). He gives
up on those who insist on perverting the knowledge of Him. That
means He unleashes these people to fulfill their wildest dreams
and enjoy the consequences thereof. The wrath of God in history is

seen when God takes His hand of restraint off and says, "You want it, you've got it."

He lets them enjoy the fruit of what they want so badly. He says, "You want independence from Me? You've got it. You want to live your own life? You've got it. You want to be your own god? You've got it—and everything that comes with it."

It's like the child who says, "Mother and Father, I don't want you to be over me anymore. I want my freedom!"

And you say, "You've got it. Cold, harsh world, here he comes."

God says, "You've got it." Romans 1:24 says "God gave them over in the lusts of their hearts to impurity." He also give them up to "degrading passions" (v. 26). We see a "devolution" here. First God gave them up to general lusts to fulfill the desires of their hearts. Then the lusts begin to take specific shape because now they come up with wild stuff.

IN THE RIGHTEOUS REVELATION OF HIS WRATH, HE WITHDRAWS HIS RESTRAINT AGAINST SIN AND ITS CONSEQUENCES, AND EVIL BEGINS TO SPREAD.

What kind of stuff? "Women exchanged the natural function for that which is unnatural" (v. 26). That's lesbianism. "And in the same way also the men abandoned the natural function of the woman and burned in their desire toward one another, men with men committing indecent acts and receiving in their own persons the due penalty of their error" (v. 27). That's homosexuality. One penalty or payment for their sin is called AIDS.

Because of this, innocent people have to suffer early and agonizing deaths through things like AIDS-contaminated blood transfusions because people have come up with every kind of device imaginable to fulfill their passions. God says, "You want it, you've got it!"

So we've come up with all manner of sin and with it, the sexually transmitted diseases that devastate us today. Paul says, "All of this doesn't come just because it is blowing in the wind. God releases it. In the righteous revelation of His wrath, He withdraws His restraint against sin and its consequences, and evil begins to spread. New diseases show up. Crime increases. Respect for life deteriorates. Life loses its value."

But we still haven't hit bottom. We have not arrived at the worst stage yet. Stage one is what I called above "general passions," a do-your-own-thing approach. But then people go wild and devise insane ways to satisfy their lusts: stage two. Then they get so used to what they're doing that they wind up at stage three. Look at verse 28: "And just as they did not see fit to acknowledge God any longer, God gave them over to a depraved mind, to do those things which are not proper."

God will let people get so crazy in their sin that they can no longer think right, perceive right, or act right. They go stark-raving mad spiritually, morally, physically, ethically, and every other way. This madness shows itself in so many horrible ways that Paul merely needs to list them and we get the message (vv. 28–32). These degradations don't need to be illustrated.

Given what happens in this country in an average twenty-four-hour span, it's interesting to see that breakdown in society, murder, and rebellion against parents show up in sin's "Hall of Shame." But even these aren't the lowest man can go. The real kicker comes in verse 32, the capstone of this section: "And, although they know the ordinance of God, that those who practice such things are worthy of death, they not only do the same, but also give hearty approval to those who practice them."

You know you've hit bottom in God's wrath when people do insane things and other people seek to legitimize and legalize them. When they start talking about legalizing homosexuality, you know your world has gone mad, under the wrath of God. When you see TV talk show hosts trotting out the most perverted guests they can find, and the audience clapping and approving of what they're doing, the wrath of God is being revealed before your very eyes.

So God has backed off and said, "You want to go crazy? Go crazy! The payment in society will be devastating. The loss of life will be devastating. The chaos will be devastating. The diseases will be devastating. You want to leave me out? Have a ball to the grave."

When it gets this bad, it doesn't matter who's on the school board or the city council—or in the White House. When the wrath of God is your problem, the goodness of God is your only solution.

How can people deny and pervert the truth of God this badly? Because they don't like the God of Romans 1. They want a God who looks and acts like them, who says, "Well, I understand. You know, everybody sins." They want an "I'm OK, you're OK" God.

But the God of the Bible presents the greatest possible threat to their sinful lives. This God reveals His wrath against unrighteousness wherever it is found.

GOD'S WRATH
DISPLAYS HIS JUSTICE IN ETERNITY

We see God's wrath executing His justice in history right now, but this is not the end of it. The wrath of God will continue in eternity:

> But because of your stubbornness and unrepentant heart you are storing up wrath for yourself in the day of wrath and revelation of the righteous judgment of God. (Romans 2:5)

Stored-up Wrath

Sometimes we get upset because evil people seem to keep getting away with evil. No, their sin account keeps growing. Many people will never have much trouble in this life. But if you could only see the bill awaiting them in eternity! The psalmist pictured the wrath of God like a bow being drawn back (Psalm 7:12). The more sinners sin, the further God pulls back the bow.

You know the farther a bowman pulls back the arrow, the harder it will hit and the deeper it will penetrate. God says that when He lets His arrow go, it's going to penetrate the unrighteous with great agony. That's why the Bible cautions us not to become envious of the wicked. Never get all upset because bad folks have it good and good folks have it bad down here. God just hasn't let His arrow go yet.

Evil people are storing up God's wrath, and the Bible says that God will let His arrow fly at the judgment. This will usher in eternity, which will mean hell for those under His wrath. Hell is not a popular subject. I would prefer that it not be part of the deal, but I'm not making the rules. And God has said there is a place where those who reject Him will be housed forever.

So critical is this doctrine that John the Baptist warned, "Flee from the wrath to come" (Matthew 3:7). Jesus said that in hell, "their worm does not die" (Mark 9:48). In other words, there is no death there, no time when the conscience is at ease. Hell is a place of desolation and great pain.

In Revelation 20:10–15, John describes the great and final judgment when Satan and those who reject Christ will be thrown in the "lake of fire" along with "death and Hades" (the abode of the dead, a "holding tank" for those awaiting judgment). The lake of fire is eternal punishment, for its inhabitants will be "tormented day and night forever and ever" (v. 10).

That isn't a pleasant picture, and many people deal with it simply by saying, "I don't believe that." You'd better be sure, because no one can afford to be wrong about this one. If you miss this one, you'll get a bill that can never, ever be paid. It's like some people's credit card bills. They never have enough to pay them off, so those bills just keep coming around every month. In hell, the payments never stop!

Eternal Wrath Illustrated

The Bible's most descriptive story about eternal punishment isn't designed to make us feel very good. But when you have life-threatening cancer and need radical treatment, making you feel good is not the doctor's first goal. Sin is a cancer, and God's eternal wrath will be the outcome of it unless we have radical surgery to remove it.

The story I'm referring to can be found in Luke 16:19–31, and since it fell from the lips of Jesus we need to give it careful attention. It's the account of the rich man and Lazarus. When both men die, Jesus peels back the corners of eternity and gives us a look at both sides. Lazarus was carried by angels who put him in Abraham's bosom, what we would call paradise or heaven.

The rich man, called Dives by tradition, went to Hades (v. 23), the abode of the evil dead, as I mentioned above. But first, Jesus noted his burial in verse 22. I am sure they had a big funeral for this guy. I bet the limousines were all lined up out front, with a police escort waiting to lead the procession down the middle of Main Street.

At the funeral, they had to cut the eulogies short, because so many people wanted to talk about how much money Dives had given to charity and how nice he was, and what a great credit he was to the community. But the rich man couldn't enjoy all that, because he was in "agony" in the flames (v. 24). That means he could feel.

He could see, too. Jesus says that Dives looked up "and saw Abraham far away, and Lazarus in his bosom" (v. 23). He saw what he was missing. The great tragedy of hell is not only what you are going through, but what you could have had and are missing. This definitely gives the lie to the notion that hell is where the party is. God throws the party in heaven.

Dives then asks Abraham to send Lazarus with just a fingerful of water to ease his pain. You would have thought he would ask for a bucket of water or even a whole lake, but he doesn't. He wants a finger's worth of water. Now whenever you feel like one drop of water will change your existence, you are in bad shape.

But Abraham answered, "I'm sorry. A great gulf is fixed between us and you. We can't come over there and you can't come over here" (see vv. 25–26).

Eternal Wrath Experienced

Do you know the worst part of hell? It will be the eternal torment of remembering that on such-and-such a day, the person sat in church, heard that preacher say this place was real, and didn't do anything about it. Hell is knowing that you could have but never did address the issue of your eternal destiny. You didn't take seriously the wrath of God.

No help came for Dives. He remained fully conscious. He had his memory, his conscience, and all of his physical senses intact, but it was all agony.

A man once told me, "I'm not into that hell stuff. I don't believe in the wrath of God. But even if hell is true, I'm going to turn the place out because all my 'homies' are going to be there. We are going to go down there, get with the devil, and boogie down."

He obviously didn't get the picture, so I said, "Do me a favor. When you go home today, turn on a burner on your stove and wait till it gets real hot. Then sit on that burner and try to get a party going at the same time. Let's see how you do."

He does not understand that hell is a place of solitary confinement. Hell has no fellowship, no parties, no get-togethers, no buffets. God will eternally quarantine all those who are not rightly related to Him in the pit of the universe so they won't mess up the enjoyment of heaven for those who are rightly related to Him.

The Bible does teach that hell has degrees of punishment. Jesus says those who knew more will be worse off than those who knew less (Luke 12:47–48). In other words, a person who rejects Christ at

Oak Cliff Bible Fellowship Church in Dallas is going to be more severely punished than someone who has not had our opportunities. The second person may have rejected God, but he or she did so with far less information.

But even though hell has degrees of punishment, I don't want even the slightest of those degrees! Have you ever thought about how long eternity is? It will keep you awake at night. Here's an illustration that gives you some idea of what eternity is like.

If you emptied the Pacific Ocean, the largest body of water in the world, and piled it full of sand as high as Mount Everest, the highest mountain in the world, you would have a pretty big sand pile. Now suppose you got a bird and trained it to pick up one grain of sand every million years. How long would it take that bird to empty that sand pile? A long time. We probably don't have numbers to count that high.

But guess what? When that bird has picked up that last grain of sand, you will have only spent your first second in hell. That's what I call an eternity!

A tombstone in an old cemetery reads this way:

> Pause stranger when you pass me by.
> As you are now, so once was I.
> As I am now, so you will be
> So prepare for death and follow me.

Someone came by one day and read the inscription, then picked up some chalk and wrote underneath it:

> To follow you, I am not content.
> Until I know which way you went.

You'd better know who you are following because the issue is your eternal destiny. Don't follow your relatives to hell. Don't follow your friends to eternal torment. Don't let people lead you down the path to eternal destruction, because God is a God of wrath.

GOD'S WRATH
COMES WHEN HIS PATIENCE IS IGNORED

God does not just come out of nowhere and lower the boom on unsuspecting people who had no chance to do anything about their eternal destinies. In his discussion of God's sovereignty, Paul points out that God endures "with much patience" even those people who are "vessels of wrath prepared for destruction" (Romans 9:22), people we might call hell-bent.

Wrath and Mercy

As we saw earlier, God is long-suffering. "The Lord . . . is patient toward you, not wishing for any to perish but for all to come to repentance" (2 Peter 3:9). God is not wrathful because He wants to injure. He's wrathful because He's just. That's what we have to understand. His sense of justice demands that He react to sin.

GOD IS A WRATHFUL GOD, AND WHEN THE CLOCK STRIKES MIDNIGHT, IT'S OVER.

But God's wrath is preceded by so much patience. Remember the 120 years He put up with a rebellious world before sending the Flood? I can identify with long-suffering because it's a strength I have. My wife has only seen me angry twice in twenty-four years. I just don't get angry very easily.

God's patience lasts a lifetime. He waits on us, He forgives us, He doesn't give us what we deserve, He holds back His wrath toward us. He says, "Come to Me now." But we keep putting Him off, not submitting and turning to Christ.

We say, "Not now. Tomorrow. Before I die." And the clock runs out. I don't know how old you are, but I know that youth is relative when it comes to facing God's wrath. You see, you can only measure how young you are against your death date, not your birthdate. A person who is going to die at the age of twenty-five is old at fifteen. But if that same person lives to be ninety, he or she is still young at fifty.

The End of Patience

But you say no one knows his death date. You're right—and that's why today is always the day of salvation (Hebrews 4:7–15). You don't put this thing off. Put something else off, but not this. God is patient, so come to Him while you can.

How patient is God? Numbers 14 tells about the unbelief of Israel when the people refused to believe God and take the Promised Land. God was hot. He wanted to destroy those rebels and start over with Moses (vv. 11–12). But Moses reminded God of His patience, and He granted the nation a stay of execution, so to speak (vv. 18–20).

But read the rest of Numbers 14 and you'll see that God did judge His people. Too many make the mistake described in Ecclesiastes 8:11, which says that people take God's delay in judging sin as an excuse to sin more. They figure they're home free. They think God has slackened up (2 Peter 3:9). So instead of saying, "Boy, God has been patient with me, I had better repent!" they say, "God is so easy-going He's not really going to do anything."

Kids make this mistake all the time. You haven't spanked them yet, so they figure you aren't ever going to do anything. Because God hasn't done anything yet, we think He's never going to do anything about sin. But that's not the case. God is a wrathful God, and when the clock strikes midnight, it's over.

Hebrews 9:27 says, "It is appointed for men to die once and after this comes judgment." Not a second chance, not a lot of slack, not a reprieve, but judgment. Romans 2:4 says it this way: "Do you think lightly of the riches of His kindness and forbearance and patience, not knowing that the kindness of God leads you to repentance?" If He hasn't judged you yet, you should be running to Him in gratitude and repentance.

The Bible pictures the unsaved as dangling over hell. In Luke 13:1–5, Jesus makes clear that the unsaved are just one heartbeat, one act of violence, or one accident away from God's judgment. His examples show that the blow could fall at any moment. The lost are being held only by the grace of God, and when He releases His grip, they are gone. It doesn't matter how young or healthy they are. When God lets go, they're gone. But the Bible also tells us of an escape.

ESCAPING GOD'S WRATH

A choice must be made. Anyone who goes to hell goes by his or her choice, not because God is an ogre. God made hell for Satan and his angels, not for people, the Bible says. His justice demands payment for sin, but in His mercy He provided a substitute to take our punishment for us.

God's Substitute

This is good news! God's system of justice allows for a substitute.

There once was a king who ruled over a very wicked people. So he made a law which said, "Anyone who violates the law will have both eyes put out." The first young man to violate the law was brought to the king for judgment—but when the king looked up he cried out in anguish, because it was his son.

This king was in a dilemma. Justice demanded that he put the boy's eyes out. But his love said, "This is my son. I can't put my son's eyes out." How did he balance justice and love? The king put out one of his son's eyes and one of his own eyes. So whoever saw the two of them together saw justice and love in operation: justice, because two eyes were put out as the law demanded; and love, because the king loved his son enough to give his eye for him.

That's a nice illustration, but God went one step further. Jesus paid it *all.* He took all of our sins, our rebellion, and our guilt, and paid for them all on Calvary. And it cost Him His life, not just an eye. Jesus paid it all.

That is why God will not tolerate people rejecting Christ. He will not tolerate it because an eternal God let His eternal Son pay an eternal price for our eternal sin that eternal people might live with Him eternally. But if we reject the God who paid the price through His Son for our sin, then we will face the eternal consequences.

God paid too high a price for us to fool around and play games with His wrath. He said, "I'm telling you in advance, I'm a wrathful God. But I'm going to do something Myself to satisfy My wrath, because nothing you could do could ever satisfy Me. My Son will become a man like you, except without sin, so I can forgive you of your sin. But once My Son does this and I raise Him from the dead to let you know this is real, don't mess with Me! Take Me very seriously. Don't presume on My goodness."

That's why 1 Thessalonians 1:10 says Jesus "delivers us from the wrath to come." According to Romans 5:8–9:

> God demonstrates His own love toward us, in that while we were yet sinners, Christ died for us. Much more then, having now been justified by His blood, we shall be saved from the wrath of God through Him.

Saved from Wrath

You are saved from the wrath of God through Christ, not through attending church, by being a nice person, or by doing good in the community. You will be saved from the wrath to come only by the eternal provision of Jesus Christ.

You say, "But I'm already a Christian. I'm already saved. None of this applies to me."

True, if you are a Christian, you will never experience the wrath of God. You may undergo His discipline, but you will never face His wrath.

But this does apply to you if you've got a brother or sister or aunt or uncle or anyone else who does not know Jesus Christ. You can't just let the person die without Jesus Christ, without hearing from your mouth the need to flee from the wrath to come.

You don't want your family, friends, and co-workers going to a lost eternity saying, "But I worked next to her for twenty years and she never told me about this. I was his relative, we went to family reunions together every year, and he never warned me about hell. I lived next door to the man, and he never said anything to me about this."

The wrath of God applies to you if there will be people in hell you and I knew and loved and worked beside, but who never heard how they could flee His wrath because we never opened our mouths to be a witness. Our job is to tell a lost world about Jesus Christ so their blood won't be on our hands (Ezekiel 3:15–19).

I don't want to stand before Jesus and have Him look at me and say, "Where are all your friends? Where is your family? They're not here because you didn't tell them. You were scared to witness. But you weren't scared to talk about everything else. Why was I too big a problem to talk about?"

A pastor who wanted his congregation to understand that people were dying and going to hell got up one Sunday morning and said, "It bothers me that you people aren't sharing your faith. And millions are dying and going to hell. You don't give a [expletive]."

Then he said, "Right now, most of you are more concerned that I used that word than that millions of people are dying and going to hell. You are upset about that when it ought to be setting your feet afire that you've got relatives and neighbors and co-workers to call this afternoon and tell about Jesus."

Pardon Rejected

I don't recommend this pastor's method, but we've got to get our priorities straight. So I have two messages. If you are a Christian, you'd better start talking because people will lose out on this deal if you keep quiet. If you are not a Christian, you'd better run to Jesus today because He is offering you a pardon and the clock is ticking.

In 1829, a Philadelphia man named George Wilson robbed the U.S. mail and killed someone in the process. Wilson was arrested, brought to trial, convicted, and sentenced to be hanged. Some friends intervened on his behalf and were finally able to obtain a pardon for Wilson from President Andrew Jackson.

But when informed of this, Wilson refused to accept the pardon. The sheriff was unwilling to carry out the sentence. How could he hang a pardoned man? An appeal was sent to President Jackson. Perplexed, Jackson turned to the U.S. Supreme Court to decide the case. Chief Justice John Marshall ruled that a pardon rejected is no pardon at all. George Wilson would have to face his sentence. Wilson was hanged, although his pardon lay on the sheriff's desk.

God forbid that at the judgment, He should ever have to say that about us or anyone we care about! We need to warn people to escape God's wrath and embrace His forgiveness.

Responding to the Wrath of God

I told you this was a tough subject to talk about. But since the Bible doesn't stutter or blush about it, neither should we. The suggestions below are designed to help you do something about the wrath of God:

1. Have you got a family member or friend who is dangling over the open mouth of hell? Get on the phone, pick up a pen and paper, make a lunch appointment, or do whatever else you have to do to get with that person and share the truth of God's love—and wrath—with him or her.

2. Sometimes as Christians we get upset because the wicked in our world seem to have things their way. If you've ever felt this way, you're in good company. Read Psalm 73 carefully. The psalmist began lamenting the ease of the wicked and got himself really worked up about it. But notice the first word of verse 17: "Until. . . ." Thank God that this world isn't the last word, and that you belong to Him.

3. Let me give you another line of thought you can use in your witnessing when someone rejects the idea of God's wrath. Ask that person how he would feel if he gave someone a gift that cost him dearly, only to have the recipient snort in disgust, throw the gift back in his face, and walk away.

Most people wouldn't have any problem admitting they would be hurt and angry. Now take your friend a step further and ask him to imagine this happening again and again and again as he kept offering his priceless gift to the receiver. How many times would he allow himself to be rejected and insulted before he would withdraw his offer? We can't appreciate God's wrath until we see what a great offense our rejection of Christ is.

4. I know I asked you earlier about your salvation, but it's so important I want to urge you again. If you have any doubt about where you stand before God, flee His wrath and embrace the pardon offered in Jesus Christ. Don't put it off. Don't count on your church membership or good deeds to save you. Don't guess about your eternal destiny!

14
THE LOVE
OF GOD

veryone wants to be loved. Love is the crying need of the human heart. But when you ask people to define love, they hem and haw, trying to come up with words that work. For some it's a fuzzy feeling in the pit of the stomach. For others, it's a deep caring. For others, it's excitement over something they value highly.

The concept of love has been so used, abused, and misused today that you can put almost anything under it, and it will work. That's because most people are desperately looking for love in all the wrong places. They know they need it, they know they've got to have it, but where to find it and how to know it's authentic, that's another question.

If you feel like that, or know someone who does, I have good news for you: God is love. I know you've heard that many times before, but I hope that by the end of this chapter, that little phrase will take on a new world of meaning to you. Let me start with a definition: The love of God is His joyful self-determination to reflect the goodness of His will and glory by meeting the needs of mankind.

That's a big definition, but I believe it includes the key elements of what the Bible means by God's love. And the Bible makes this absolutely clear: *No* definition of love means anything unless it is rooted in God. No matter how you define love, if you can't root your definition in God, it is flawed. It will either be incomplete or imbalanced, but it will not be correct because God is the definition of love.

So whether it's your love for your spouse, your children, your friends, or anyone else, it must have an anchoring point or it will drift in one of two directions: into emotional sentimentalism or into unfeeling duty. Your love will not find the harmony and wholeness it can enjoy until you anchor it in God. Let me illustrate four truths about the love of God that will help us understand love in any dimension.

THE JOYFUL OVERFLOW OF GOD'S WILL AND GLORY

Turn to Ephesians 1 and you'll see this fundamental principle of God's love: It includes His obsession with His own glory. The early verses of Ephesians 1 highlight the glory of God in relation to His love:

> [God] chose us in [Christ] before the foundation of the world, that we should be holy and blameless before Him. In love He predestined us to adoption as sons through Jesus Christ to Himself, according to the kind intention of His will, to the praise of the glory of His grace, which He freely bestowed on us in the Beloved. (vv. 4–6)

God's Love and His Glory

These verses make clear that God's activity in love always coincides with His will, which verse 6 shows to be "the praise of the glory of His grace." The working out of God's will in love results in His glory. And Paul doesn't stop there, because this is important. Again in verses 12 and 14, he caps off God's work in saving us and sealing us with the Holy Spirit by saying all of it is for "the praise of His glory."

Therefore, to understand fully the love of God, we must understand God's purpose in the universe, since He *is* love. That's why we can't begin a study of the love of God simply by jumping into 1 Corinthians 13 or 1 John and describing what love does or what it looks like. We need to back up and understand that God's eternal passion is to accomplish His will in such a way that when all has been said and done, He is glorified.

How does this fact relate to God's love? Stay with me for the next page or two and I'll show you. First, we need to realize that God did not *become* love after He made the world and mankind. As one of His attributes, God's love is eternal. In other words, God was love before there was man or anything else outside of God to love. In and of Himself, God is love.

Now if God's love existed before the foundation of the world because *He* existed before the foundation of the world, what was there for God to love in eternity past? We can draw only one conclusion: The object of God's love was Himself. God is absorbed in His own glory.

At first glance, that strikes some people wrong. Something doesn't sound right about it. It sounds like God's got the big head. But here's one place where human logic doesn't work.

If you and I get absorbed in our own glory, we've got a problem. First, because we focus on untrue things. We begin to deceive ourselves. Second, we start forgetting about things we can't do. We begin to think we can leap tall buildings. Third, we focus on things that are flawed by sin. We begin to mess with stuff better left alone.

God can pursue His own glory because He has *perfect* glory. God does not pursue His glory to gain something He lacks. God has everything He needs. He pursues His own glory because He could aspire to no greater goal than Himself. He is the apex of everything.

Since God's love precedes creation, the only way God could express His love was within Himself. Therefore, for God to love, He must seek Himself. And in order for God to seek Himself, He must seek His own will and glory.

This may be a little heavy here, but if we let God be God we will be halfway to unraveling what sounds like a complicated truth. Remember earlier I said that if anything in the universe was greater than God, then that entity would be God.

But since nothing greater than our perfect God could possibly exist, it shouldn't surprise us that His glory is the focus of His love. In fact, as we also learned earlier, God finds great delight in achieving His will. He doesn't blush about pursuing His own glory. The Bible talks a lot about the delight God gets out of doing things for His own glory.

God's Love and You

Make no mistake. Nothing I've said about how much God loves Himself and delights in His glory is meant to imply that God is selfish with His love, hoarding it for Himself. God forbid! But the only reason God can be for you is that God is for Himself. You see, if God were only for you and not for Himself, there would be limits on what He could do.

But since God is pursuing His own glory, when He brings you under the umbrella of His love, you are in the very best position possible. Why? Because as God unfolds His will to achieve His glory in your life, you get to enjoy the blessings of His grace, power, purpose, and joy.

It's sort of like the man sprinkling his yard on a hot day. The neighborhood kids all show up in their bathing suits, and since this man happens to love kids, they get to run in the sprinkler all afternoon. He even goes in and fixes them a snack and brings it out to them.

That's not a perfect illustration, but you get the idea. When you get the love of God, you will be loved like you've never been loved before—or ever could be. God loves you with the greatest possible love that exists, which is His love for Himself and His passionate concern for His own glory. "From Him and through Him and to Him are all things" (Romans 11:36).

In Isaiah 43:7, God Himself speaks of Israel, "whom I have created for My glory." He also says that in bringing them back from captivity, He would do something so marvelous that even the "beasts of the field" would glorify Him for it (v. 20). And He promises to wipe out their sins for His own sake (v. 25). This same God loves Israel "with an everlasting love" (Jeremiah 31:3).

You can't miss the connection between God's love and His glory. God does what He does for His glory. And He's been at it for all eternity. When God created the world, He simply went public with His glory. When God created, He said, "Let me create things outside of Myself that can bring Me glory."

So God spun the universe into existence. In an act of love, He created the world because the most loving thing He could do was to create something that could reflect His glory. God loves us so much that He has given us the privilege of basking in His glory.

GOD'S JOYFUL LOVE

Let me sum up this first section by saying it once again: When we talk about the love of God, we are talking about the joyful overflow or expression of His will and glory. In His own Person, God is perfect love. In His great prayer in John 17, Jesus spoke of the love His Father had for Him before the world began (v. 24). A love relationship exists between the members of the Trinity.

*W*HAT GOD DID FOR US IN CHRIST IS THE STARTING AND ENDING POINT OF ANY DEFINITION OF LOVE.

Since God's love is the overflow of His will and glory, whenever His will is done or His glory expressed, God is joyful about it. Jesus said heaven experiences great joy when a sinner repents. Heaven itself is a place of perfect joy. To put it in common terms, God is excited about His glory. You won't fully understand His love until you see that.

GOD'S LOVE MANIFEST

God's love finds its fullest manifestation in Christ's provision for the salvation of sinful men. The apostle Paul says this in Romans 5:

> Therefore having been justified by faith, we have peace with God through our Lord Jesus Christ, through whom also we have obtained our introduction by faith into this grace in which we stand; and we exult in hope of the glory of God. And not only this, but we also exult in our tribulations, knowing that tribulation brings about perseverance; and perseverance, proven character; and proven character, hope; and hope does not disappoint, because the love of God has been poured out within our hearts through the Holy Spirit who was given to us. . . . But God demonstrates His own love toward us, in that while were yet sinners, Christ died for us. (vv. 1–5, 8)

Paul is saying, "If you want a visible definition of love, look at what God did for us in Christ." If you really want to understand love, don't listen to "rap" music. Don't listen to people who throw the term "love" around. If you want to get to the depths of what it means to love and be loved, look to the death of Christ, because there God's love came to mankind.

With the cross of Christ as the ultimate definition of God's love, I want to suggest six elements of true love. If you want to know whether you love God, this will tell you. If you want to know whether you love your mate or anyone else, this will tell you. What God did for us in Christ is the starting and ending point of any definition of love. Love must have these six criteria to be genuine. True love is:

Visibly Expressed

True love does not just say, "I love you." That's rap. True love is always visibly expressed. God expressed His love in creation. You can look around you and see proof of God's love. But as we just discussed, creation isn't the greatest demonstration of His love. God showed His love most clearly in redemption, Jesus Christ hanging on the cross for all to see. That's the message of Romans 5:8.

Invisible love is no love at all. If people have to read your mind to know you love them, they will never really know they've been loved. True love always can be pointed to. Its activity constantly says, "I love you." So the question is, how are you demonstrating your love? God so loved that He gave us His Son (John 3:16). No demonstration of your love can ever be too costly compared to that!

Always Sacrificial

True love is always willing to pay a price for the benefit of another. John 3:16 reminds us how deeply sacrificial God's love is. If you want to measure your love for someone, or his or her love for you, look at the price tag each person is willing to pay for love. If a man will not sacrifice anything for the woman he claims to love and wishes to marry, he's not the one. If he doesn't want to be inconvenienced, he's not the one. True love is sacrificial.

A tremendous price tag is attached to true love. Just look at the price paid by Jesus Christ. Too many people, though, do not understand or appreciate the price of Calvary. That's why God doesn't get much love back from us. Some people even dare to question whether God loves them. But He says, "Look at the price I paid for you. Look at the fact that when you were hopeless, when you were sinful, when salvation was totally out of your reach, I gave My Son for you. That's how much I love you."

It's safe to say no one else has ever loved you like that. Probably no one else has ever stepped forward to put his or her life on the line so that you might live. No one else has volunteered to take all the strokes of your punishment—especially someone you had mistreated or hurt. We're not into suffering that much.

That's why Jesus Christ so uniquely demonstrates God's love. I want to spend some time on this, because Christ's sacrifice is crucial to our understanding of God's love, and because we take it for granted far too much. It's good to remember that although Jesus' sacrifice for us culminated in His death on the cross, a lot preceded Calvary.

First of all, the perfect, spotless Lamb of God had to live more than thirty-three years in a sinful environment. Try to imagine having to live thirty-three years in a house that has never been cleaned. The house has horrible filth on the carpets, a stench in every room—and you're stuck there for thirty-three years!

God loved us so much that His Son was willing to live in the stench of a sin-contaminated creation to bring about our salvation. You have to realize how holy God is to appreciate that for Jesus Christ, earth was a stench-filled environment. In the midst of the contamination, He lived a perfect, sinless life. But then sinful men laid their smelly hands on Christ and took Him away.

They falsely accused Jesus, and then they scourged Him with a horrible, short-handled whip that today we would call a "cat-o'-nine-tails." Threaded into the thongs of this Roman scourge were jagged pieces of metal and sharpened bone. The scourging Jesus endured for you and me was not just a whipping that left welts on His back. With every lash, those pieces of metal and bone would dig in and lift out chunks of flesh when the whip was pulled back.

That's why Jesus fell trying to carry the cross to Calvary. He was weak from the beatings and the scourging, and the rubbing of that old rugged cross against the deep wounds in His back made it impossible for Him to carry the weight. The only reason He did so was that you and I were on His mind. Otherwise, as the song says, "He could have called ten thousand angels" to deliver Him.

When He got to Calvary, Jesus was nailed to the cross with spikes through His wrists, not His hands as we so often hear. A spike through the palm would not bear the weight of the body, because the hand would tear away.

Jesus' feet were placed on top of one another, and a third spike was driven through one arch, then the other arch, and into the wood. The lifting up of the cross and dropping it with a thud into the hole dug for it must have caused Jesus unbelievable pain. How painful was it? The psalmist said by way of prophecy that all of Christ's bones were out of joint (Psalm 22:14). But He stayed pinned to that cross because you were on His mind.

Then Jesus was offered wine mixed with gall, a narcotic mixture designed to dull the senses and make the excruciating pain of crucifixion a little more bearable. But what did Jesus say? "No. Don't drug Me. I will take the full pain of the punishment. To set sinners free, I have to take their full hell. Don't dull My pain."

Loving God's way involves sacrifice. It costs you something to love. True love is never free. When it comes to love, you must always count the cost and ask, "Do I want to pay the tab?"

Always Beneficial

True love always seeks to benefit the one loved. It does not ask first, "What am I going to get out of this?" but "What am I going to put into this so that the one I love can get something out of it?" Godly love "does not seek its own" (1 Corinthians 13:5), but rather that which is beneficial to another.

Of course, being sinful creatures we think selfishly and want to know, "What's in it for me?" The fact is, there is something for us in true love. Love does not cancel out your own interests, but your benefit is not the focus. Instead, you want to make sure you accomplish a beneficial goal for someone else.

Romans 5:9 reveals a tremendous benefit that Christ purchased for us when He demonstrated God's love. He died for us to save us from "the wrath of God." He had our interests in mind.

Unconditional

God's love is not tied to the worth of the person being loved. If that were the case, none of us would have been saved because Romans 5:8 tells us what our "worth" was before God: "we were yet sinners."

Jesus didn't wait until we got better to die for us. He died when we were in our most unlovely state. The person who doesn't deserve love actually needs love more, not less. If you know someone unworthy of love, that's great! You now have a chance to emulate Christ, because the essence of His love is unconditional.

If your love truly reflects God's love, it is not predicated on the other person's earning it, but on your decision to give it. In Deuteronomy 7:7–8, God tells Israel, "[I] did not set [My] love on you nor choose you because you were more in number than any of the peoples . . . but because [I] loved you and kept the oath which [I] swore to your forefathers." God decided to love Israel.

True love does not have to be earned. If it did, God would have stopped loving us a long time ago.

Judicial

The fact that God's love is unconditional doesn't make it weak and accepting of everything. Here we find a major difference between divine love and what so often passes for love among people. Remember that silly line from the famous sixties' movie *A Love Story?* "Love means never having to say you're sorry." Sorry, but that's poor love and even worse theology.

GOD'S LOVE IS ALWAYS VISIBLE, SACRIFICIAL, BENEFICIAL, UNCONDITIONAL, JUDICIAL, AND EMOTIONAL. WE'LL SPEND THE REST OF OUR LIVES TRYING TO LIVE UP TO THAT STANDARD.

God's love always makes judgment calls. Paul put it this way: Love "does not rejoice in unrighteousness, but rejoices with the truth" (1 Corinthians 13:6). Love hates what is wrong and embraces what is right.

Some people believe that if you love them, you have to accept anything they want to do. No, love always makes judgment calls. God is very concerned about right and wrong. That's why parents who love have to spank sometimes. In Hebrews 12:6 the writer says, "Whom the Lord loveth, He spanketh" (Evans translation). Love does not tolerate wrong, so the loving thing to do is to correct. You do not love when you do not correct.

In fact, God says, "If I don't correct you, it's because you are not My child." So if you go year after year rebelling against God and never get a spanking, your problem isn't that God hasn't gotten to you yet. Your problem is you are not saved. If you are the devil's child, God may not mess with you. But He says, "If you are My child, I'm going to wear your backside out because I love you."

Emotional

Don't let anyone tell you that love does not feel. True love always feels. Emotion by itself doesn't equal love, but you can't have true love without feeling. God feels His love. The Bible says He delights in the works of His hands. He takes great joy in His love for us. Paul says that love "rejoices" when the truth wins out (1 Corinthians 13:6). Sometimes we emphasize the caring aspect of *agape* love so much we negate the emotion of it.

In fact, Paul told the Philippians that he longed for them with "the affection of Christ Jesus" (1:8). Any definition of love is incomplete that does not include joy and deep feeling. It doesn't mean you feel good all the time, but it means that your love is marked by an overriding principle of joy.

The Bible says that "for the joy set before Him, [Jesus] endured the cross" (Hebrews 12:2). True love always feels. But please note this crucial distinction: Feeling doesn't necessarily mean you love; but if you truly love, you will feel.

So God's love is always visible, sacrificial, beneficial, unconditional, judicial, and emotional. We'll spend the rest of our lives trying to live up to that standard.

GOD'S LOVE
AND OUR WELFARE

The love of God reflects in His determination to see to the comprehensive welfare of His children. This takes us back to Romans 8 again. Your Bible should just about fall open to this incredible chapter by now:

> What then shall we say to these things? If God is for us, who is against us? He who did not spare His own Son, but delivered Him up for us all, how will He not also with Him freely give us all things? (vv. 31–32)

If you think about this for a minute, you may be shouting right now. These are rhetorical questions. If God is for you, who can be

against you? Answer: nobody! Not your employer, your circumstances, or your enemies. If He did the hard thing and gave up His
Son for you, will He not also freely give you any good thing you
need? Answer: of course He will.

Nothing Overlooked

This means that when God loves, He loves in such a way that
He is not just concerned about getting you to heaven. He cares
about your comprehensive well-being, every minute detail of your
life. He checks into all the nooks and crannies of your existence. No
area goes unloved by God because if He gave you Jesus, He's not
going to hold back anything else. He has invested too much in you
to overlook anything.

Since this is true, God's love for us has some exciting implications. Paul asks rhetorically in verse 35: "Who shall separate us
from the love of Christ? Shall tribulation, or distress, or persecution, or famine, or nakedness, or peril, or sword?"

Notice Paul did *not* say these trials would not come. That's
something we read into the text. In fact, Jesus told us, "In the world
you have tribulation, but take courage; I have overcome the world"
(John 16:33). Paul agrees. In Romans 8:36 he quotes Psalm 44:22,
saying we will have one trial after another because of who we belong to.

So where do we get the courage to overcome? Knowing that
God's love won't desert us during those times. More than that, it
will bring us out as overwhelming conquerors on the other side (v.
37). And if you need a little more steel in your backbone, read the
last two verses of Romans 8. Then go back to verse 1. God started
you off with "no condemnation" and keeps us with "no separation"
(v. 39). God loves you all the time.

Closing the Loop

Therefore, when your life is falling apart, when your world is
crumbling, you can appeal to the love of God. Now this may raise a
few questions in your mind, because when we look around, things
don't look as good as Romans 8 makes them sound, right? Why
don't we experience the love of God more or feel it more deeply,
since feeling is involved? Why don't we have a greater sense that
God loves us like this passage says He loves us?

There is a reason. We don't sense God's love more because we
break the loop of His love. I said earlier that love of God is the

overflow of His glory. You and I live in a world where our negative circumstances often obscure His love. But when we live for His glory (which is what He loves), when we are passionately consumed with living for God's glory, then we close the loop of His love.

The "secret" is in our passion to live for God's glory. The psalmist said, "Delight yourself in the Lord" (Psalm 37:4). Find your chief joy in life in Him. Paul wrote, "Rejoice in the Lord always; again I will say, rejoice!" (Philippians 4:4). In other words, when we seek God's glory in every circumstance of life, when we take what He does in our lives and aim it back toward His glory, God finds great joy in our taking His glory seriously.

And when God finds great joy in us, He allows us to experience His joy. When you have God's joy, the numbers in the bank account don't matter as much anymore, because you sense His welfare. A great illustration of this appears in 2 Corinthians 8. The Christians in Macedonia were undergoing "a great ordeal of affliction" (v. 2). Their pockets weren't just empty. They had holes in them. These people weren't poor. They were "po' folk"!

But the Macedonian Christians were so full of the grace of God, so zeroed in on His glory, that they begged Paul for the opportunity to support other saints in need. God had become so alive to them, His overflowing joy so dominant in them, that even in their ordeal and poverty, they were eager for the chance to serve Him more. May God give every pastor about ten pews full of folks like this!

God's Joy

True love is only activated when the glory of God is the goal of our lives, because that's what His love is designed to achieve. If you live only for yourself and not for the glory of God, He will not share His joy with you.

If you are not living for God's joy, marriage won't help you. You will have a husband or a wife and no joy. The idea is to become dominated with God's joy whether you have a mate or not; whether you have a job or not; whether you have money or not; whether your circumstances are good or not. Remember, God can "freely give us all things." That presents no problem for Him. But there's more to it than just having smooth sailing.

Salvation is like taking a deranged person into your house and making him heir to everything you own. God took sin-deranged human beings into His family and made them heirs to the throne of

Jesus Christ. We couldn't think straight or talk straight. He should have left us nothing, but He turned around and signed the whole thing over to us. If we only knew the benefits that come with knowing Christ. It's not just fire insurance.

Consumed with His Love

Knowing Christ means we have His guarantee that in every situation in life, He loves us. When our world falls apart, we can say, "Lord, I don't know why I'm going through this. I don't understand it, but I'm sure glad to know You love me. How can I glorify You right now?"

You say, "How do I know God is loving me at times like that?"

Because when you "exult" in your trials and bear up under them with perseverance, God pours His joy into your heart in such abundance that it just spills all over the place (Romans 5:1–5). His joy consumes you. This means you don't have to fear anymore. "Perfect love casts out fear" (1 John 4:18). Are there legitimate reasons for concern? Of course. But you don't let these things consume you. Why? Because God loves you.

WHERE YOU HANG OUT WILL DETERMINE WHAT YOU SMELL LIKE. IF YOU HANG OUT WITH GOD, YOU'RE GOING TO SMELL LIKE LOVE!

We're like the little boy who got separated from his mother in the mall. He was looking around for his mommy, and getting scared. He began to cry because everyone was a stranger and everything looked so confusing and every store was packed and he didn't have his mommy. But all of a sudden, his mother found him and picked him up. His eyes began to dry, not because his surroundings were changed, but because of whose arms he was in.

When you have someone holding you who loves you, it doesn't matter anymore what everyone else does. When you are in the arms of a loving God, when you have become consumed with His love and you share in His joy, it's all right. He holds you and says, "Don't cry. I'm here. I'm here." He loves you.

GOD'S LOVE
IS THE MEASURE

We measure authentic love for others against the love of God. John, "the apostle of love," says this: "Every one who loves is born of God and knows God" (1 John 4:7). "Born of God" is salvation; "knows God" is intimacy.

John is saying, "If you have learned love, you learned it from God because He is the only One who can give you this kind of love." You can't learn this kind of love from watching "As the World Turns." "All My Children" won't teach you this.

John goes on to say in verse 8: "The one who does not love does not know God, for God is love." You can't have God and not have love. If you are getting close to God, it's going to rub off on you. If you hang out in a flower shop, you smell flowery. If you hang out in a perfume shop, you smell sweet. Where you hang out will determine what you smell like. If you hang out with God, you're going to smell like love!

So if you are hateful, ornery, irritable, or frustrated; if you are not a "happy camper," your problem isn't that people keep messing with you. Your problem is you don't know God. I am convinced that a lot of the problems I see in relationships, especially between husbands and wives, come because someone doesn't know God here. When God consumes you, He says, "You will love."

Loving Others

That's the beautiful thing about admitting, "I can't love so-and-so." You are absolutely right. You can't, but that's not the question. The question is, can God love this person? Then you'd better get hooked up with Him. If it's a 100-degree day, to sweat you just need to stand in the presence of the sun.

When you stand in the presence of a loving God, you will radiate love just because you are there. But we want to keep running into "spiritual air conditioning." We want to insulate ourselves from the hot sun of God's love which transforms us.

In 1 John 4:19–20, John concludes, "We love, because He first loved us. If someone says, 'I love God,' and hates his brother, he is a liar; for the one who does not love his brother whom he has seen, cannot love God whom he has not seen." Now I didn't call anyone a liar. God did. Anyone who says he loves God and can't love others is lying through his two front teeth. John says, "You can't be consumed with God and not love other sinners. He doesn't like what they do, but He loves sinners."

When you get consumed by the love of God, it overflows you and spills out onto others. If God has poured His overflowing love into your heart, others can't help getting hit by the splash!

Getting in the Game

But too many of us sit on the spiritual sidelines when it comes to this thing called love. I love watching football. When I see a great play, I respond. I really enjoy watching other people play the game.

But I love something else even more: playing football myself. There's something about putting on the shoulder pads and picking up the ball, even if it's just to play around with my kids. In fact, while I'm watching a football game I often pick up a football and just toss it from hand to hand. I want to get in on the action.

Sometimes I tackle my boys. And if I'm really into it, I tackle my girls. I've got to tackle someone—except my wife. One day I bumped against Lois during a living room football game and she said, "You'd better stop that." The game was over. Lois prefers to remain on the sidelines.

Too many of us are spectators to the love, grace, glory, and goodness of God. It's time to get on the field by living God's love the way it was meant to be lived—which is to turn everything back to His glory. It is to ask God, "How can I glorify you?" and then bask in His glory. That will bring Him delight. Then He will allow you to experience His delight, and you will feel the joy of His love.

The Hanging Tree was a classic Gary Cooper western film. A young man had been shot and was dying. Cooper took his knife, dug into the young man and pulled out the bullet, stopped the bleeding and bandaged him up, and the boy made it. He looked at Gary Cooper after he got well and asked, "Sir, for what you have done to me, what should I do for you?"

Cooper said, "You're going to be my servant for the rest of your life, because that's how long you would have been dead if I hadn't saved you."

God looked down at us, saw our wound, and went to great pain to dig out the bullet of sin so that you and I could enjoy His grace. What should we do in return? Serve Him for the rest of our lives and even throughout eternity, because that's how long we would have suffered if He hadn't acted in love to save us!

Responding to the Love of God

Are you ready to get into the game? Do you want the love of God to fill and overflow you, bringing you His joy and glory and spilling over into the lives of the people around you? Great! Grab a helmet and get out there. Here's a "game plan" to get you started:

1. Besides your words, can you point to something you've done in the past week to demonstrate your love to your spouse, your child, or some other loved one or friend? If you have to scratch your head to come up with something, it's time to get busy.

2. If you're like most of us, somewhere along the way God has brought an unlovely person into your life. Unloveliness has nothing to do with his or her appearance. The person just makes it very hard for you to love. Try a "sneak attack." At your next opportunity, startle that person with an act of kindness or a helping hand at the moment he or she least expects or deserves it. You may have to scratch your head a while to plan this one, but God will make it worth the effort.

3. Since God has promised to carry you from spiritual birth (no condemnation) all the way to heaven and His presence (no separation), *nothing* in between can take you out! If that assurance makes you just a little bit happy, why not spend the next few minutes telling God how wonderful His love is? You have my permission to shout.

4. You may be carrying a heavy load right now. At times like this, the *daily* presence and assurance of God's love means the most. No matter what the load or how long you've been carrying it, do you believe God can give you the grace and strength to carry it one more day or week or month? Do you believe He's eager to give you what you need? Then ask Him for it today, and tomorrow, and the next day. . . .

15
THE GRACE
OF GOD

What would you think if you went to buy a car and the salesman told you you either had to push the car everywhere you went or pay extra for an engine? You'd know something was wrong because cars come equipped with their own supply of power to get you where you're going. The engine is part of the purchase price of the car.

You do have a responsibility to turn on the ignition and steer, but your effort does not supply the power for the trip. When I see so many Christians failing in their Christian life, living defeated lives day after day, month after month, and year after year, it soon becomes apparent they "push" their Christian lives. They don't realize that the power for the Christian life is already under the hood.

That power is the grace of God, His inexhaustible supply of goodness by which He does for us what we could never do for ourselves. Some of us live under the misconception that we have the power to pull off the Christian life. If that were true, we would be no different than a non-Christian who keeps the Ten Commandments. It's all human effort.

But God has supplied every true believer with a magnificent provision: His inexhaustible supply of goodness called *grace*. We can't earn it, we don't deserve it, but He has made it abundantly available. If Christians need to grasp any truth, it is grace. Grace is not well understood today because the word has been used so flippantly or without a proper understanding of what's involved in it.

One reason most people have problems understanding grace is that they have a misconception about God. Because people do not see God as a holy God, they don't see where they need His grace. They expect to wake up tomorrow morning the way they did this morning, because that's just part of the deal. But many people were here yesterday and aren't today.

Grace means God doesn't have to do anything. We have seen that He is totally self-sufficient and in need of nothing. Grace means that all you are and all you have comes because He chooses to give it, not because you can demand it or deserve it.

Man has devalued God and made Him into merely a glorified man. The God of most people today does not look like the God of the Bible. We have created a God who accepts wrong, who doesn't judge sin, and who does not have retribution as one of the moral laws of His universe. We pay a high price for this God, because we have the attitude, "It's OK to do wrong as long as you don't get caught."

Look how hard it is today to exact punishment for crime. Two boys admit to killing their parents, and the jury can't convict them. A teenager in Fort Worth murders his two unarmed cousins and claims "urban self-defense" because he says they were planning to kill him. His attorney uses that defense, and the first trial ends in a hung jury.

This permissive attitude is reflected in our society's view of the death penalty. It's seen in parents not wanting to correct their children. All of this shows a warped view of God. He is totally holy, totally pure, set apart from all sin and therefore, He owes sinful man nothing. Anything we get from God, we get because of His grace.

We have to understand that. God owes us nothing. Yet in grace, He has given us an inexhaustible supply of His goodness.

GRACE IS POSSIBLE
BECAUSE OF CHRIST

The grace of God is possible because of the sacrifice His Son made for the salvation of sinful mankind. We are only alive today and not consumed because of what Jesus did. And we will only go to heaven because of what Jesus did.

If it were not for the sacrifice of Jesus Christ, we would have been wiped out in judgment. But Christ's death on the cross freed God up to shower us with His grace rather than pour out His holy and justly deserved wrath on us. We got more of God's goodness than we'll ever be able to experience down here.

In fact, the essence of heaven is the uninterrupted enjoyment of God's goodness. We will have glorified bodies that won't get tired because God doesn't want one second to go by without us thoroughly enjoying His goodness.

But God's goodness is only available in heaven and on earth because of grace. The reason we worship the Lord Jesus Christ is that because of Him, God's grace was unleashed. We worship Christ because He dealt with the one thing which kept God from extending His grace to us: our sin.

Look at Romans 5, which contrasts the first Adam with the last Adam (Christ). Paul says, "Just as through one man sin entered into the world, and death through sin, and so death spread to all men, because all sinned" (v. 12). In other words, "In Adam all die" (1 Corinthians 15:22). We will die because Adam sinned. We were "in Adam" when he sinned. Adam was our titular head; that is, he was our representative.

Now someone may say, "Wait a minute. I didn't choose Adam to represent me. I want to represent myself in this thing. I'm a pretty good person."

But God says, "If you want to represent yourself, you've got a problem. You've sinned too, just like Adam. You haven't done any better than he did."

We often hear people say, "Oh, if Adam hadn't done it." But the fact is, if Adam hadn't sinned, we would have done it anyway. I like the story of the forester named Sam. Sam chopped down trees every day, and every time the boss came by he would hear Sam saying, "Oh Adam! Ohh Adam! Ohhh Adam!"

One day the boss asked, "Why do you moan, 'Oh Adam!' every time you're out here chopping trees?"

Sam replied, "Because if Adam hadn't sinned, I wouldn't have to do this backbreaking work, which is part of the curse."

So the boss said to Sam, "Come with me." He took Sam to his palatial home with a tennis court, swimming pool, maid, and butler.

"All this is yours, Sam," he said. You never have to complain again. I give all of it to you, a perfect environment."

Sam couldn't believe it. The boss said, "Now you can enjoy everything all the time, only don't do one thing. A little box sits on the dining room table. Don't touch it."

Sam went out and played tennis every day, swam, and had his friends over, but after a while he got bored. There was only one thing in that house he didn't know about: that little box on the dining room table. He walked by, checking out the box, but then he reminded himself, "You can't touch it. Don't touch it."

But every day Sam walked by and saw that box. One day, he finally gave in. "I've got to find out what's in that box." He went over and opened the box, and out flew a little moth. He tried to catch it, but he couldn't.

When the boss found out that the box had been tampered with, he sent Sam back out to the forest to chop trees. The next day, the boss heard him groaning, "Oh Sam! Ohh Sam! Ohhh Sam!"

Even if Adam hadn't messed up, we would have because "all have sinned" (Romans 3:23). We would have to face the issue of death anyway. Turning back to Romans 5, listen to what Paul says about the grace of God in Christ that takes the sting out of death:

> But the free gift is not like the transgression. For if by the transgression of the one the many died, much more did the grace of God and the gift by the grace of the one Man, Jesus Christ, abound to the many. . . . For if by the transgression of the one, death reigned through the one, much more those who receive the abundance of grace and of the gift of righteousness will reign in life through the One, Jesus Christ. So then as through one transgression there resulted condemnation to all men, even so through one act of righteousness there resulted justification of life to all men. (vv. 15, 17–18)

Thanks to God's "gift of grace" in Christ, we as Christians don't have to fear death. The Bible describes the death of a Christian as "sleep" (1 Corinthians 15:51). Non-Christians die, Christians sleep. The moment you close your eyes, "To be absent from the body [is] to be at home with the Lord" (2 Corinthians 5:8). You will never feel death because less than a second after you die, you will be in the presence of God. Death means immediate transferal into glory.

Common Grace

The work of Jesus Christ also brings general benefits to all people. Original sin means that we are all born into this world with the mark of condemnation on us. But the atonement of Jesus Christ for the sins of all men has neutralized the effects of the Adamic curse and satisfied the demands of a holy God, so that God is now free to be good even to sinful people.

Please note, I did not say that all people are automatically saved by Christ's death. Every person will be judged on the basis of what he did with Christ. Those who reject Him will face condemnation. I'm not talking about salvation benefits, but what is often called "common grace."

For instance, Jesus says that God causes the sun to shine and the rain to fall on the unrighteous as well as the righteous (Matthew 5:45). That's part of God's common grace to all. So is the air. You don't have to be a Christian to get oxygen. God gives common grace to all. But He reserves His special grace for His own.

Special Grace

Kids from the community frequently come over to the Evans house. We enjoy it, and we share what we have with them. They play and have something to drink, get lunch, or whatever. But special benefits are available only to my kids. God gives common benefits to the whole human race, but the benefits of His special grace come only to His children. Again, these flow to us through our relationship with Jesus Christ.

Everything good comes from God, and only because Jesus Christ freed Him up to give it. Non-Christians will not always thank God for the air, water, and sunshine that keep them alive, but everyone who names the name of Christ should wake up each morning thanking God for His grace. We know it's all because Jesus Christ satisfied the demands of a holy God. So first of all, grace is possible only because of Christ.

GOD'S GRACE
BRINGS US MERCY

God's mercy is distinct from His grace in that grace means giving a person something he doesn't deserve, while mercy is identifying with someone's misery. According to Ephesians 2:4–5:

> God, being rich in mercy, because of His great love with which He loved us, even when we were dead in our transgressions, made us alive together with Christ (by grace you have been saved).

Here Paul beautifully juxtaposes grace and mercy. In mercy, God's heart went out to us in our helpless condition. In grace, He gave us what we didn't deserve—salvation. Mercy is what a mother shows when she cuddles her sick child.

GOD'S GRACE MUST DEAL WITH SIN BEFORE GOD'S MERCY CAN QUELL THE MISERABLE EFFECTS OF SIN.

Every misery we experience in life is to some degree related to sin: either our own sin, someone else's sin, or just the contaminated, sinful world in which we live. Because He's "rich in mercy," when God sees our pain, He feels it. He experiences it with us. But grace must precede mercy because God can't help us with our misery until He first deals with our sin.

Often someone will come to one of the staff members in the counseling ministry at our church in Dallas and say, "Help me! This problem is making me unhappy, discouraged, depressed, and frustrated. It's making me miserable." We have to tell that person he or she can find no divine relief for misery, no matter who the counselor is, unless the sin question has been addressed.

That's because God's grace must deal with sin before God's mercy can quell the miserable *effects* of sin. Once God has dealt with us in grace, He can act toward us in mercy. You wouldn't think much of a doctor who was willing to deal with the symptoms of a serious illness without looking at the disease that caused those symptoms. If you want God's mercy to deal with your misery, you've first got to accept His grace to deal with your sin.

That's why John wrote to Christians, "If we confess our sins, He is faithful and righteous to forgive us our sins and to cleanse us from all unrighteousness" (1 John 1:9). Confession of your sin frees God to show you His mercy. If you are miserable, you need God's mercy. But you can't have His mercy until you have allowed His grace to take away your sin. Once you've come clean with God, He is able help you with the things that bring hurt.

One day a Sunday School teacher asked a little boy, "What's the difference between grace and mercy?"

The boy said, "Well, I asked my mommy for a peanut butter sandwich, and she made it for me. That was grace. But she put jelly on it too. That was mercy."

Mercy happens when God gives you the jelly; when He not only deals with your need, but goes overboard and deals with the effects of that need in your life. Mercy is when He provides sweetness to your experience. We need that because many of us have made decisions or had experiences which have messed us up.

Maybe abuse by a parent, some rebellion on your part, or something that you shouldn't have done has caused you real problems. It could be emotional, mental, or physical problems that have created misery for you. God is free to help you because He is full of mercy, the result of His great grace. The Bible says that God's mercies are "new every morning" (Lamentations 3:23). Every day, God has something new to show you as He deals with some aspect of your life.

The problem is we aren't looking for it, so we seldom see it. If we would be fully aware of what God does in one twenty-four-hour period, we'd be amazed at how many things He does to relieve some of the burden for us. We dismiss so much of what happens to us as ordinary or even chance. But the verse just before the one I quoted above says, "It is of the Lord's mercies that we are not consumed" (Lamentations 3:22 KJV).

Every day that you wake up, it's by the mercy of God. We've all made promises to God: "Lord, if You'll get me out of this . . . if You'll solve this problem . . . if You'll raise me from this sickbed . . . if You'll give me a good doctor's report . . . I'll serve You the rest of my life."

We fail to keep many of our promises. So why doesn't God take us out? Because of His mercy. And why can God show us mercy? Because of grace. Because He looks at Jesus Christ and is so satisfied He's able to deal with us in mercy and pity us in our pain. No one wants what he or she deserves. Does a guilty person throw himself on the *justice* of the court? Of course not. He throws himself on the *mercy* of the court.

That's what we do when we cry out to God and say, "Lord, I messed up. It was my sin that got me in here, or the sin of someone else, but I plead the blood of Jesus Christ. Have mercy on me!"

The Israelites cried out to God from the misery of Egyptian slavery, and their cry reached not only His ear, but His heart. So He sent Moses to deliver them (Exodus 3:9–10). Those Israelite slaves wanted mercy. So should we.

I'm reminded of the badly aging Hollywood star who had her photograph taken. When she saw the picture, she said to the photographer, "That picture doesn't do me justice."

The photographer looked at her and said, "Lady, with a face like yours, you don't need justice, you need mercy."

With lives like ours, we don't need justice, we need mercy. God is free to pity you in your pain, walk with you in your struggle, and hurt where you hurt because His great grace has unleashed His great mercy. Mercy means God mixes it up with you in the hurts of life.

GOD'S GRACE
IS SUFFICIENT FOR EVERY NEED

You should memorize this verse: "And God is able to make all grace abound to you, that always having all sufficiency in everything, you may have an abundance for every good deed" (2 Corinthians 9:8). God's got something for everything you need. There is no such thing as insufficient grace.

Most of us have suffered the embarrassment of bouncing a check because of insufficient funds. But God has no problem covering His checks. The Bible says that God's grace is so inexhaustible, so awesome in its supply, it never runs out. Grace is designed not only to save you, but to keep you. When you became a Christian, God supplied you everything you need for spiritual life and growth.

That's why Peter says, "Grow in the grace and knowledge of our Lord and Savior Jesus Christ" (2 Peter 3:18). Peter is saying, "Grow in your understanding of grace. The more you understand about grace, the more you enjoy the Christian life." Don't let anyone stop you from growing in your understanding of the awesome supply of God's grace.

The story is told of a man who paid for an ocean cruise. The fare took all of his money, leaving him nothing for meals on the week-long trip. So he brought peanut butter and jelly sandwiches with him, and while his fellow passengers enjoyed sumptuous meals and buffets every evening, he went to his cabin in embarrassment and ate his meager meals.

The man was miserable knowing that everyone else was eating this incredible food, but he knew he couldn't enjoy any of it because he had used all of his money for his ticket. At the end of the cruise, as the man was leaving the ship, one of the porters asked him, "How did you enjoy the cruise?"

He said, "Well, I loved the ride, but I was always hungry because I couldn't afford any of the food."

The porter looked at him in astonishment and replied, "Sir, the meals were included in the price of your ticket! You were miserable for no reason at all."

I think when a lot of us get to heaven, God will say, "You were miserable for no reason at all. All of your answers were available in My grace. But you didn't grow in grace and never came to understand My sufficiency." When you met Jesus Christ, everything you need for your Christian life was included in the salvation "ticket" He gave you. But if you don't grow in grace you don't know all the goodness God has supplied for you.

Many "millionaire" Christians live pauper lives because they haven't grown in their understanding of God's great, inexhaustible supply that was provided in Christ. Don't let anyone stop you from maximizing your Christian experience. Would anyone do that? I don't want to shock you, but you need to know that some Christians think their calling is to make you spiritually miserable. They aren't going anywhere spiritually, and they want company. But God says, "My grace is sufficient."

Paul learned this truth in the midst of a problem:

> Because of the surpassing greatness of the revelations, for this reason, to keep me from exalting myself, there was given me a thorn in the flesh, a messenger of Satan to buffet me—to keep me from exalting myself! (2 Corinthians 12:7)

We are not quite sure what Paul's thorn was, whether a physical ailment like bad eyes or even a person who was trying to discredit him. Whatever it was, he struggled with it. It was number one on his prayer list for some time. He tells us:

> Concerning this I entreated the Lord three times that it might depart from me. And He has said to me, "My grace is sufficient for you, for power is perfected in weakness." (vv. 8–9)

I'm confident you have a "thorn" somewhere in your life. Maybe your thorn is a person who keeps pricking you, a problem you can't get over, or an illness the doctors can't heal. God says His grace doesn't always remove these things, but it does empower you to overcome them. God's grace is not just a "disappearing cream" you rub on problems. It raises you above the problem and gives you power at the exact point where most people would quit.

God's grace enables us to love people we would normally hate, to have patience where we would normally give up. Grace gives us power we didn't have before. Grace does not only remove problems. Sometimes it helps us plow through them. But it's still grace, because we couldn't have done it without God.

My question to you is, what did you do last week, last month, or last year that only God could have pulled off? If you can't point to something in your life that only God could have done, you are not growing in grace. You still live in your own power. You push your car rather than letting grace do the work.

GOD'S GRACE
TRAINS US FOR VICTORY

The grace of God also trains us in how to live the victorious Christian life. Paul says in Titus 2:11: "For the grace of God has appeared, bringing salvation to all men." The appearance of God's grace Paul talks about is the coming of Jesus Christ to earth to die for us and bring us salvation. But look at what else God's grace does for us:

> ... instructing us to deny ungodliness and worldly desires and to live sensibly, righteously and godly in the present age, looking for the blessed hope and the appearing of the glory of our great God and Savior, Christ Jesus. (vv. 12–13)

Grace instructs us in how to live. You see, grace is much more than just a concept. It is an environment in which we live and move. In his tearful good-bye to the elders at Miletus, Paul commended them to "the word of [God's] grace, which is able to build you up" (Acts 20:32). He said this in the context of their responsibility to the church, to guard God's flock. These men were going to need real spiritual strength to do their jobs.

That's what grace does. Grace will give you victory where you didn't have victory. Grace will give you power where you didn't have power. Grace will give you the ability to keep on keeping on when you want to give up.

Grace teaches us how to live. It not only gives us the right information, but the right enablement with it. With grace comes power. A lot of people can give out right information. After all, we're on the "information superhighway." Trouble is, this highway has no gas stations. Where do we get the power to pull this off?

"Grace gives it to you," Paul says. He explained it to the Galatians this way:

> I have been crucified with Christ; and it is no longer I who live, but Christ lives in me; and the life which I now live in the flesh I live by faith in the Son of God, who loved me, and delivered Himself up for me. (2:20)

In other words, "I have exchanged my life for Christ's life living in me." Notice he goes on to say in verse 21 that this kept him from "nullify[ing] the grace of God.'"

Living the Christian life in your own power nullifies the grace of God. If you try to pull yourself up spiritually by your own good works, by positive thinking, or by sheer determination, you cancel out God's grace.

It's no accident that Paul wrote this way to the believers in Galatia. In the very next sentence he said, "You foolish Galatians, who has bewitched you, before whose eyes Jesus Christ was publicly portrayed as crucified?" (3:1). They were being tricked by people who had exchanged inner spiritual power for outward religious conformity. If you're making that same exchange today, you have been tricked.

What's the solution? Paul reveals it in Galatians 5:1: "It was for freedom that Christ set us free; therefore keep standing firm and do not be subject again to a yoke of slavery."

Here's an expanded Evans translation: "Don't let anyone enslave you. When you were set free by Christ, you were free to do what you ought to do. You were set free by Christ to enjoy Christ's life in you. Don't let anyone put a magical spell on you. Don't let anyone enslave you to thoughts, actions, or patterns that are not in agreement with Christ. You are free now. Don't let anyone tie you up." Jesus told His disciples, "Apart from Me you can do nothing" (John 15:5).

Some Christians are tied up in knots trying to live by other people's religious rules rather than by grace. Paul says, "Let grace govern your lives, not people." Galatians 5:2 shows how critically important this is. "Behold I, Paul, say to you that if you receive circumcision, Christ will be of no benefit to you." Verse 4 carries on the startling thought: "You have been severed from Christ, you who are seeking to be justified by law; you have fallen from grace."

So it's possible for us as Christians to go back to an external rule of conformity, and in so doing to cancel out the power of Christ in our lives. Some of us who are trying to do good have cut off the power of Christ because we operate by our external conformity and determination rather than by the inner dynamic of grace.

What does it mean to fall from grace? It means you no longer live by the grace standard, but by the flesh standard. You try to do in the flesh what can only be done by the power of God. To the degree that you are in deep relationship with Christ, you will have the power to live the victorious Christian life.

RULES ARE NECESSARY, BUT THE POWER TO OBEY THEM MUST COME FROM WITHIN.

It's much like marriage. To newlyweds, it's pure joy to do things for one another. The new wife asks, "Darling, what can I make for you this evening?" The new husband goes out of his way to make sure his bride doesn't lift anything heavy or strain herself in any way. The daily chores that come with married life aren't a burden but a delight, because the energy to do them is generated from within, from the power and newness of that love relationship.

But what happens five years later? He's lucky to get a meal. She's lucky he doesn't take off and drag her down the driveway while she's trying to get in the car. If the work still gets done, it's because they have to, not because they want to. What happened? The internal motivation has been replaced by external conformity. Whenever that happens, you have no joy or peace. You just have a job.

Like a joyless marriage, the Christian life becomes miserable whenever you try to live it by your own determination rather than by the supply of divine energy from within. The Christian life can only be lived when you remain in vital relationship with Jesus Christ, your power source. That's why Paul goes on to say in Galatians 5:16: "Walk by the Spirit, and you will not carry out the desire of the flesh."

Now don't get me wrong. Nothing is wrong with rules. Rules are necessary, but the power to obey them must come from within. The idea is not to get rid of legitimate rules, but to get back into relationship with Christ so that we will have the proper motivation to do the right thing.

Grace never means people hold no responsibility. That's called lawlessness. The difference between living under grace and living under law is that under grace we are motivated to obey by the proper power source, which is the Spirit. That's the engine underneath the hood. The Bible calls it "the filling of the Holy Spirit" (see Ephesians 5:18). By the way, the verb there indicates that filling is to be a continuous process.

But it's like filling your car with gas. Your tank may be full now, but if you just keep going and going, you will run low on gas. We just keep living the Christian life without continually being refueled by our relationship with God, and then we wonder why our lives become stalled spiritually.

I can relate to this because I regularly drive on fumes. I can usually tell how far past empty the gas tank needle can go before I need to fill up. One time, though, I guessed wrong and ran out of gas on Interstate 35 in Dallas. I started to chug along and finally had to pull over to the side. I looked down and sure enough, I was out of gas. Now I was really frustrated.

But it was really bad when a couple of my church members drove by, waved, and didn't stop. In fact, one of them had the window down and said, "Hi, Pastor." They really gave me a hard time about it.

If you don't keep your spiritual tank full, don't be surprised if you wind up on the side of the road. We have got to keep a "tiger in the tank" so to speak, if we want to know the enabling power of God's grace. We ought to be constantly saying, "Boy, I don't know where I got the ability to do that." Just saying it will remind you where you got it—the grace of God.

So as our relationship with Christ is cultivated, we grow in grace. Then the supply of grace, energized by the power of the

Holy Spirit, gives us spiritual victory. At that point we can say with Paul, "By the grace of God I am what I am" (1 Corinthians 15:10). When grace starts operating, we'll begin to sing when it's not Sunday, serve without being asked, and know how to speak to others with a voice of grace (Colossians 4:6). We give grace because we've got grace.

GOD GIVES GRACE ON HIS TERMS

The grace of God is only experienced by those who receive it on His terms. James 4:1–2 says:

> What is the source of quarrels and conflicts among you? Is not the source your pleasures that wage war in your members? You lust and do not have; so you commit murder. And you are envious and cannot obtain; so you fight and quarrel. You do not have because you do not ask.

The first way you get God's grace is by asking for it. But too many of us try to make things happen on our own, fussing and fighting to get what they want. How many husbands and wives fight to change one another? Or struggle to make this happen and that happen? "You are warring," James says, "when all you have to do is ask."

It is of course possible to ask "with wrong motives, so that you may spend it on your pleasures" (v. 3). We tend to think of this as asking for material things. We think, "Sure, I can understand God not giving me a sports car." But this can apply to all kinds of prayers we make that are designed not to glorify Him, but to benefit us.

I keep coming back to children as an illustration, because so much of what we do as Christians is similar to what our kids do. Kids ask mostly for things for themselves. And when they get them, they're usually not too eager to share.

James says, "One reason you are defeated and don't have a lot of things necessary for you to be victorious is that you don't ask. And when you do ask, you ask too often only to benefit yourself. You are using human methods. Ask, but with the right motives."

Then he says in verse 4:

> You adulteresses, do you not know that friendship with the world is hostility toward God? Therefore whoever wishes to be a friend of the world makes himself an enemy of God.

You can't love the world and love God at the same time. You have to make a choice. No compromise is possible. "You can't have the world and God too; that's spiritual adultery," James warns. Our God is jealous of His work in us (v. 5). He won't share us with another spiritual suitor—and He shouldn't have to!

Then James makes a statement about grace: "But He gives a greater grace. Therefore it says, 'God is opposed to the proud, but gives grace to the humble'" (v. 6).

If you think you can do it yourself, God says, "OK, do it yourself. If you can't do it yourself, come to Me." That's humility. Humility recognizes that I have a need I can't meet by myself. It says, "God, I need You to meet it for me." As long as you think you can do it yourself, that's pride. And God opposes the proud.

You don't want God opposing you. He will make it impossible for you to do what you want to do through the methods you are trying to use. He's going to resist you because God will resist His children who operate independently of Him, who don't ask, who compromise with the world. But the humble cry, "I can't. I need You. I'm desperate!" To them He gives more grace.

Hebrews 4:16 says, "Let us therefore draw near with confidence to the throne of grace, that we may receive mercy and may find grace to help in time of need." You can go to a place called the "throne room of grace." It's like a bank. It stores up whatever you need to pay whatever bills you need paid. In this throne room God dispenses grace, but only upon request.

When was the last time the bank called you and asked, "Do you need some money?"

No, it's generally you going to the bank saying, "I need some money."

God says, "I've got a throne room called grace. Do you need grace? Then draw near that you may receive mercy and grace in the time of need." How long do you stay there? Until you get what you need. If it's important enough, you will stay.

When chain saws first came out, a man who was used to chopping trees by hand went to a hardware store. The proprietor said, "We have a new power saw. With this saw, you can cut down thirty trees a day instead of the three you're doing now."

The man said, "Are you serious?"

"Yes, thirty trees a day with this power saw."

"I'll take one." He bought the power saw, but came back mad a week later. "Why did you sell me this piece of junk?"

The proprietor asked, "What's wrong?"

"It took me a week to cut down one tree with this piece of junk. I was better off using my old axe!"

The proprietor said, "Let me see it." He took the saw, pulled on the cord, and it started right up with its motor roaring.

The man jumped back and asked, "What's that noise?"

You don't buy a power saw so you can go out and put even more human effort into cutting down trees. You buy a power saw to let the motor do the cutting. God didn't save you so you could continue trying life on your own. He saved you to display His power and His strength in your life.

What a shame to have God's Spirit but only to chop down one need in your life, when enough power has been made available to chop down a hundred needs. This is the provision of God's grace.

Responding to the Grace of God

God's grace is available in abundance to us. If God saved us by His grace, why would He withhold any other grace? James notes the conditions under which greater grace is available. These suggestions may help you to put God's grace to work in your life in a new way, or at least point you in the right direction:

1. Here's that verse I want you to memorize: "And God is able to make all grace abound to you, that always having all sufficiency in everything, you may have an abundance for every good deed" (2 Corinthians 9:8).

2. Let me repeat a question I asked earlier. What have you done in the past week, month, or even year that can only be explained as the power of God working through you? If you have trouble answering that, it may be time to get alone with God and allow His Spirit to do some heart searching.

3. Anytime is a good time to measure your growth in grace. Before too much longer, take some time to put your life up against a "spiritual growth chart" like Galatians 5:22–23, the fruit of the Spirit, and mark your progress. For every sign of new growth you see, thank the Lord. For every area of growth needed, humbly ask for His grace.

4. Based on what we have learned from James 4 about asking with the wrong motives, we probably ought to thank God more often for *un*answered prayer. Have you prayed any prayers like that lately? Is it possible you're praying for something right now that would not be good for you or glorify God? Those questions are worth thinking seriously about.

16
THE INCARNATION OF GOD

esus Christ is one of a kind. No one is like Him. He never wrote a book, yet the book that tells His story, the Bible, has outsold every other book in human history. More books have been written about Jesus than about any other person. He never wrote a song, but more songs have been written about Jesus than anyone else. He never traveled more than a few hundred miles from home, yet you can go almost no place where His name is not known.

No book that claims to talk about our awesome God would be complete without a study of the incarnation of Jesus Christ, the God-man. So it's appropriate that we close this section of the book by considering the supernatural birth of Jesus Christ. The incarnation is also a fitting close to this portion of our study because, as you'll see, in the process of sending Jesus Christ to this earth, God displayed many of the attributes we have just spent so many chapters studying.

The prophet Isaiah captures the uniqueness of Jesus' birth when he writes: "Behold, a virgin will be with child and bear a son, and she will call His name Immanuel" (Isaiah 7:14). When Matthew quotes this prophecy, he adds this crucial phrase concerning the name Immanuel: "which translated means, 'God with us'" (Matthew 1:23).

"God with us." The theological term for it is the "incarnation" or "enfleshment" of God. The term *incarnation* comes from the Latin word meaning "flesh." Very simply, God became a man. It's easy to say that, but it will take eternity to understand and grasp it fully.

However, the Bible teaches the incarnation of Christ so clearly that simply to admire Christ as a great person, a great prophet, or a great leader devalues Him terribly. It's an insult to Him, for He is nothing less than God become man! In one of the greatest miracles ever, the Son of God took on human flesh. He became like us in order to bring us back to Himself.

I like the way Isaiah put it in Isaiah 9:6: "For a child will be born to us, a son will be given to us." Notice that the child is born, but the Son is "given" because the Son was not born. The Son existed before the child. Jesus the Son of Man was born, but Jesus the Son of God was given because Jesus is eternal God. Notice how Isaiah continues:

> And the government will rest on His shoulders; and His name will be called Wonderful Counselor, Mighty God, Eternal Father, Prince of Peace. There will be no end to the increase of His government or of peace, on the throne of David and over his kingdom, to establish it and to uphold it with justice and righteousness. (vv. 6b–7a)

THE INCARNATION
REVEALS GOD'S SOVEREIGNTY

The first thing we want to note about the incarnation is that it reveals the sovereignty of God like nothing else. Every text that deals with the incarnation is saturated with sovereignty, down to the smallest details of those texts.

The genealogy of Jesus in Matthew 1:1–17 is a good example. We tend to skip the Bible's genealogies. But God never talks just to be talking. He has a reason for everything He included in His Word. The genealogies of Jesus are vital to establish the legitimacy of His claim to be the King of the Jews and the Son of God. He had to show that He was in the line of David. Jesus had to show His "roots."

But Matthew's genealogy is also a remarkable testimony of God's sovereignty in the incarnation. Every name in these verses tells a story. In order to pull off this genealogy, God had to work all kinds of miracles throughout the Old Testament to get Christ to Bethlehem in "the fulness of the time" (Galatians 4:4). God had to work around personalities, work around sin, and match this person up with that person to accomplish His sovereign will.

Sovereignty and Omnipotence

We'll look at some of these names below, but consider this as just one example of God's sovereign work in the incarnation. He had to get Joseph and Mary to Bethlehem, David's city. So how did He do it? Simple: He used the Roman Internal Revenue Service! God prompted a Roman ruler to call for a taxation and census that forced everyone back to their home city to be counted. So Joseph and Mary arrived in Bethlehem in God's perfect time.

That's sovereignty, God controlling the affairs of nations. And it's crucial that the records of Jesus' birth were given to Matthew and Luke to record, because when the temple in Jerusalem was destroyed by the Roman general Titus in A.D. 70, all the genealogical records of the Jews were destroyed. The temple was the records building of the day, and all the records were lost. That's why no Jew can trace his genealogy back to Bible times today. But Jesus can.

God gave Matthew the record that proves Jesus is tied by royalty to David. He gave Luke the record that establishes Jesus' tie to David by means of family relationships. The genealogy in Matthew shows Jesus' connection to David through King Solomon, which means He has a legitimate right to the throne, although Luke 3:23 makes clear that Joseph was not in actuality Jesus' biological father. Luke's genealogy says that Jesus is related to David through his other son, Nathan, and through Mary. So Jesus is tied to David by family relationship.

The beauty of the incarnation includes this: the God-man who is also the King-man. How did God get these two sides together? By a little sovereign "matchmaking." By making sure Joseph met and fell in love with Mary.

Sovereignty and Grace

Now let's walk through Matthew's genealogy a bit and see how God displays His sovereignty and grace all the way along. As we walk down the hall and see the "portraits" of these people, we see some messed-up folks. Even David was an adulterer and murderer. Solomon loved about nine hundred ninety-nine too many women. Rahab was a prostitute and a Gentile woman, a double problem because inheritance was always reckoned through the man in the Jewish world—and of course, no Gentile would have counted anyway. Manasseh had a fifty-five-year losing streak as a king.

Ruth was also a Gentile woman. She and Boaz had a son, who became the father of Jesse, the father of David. Tradition places Ham as the father of the Africans, so Africans are represented in the genealogy. All these people show up in Matthew 1 because in God's sovereign grace, He chose to use them.

THE INCARNATION
REVEALS GOD'S HOLINESS

Not only does the incarnation of Christ reveal God's sovereignty and grace, it reveals His holiness. Notice Matthew 1:18–19:

> Now the birth of Jesus Christ was as follows. When His mother Mary had been betrothed to Joseph, before they came together she was found to be with child by the Holy Spirit. And Joseph her husband, being a righteous man, and not wanting to disgrace her, desired to put her away secretly.

Just because God used some people who were unholy at times to bring His Son into the world, don't ever think He was not concerned about His holiness in the incarnation. God was very concerned about it. Because He was a holy God getting ready to manifest in history His holy Son, He wanted to work through holy people. Joseph and Mary were godly young people. And the other key couple in the incarnation story, Zacharias and Elizabeth, were righteous people, as we'll see in Luke 1.

Nothing was unholy about the incarnation. Matthew says that Joseph protected Mary's virginity. Joseph and Mary had no sexual contact during their engagement. Virgins can't get pregnant, except supernaturally. Even when Joseph found out Mary was pregnant, as a "righteous man" he was going to divorce her quietly and spare her public disgrace. Joseph was committed to a moral code which would not allow him to compromise, because God is holy. Happily, Mary lived by the same code.

THE INCARNATION
REVEALS GOD'S POWER

The virgin birth of Jesus, His incarnation, also reveals the incredible power of God. For this I want to leave Matthew's account for a while and turn to Luke 1, where we meet Zacharias and Elizabeth, relatives of Mary and Joseph. They were "righteous in the sight of God," but were childless after many years of trying to conceive (vv. 6–7).

The Visitation to Zacharias

Zacharias was a priest, one of twenty thousand priests in Israel in that day who served in the temple in "divisions" or rotations of twenty-four at a time (see v. 8). Only one of those priests got to be the high priest each year and to go into the temple to burn the incense offering. With that many priests, you can imagine the chances of being selected. If a priest got to do it once in a lifetime, he was fortunate. But in God's plan, Zacharias was chosen to burn incense that year.

While he was in the temple, "an angel of the Lord appeared to him" (v. 11). Zacharias was scared, for two good reasons. First, an angel appeared out of nowhere. But he was also afraid because he was offering a sacrifice in the Holy of Holies. An angel would appear there for only one reason. Zacharias figured he had done something wrong in the sacrifice, and he was getting ready to check out. He was scared to death.

But the angel says to him, "Do not be afraid, Zacharias, for your petition has been heard, and your wife Elizabeth will bear you a son, and you will give him the name John" (v. 13).

Zacharias thought, *You have got to be kidding!* He and Elizabeth were old. They had been married a long time. They had been praying for a child for many years. They probably had even stopped praying by that point. But an angel appears and says, "It's answered prayer time."

The problem was that although they had been praying for a child, it was not yet time in the program of God. Zacharias and Elizabeth were to be part of the incarnation drama. God didn't just want to give them a child. He wanted to give them the forerunner of Jesus, John the Baptist. So He couldn't answer their prayer when they were twenty or thirty because it wasn't time for Jesus to be born.

The Conception of John

We all know from the Christmas story that Zacharias doubted the angel's message (v. 18). I love the angel's answer. "I am Gabriel, who stands in the presence of God" (v. 19). In other words, Zacharias could believe Gabriel because he was standing there, and because of who had sent him.

God doesn't take kindly to people questioning His Word, so Zacharias was struck speechless for the nine months Elizabeth would carry John. The priest's silence would also be proof that Gabriel was telling the truth. In effect, Zacharias said to God, "Your saying it is not enough."

So God said, "Then let Me give you proof. You will know I said it because *you* won't be able to say it for the next nine months. That will be your sign." Shortly thereafter Elizabeth became pregnant, five months ahead of the angel's announcement to Mary. The forerunner of Jesus is growing in Elizabeth's womb. Now we are talking about the power of God!

The Visitation to Mary

But as miraculous as the conception of John the Baptist was, it was not an incarnation. John had a human father. The ultimate display of God's power was the incarnation of Jesus in the womb of the virgin Mary.

Mary is introduced in Luke 1:26–27:

> Now in the sixth month the angel Gabriel was sent from God to a city in Galilee, called Nazareth, to a virgin engaged to a man whose name was Joseph, of the descendants of David; and the virgin's name was Mary. And coming in, he said to her, "Hail, favored one! The Lord is with you."

Now this is not Mary worship. God has never called anyone, anytime, anywhere, under any circumstance, to pray to Mary. The Bible makes clear: "There is no other name under heaven that has been given among men, by which we must be saved" except the name of Jesus (Acts 4:12).

Gabriel's announcement to Mary is the announcement of the incarnation of God:

> You will conceive in your womb, and bear a son, and you shall name Him Jesus. He will be great, and will be called the Son of the Most High; and the Lord God will give Him the throne of His father David. (vv. 31–32)

The Conception of Jesus

Look at the terms used of Jesus in those verses. And just to make sure no one missed the message, Gabriel said in response to Mary's question:

> The Holy Spirit will come upon you, and the power of the Most High will overshadow you; and for that reason the holy off-spring shall be called the Son of God. (v. 35)

God was to be the Father of this Child. Why? Because Jesus had to be perfect or He couldn't be our sacrifice for sin. So He couldn't have Joseph as His biological father. But being perfect was not enough. He must also be a true man because He was coming to die for men. Jesus was not a ghost appearing in the guise of humanity. Neither was He half-God, half-man. Someone is always around to deny either Jesus' true deity or true humanity. But any such teaching is heresy.

The God-Man

So what do we have in the incarnation of Jesus? We have the God-man. He was fully God and fully man, without confusion or dilution of either His deity or humanity. Jesus is unique.

Because He was born of woman and was fully human, Jesus could get hungry. But because He was born of the Holy Spirit and was fully God, He could feed five thousand people miraculously. He got thirsty, but He also walked on water! As a man, He got sleepy. But He could get up from the greatest sleep of all, death, because He's God. He is the God-man.

Mary's Visit to Elizabeth

Gabriel had another startling piece of news for Mary, who reacted to it immediately:

> "And behold, even your relative Elizabeth has also conceived a son in her old age; and she who was called barren is now in her sixth month." . . . Now at this time Mary arose and went with haste to the hill country, to a city of Judah. (vv. 36, 39)

Mary took off to find out what was happening because if Elizabeth was pregnant, miracles were operating. I love what happened when Mary arrived and greeted Elizabeth. John leaped for joy in his mother's womb (v. 41).

I could stop here and do a chapter on abortion, because the incarnation of Jesus and the events surrounding it teach us a very vital and practical lesson. Here we have an unborn child, six months old in the womb, a viable candidate for abortion in just about any city in America. Is John a living, aware person at this point? This is not "pregnancy tissue" leaping in Elizabeth's womb. If the God who put John in his mother's womb is the same God who puts babies in the womb today, then no mother has any more right to kill her baby than Elizabeth would have had.

Elizabeth was filled with the Holy Spirit when she felt her baby leap, and she said to Mary, "Blessed among women are you, and blessed is the fruit of your womb!" (v. 42). How did Elizabeth know Mary was pregnant? The Holy Spirit revealed it to her.

This was no doubt a confirmation to Mary that she herself was pregnant, because she probably wasn't feeling anything yet. Elizabeth verified it further by saying:

> And how has it happened to me, that the mother of my Lord should come to me? For behold, when the sound of your greeting reached my ears, the baby leaped in my womb for joy. (vv. 43–44)

John the Baptist reacted to the ministry of the Holy Spirit and the presence of Jesus in the room. The incarnation of Jesus so reveals the power of God that an unborn baby stirs with excitement. And God's power is evident as the Holy Spirit brings these two women together, validating these miraculous births.

THE INCARNATION
REVEALS THE VERACITY OF GOD

The veracity of God is His truthfulness. He cannot lie. At every turn, the incarnation of Jesus reveals God's truthfulness as He sends His eternal Son to be encased in human flesh. Matthew 1:22–23 affirms:

> All this took place that what was spoken by the Lord through the prophet might be fulfilled, saying, "Behold, the virgin shall be with child, and shall bear a Son, and they shall call His name Immanuel," which translated means, "God with us."

In Matthew 2:5–6, the Jewish religious leaders told Herod that Jesus would be born in Bethlehem because God said so through His prophet, and they knew His Word could be trusted. Later in the chapter, we're told that the family went to Egypt to fulfill what God said through another prophet (v. 15). Even Herod's "slaughter of the innocents" was done in fulfillment of God's Word (v. 18).

The key word is *fulfilled*. How do we know Christianity is true and every other religion that contradicts it is wrong? How can I respond to a person who says, "Evans, who do you think you are to say the Bible is true? How can you say Christianity is true and everyone else is wrong?"

One reason I know this is that prophecy verifies God's truthfulness. These predictions were written hundreds of years before the events occurred. Could that be luck? You cannot have that kind of specificity hundreds and hundreds of years in advance unless you have a truthful God calling the shots.

Anyone who has been to a secular university knows how unbelieving professors explain these prophecies. They start with the assumption that miracles and predictive prophecy are impossible. They are left with only one possible conclusion: that these accounts were written many years after the events occurred. They only appear to be prophetic.

This is really not an explanation. It's an attempt to get rid of God because if prophecy about past events proved true, it would only be logical to conclude that God is telling the truth about the future. That idea is unacceptable to the secular mind.

JESUS IS CALLED THE SON OF GOD AND THE SON OF MAN BECAUSE IN HIS INCARNATION, HE HAS THE ESSENCE OF BOTH.

But consider just the prophecy of Micah 5:2 that Jesus would be born in Bethlehem. It was such a small town, such a specific location. If God were just sort of guessing and wanted to cover His bases in case He missed by a few miles, He could have said the Messiah would be born somewhere in the Roman Empire, or even somewhere in Palestine.

Bethlehem was small in the first century, a tiny country hamlet, a one-stoplight town. It is still small today. So why did God want Jesus born in Bethlehem? It was the city of David, to be sure, and as we've seen it was important to show Jesus' lineage to David.

But I also think God wanted the smallest possible place so there would be no doubt about His truthfulness when the prophecy was fulfilled. God's Word is true. Sign after sign validates it. Pinpointing Bethlehem was like finding a "needle in a haystack." But open up Matthew, and you find that Jesus was born in Bethlehem. Every detail of His incarnation underscores the truthfulness of God.

SON OF GOD, SON OF MAN

Jesus is called the Son of God and the Son of Man because in His incarnation, He has the essence of both. Some groups who come knocking on your door will tell you that Jesus Christ is less than God. Don't believe it. He is fully God, co-equal with the Father. The title "Son of Man" does not involve any denial of deity.

If I call myself a son of man, I am saying that I bear the essence of *Homo sapiens.* All that makes up the human species makes me who I am. I bear all the traits of humanity. Therefore, I am a child of man or a son of man. When the Bible calls Jesus the Son of Man, it means that He bears the true essence of humanity, apart from sin.

When the Bible declares that Jesus is the Son of God, it does not mean He's less than God. On the contrary, all the characteristics that make God who He is are present in Jesus. He is God too. In Jesus, we have the perfect wedding of deity and humanity, co-existing in one Person without being mixed. Theologians call this the "hypostatic union" of Christ: the nature of man and the nature of God located in one Person.

As I said above, that's why Jesus displayed all the traits of humanity—hunger, thirst, fatigue—while at the same time performing miracles to feed people, walking on water, and offering rest to the fatigued. Let me also emphasize again that Jesus is not half-God and half-man. He is the God-man: fully God, fully man, in one Person.

THE GLORY OF THE INCARNATION

We see the glory of the incarnation in that all of God was in Christ and all of man was in Jesus. That's why He is called Jesus Christ. The name *Jesus* recognizes His humanity. *Christ* is the name, or actually the title, that recognizes His appointment for salvation.

Glorious Lord

Because He is Jesus and the Christ, He is also the Lord, the "Mighty God." He is one of a kind. John 1:1 explains how it works: "In the beginning was the Word, and the Word was with God, and the Word was God." A word expresses a thought. Jesus was and is the perfect expression of God, distinct from the Father while at the same time equal with Him.

And by this Word "all things came into being" (v. 3). Jesus was a full participant in creation as a co-equal member of the Trinity. In verse 14 John gives us the glorious reality of the incarnation: "And the Word became flesh, and dwelt among us, and we beheld His glory."

God in Flesh

John says he and others *saw* the incarnate Christ. This is important because verse 18 tells us, "No man has seen God at any time; the only begotten God, who is in the bosom of the Father, He has explained Him." God became man so that men could understand Him. God "condensed" His deity into a form that we could make sense of.

Jesus Christ, God in the flesh, came to earth so that men and women could understand this glorious Being called God. This is the glory of the incarnation, that God became like us so that we could understand, know, and love Him. Without the incarnation, we would never have a revelation of God in terms we could grasp.

What a staggering thought: God becomes a man so that men can understand and know Him. But let me give you another one: God the Father has never experienced humanity. He does not know, for example, what it's like to be tired. So when you get on your knees and say, "Father, I'm tired," God the Father cannot interpret that experientially because He's never experienced it.

If you say, "Father, I'm lonely," He doesn't know what you are talking about experientially because He's never been lonely. He is self-sufficient. God the Father has never been poor, so when you say, "Father, I'm poor and needy," He can't relate to you experientially because He's never been poor.

But when Jesus became a man, He got tired, felt loneliness, and knew what it was to be poor. So when you get on your knees and pray, Jesus interprets your prayer to the Father because Jesus has been there. That's why we can go to the Father in the name of Jesus the Son. Jesus says, "Father, I know exactly what he's talking about. I know how she feels. I was lonely, I was rejected and despised. Let me tell you what that felt like."

That explains why Jesus is so precious. He makes sense of us to God, and He makes sense of God to us. That's why the only Mediator between God and man is "the man, Christ Jesus" (1 Timothy 2:5). He holds the unique position of being fully God and fully man; fully understanding both and fully experiencing both; knitting both together.

The Slave-Man

How this happened is very interesting. Philippians 2 is a magnificent declaration of the incarnation:

> Have this attitude in yourselves which was also in Christ Jesus, who, although He existed in the form of God, did not regard equality with God a thing to be grasped, but emptied Himself, taking the form of a bond-servant, and being made in the likeness of men. (vv. 5–7)

So much is in these verses that it's hard to know where to begin. Notice how Jesus' pre-existence is clearly taught. Also, His emptying does not mean He ceased being God. All He did was pour His deity into a container called humanity.

WORSHIP THAT DOES NOT INCONVENIENCE YOU IS NOT WORSHIP AT ALL. WHEN WORSHIP IS SERIOUS, YOU ARE WILLING TO PAY THE PRICE.

I especially want you to notice the word *bond-servant.* The Greek word here, *doulos,* is important because Paul is not saying that Jesus just became a man like every other man. There's a broader word Paul could have used if he had meant "mankind in general."

Instead, Jesus became a "slave-man," the lowest rank you could hold in the Roman empire. It was the bottom of the social ladder. This may be the greatest mystery of the incarnation. For the eternal God of glory, the Lord of creation, to assume human flesh would have been humiliation enough. But Jesus Christ laid aside the glory of heaven to become like a slave.

He was born in a stable to very poor parents. He lived in the utter obscurity of Galilee. Why did Jesus take such a low position in His incarnation? To let us know that no one stands outside of His grace; everyone is significant in God's sight. Jesus Christ identified with those on the bottom rung of the ladder, which means everyone has hope by virtue of Christmas morning.

Further, Paul says, as a man Jesus "humbled Himself by becoming obedient to the point of death, even death on a cross" (v. 8). He was born a slave-man, and He died as a criminal. If Jesus Christ was not the God-man, if He was not the Son of Man and the Son of God, He could not be your Savior or mine. He had to be fully God because only God can save. But he had to be fully man because only man can die. God gave us a God-man, a Savior, Jesus Christ. What an awesome plan!

Colossians 1:15 says that Jesus "is the image of the invisible God." He's a "chip off the old block." When you see Jesus, you see God.

LESSONS FROM THE INCARNATION

What do we do with this incarnation? What do we do with this God-man? Turn back to Matthew 2:1–2:

> Now after Jesus was born in Bethlehem of Judea in the days of Herod the king, behold, magi from the east arrived in Jerusalem, saying, "Where is He who has been born King of the Jews? For we saw His star in the east, and have come to worship Him."

The magi, or wise men as we usually call them, were professional astronomers. They studied the heavens. They were also looking for something, because they apparently knew that Numbers 24:17 prophesied, "A star shall come forth from Jacob." All of a sudden one night, they looked up and saw the Shekinah glory; that is, the visible manifestation of God in a brilliant light that reminded them of a star.

Worship

These wise men got so excited and wanted to worship the true God so badly that they traveled between one and one-and-a-half years to get to Jesus. If you haven't inconvenienced yourself to worship Jesus, you haven't worshiped yet. Worship that does not inconvenience you is not worship at all. When worship is serious, you are willing to pay the price. When it comes to worshiping Him, we say, "It's inconvenient, it's too far, I'm too tired."

Then we wonder why God doesn't like our worship. The wise men said, "We will pay the price tag to get there," because they took worshiping Him seriously. It wasn't a leftover attitude. It was a priority. Many of us don't appreciate the high cost of worship. You cannot come before a king without paying a price.

The religious crowd in Jerusalem wasn't interested in worshiping God. Jesus was born down the street; He had been living there for almost two years, and they hadn't even made the trek down the road to see Him. They only turned to the Scripture because the government called for it. You can't fool God about worship either. Herod tried, and God and the wise men made a fool of him.

Matthew 2:10–11 says that when the wise men saw the star, they rejoiced because it led them to the house where Jesus was. They came into the house, and when they saw Jesus they fell down and worshiped Him and presented their gifts. They understood who they were dealing with. They understood that Jesus Christ deserved to be worshiped.

Chapter 19 is dedicated to worship, but I wanted to set the stage a little bit here because we definitely should worship in response to the incarnation.

God's Will

The incarnation also teaches us something very important about God's will or guidance. With the incarnation we say, "God, if you can so arrange history and lead people to orchestrate the birth of Your Son, I can trust You fully to lead me wherever You want me to go."

God only led the wise men to Jerusalem. But they followed what leading they had, and went as far as He led them. They didn't know where to go from there, so they asked Herod, "King, do you know where He is?"

The king didn't know where Jesus was, but the preachers knew because they knew the Old Testament. So God used an ungodly king and ungodly preachers to lead the wise men to the next step. When they took the next step to go to Bethlehem, the star reappeared.

If you follow what you know of God's guidance, He will show you what you don't know until you get where you are supposed to go. Many people want to know, "How come God won't lead me?" Because God will never lead you into specifics if He can't trust you in the general. It took a lot of faith for the wise men to leave the east and head west based on a star. But you see, "He who comes to God must believe that He is, and that He is a rewarder of those who seek Him" (Hebrews 11:6).

You must be willing to follow what God says, and if you don't follow the general, He won't lead you to the specific. Many people say, "I want God to lead me." Well, are you doing what He's already told you to do?

God's Sufficiency

The wise men's gifts also teach us something of the sufficiency of God. Gold was money, of course. Frankincense was an expensive spice. Myrrh was an expensive embalming fluid. But why an embalming fluid? For the same reason that the baby Jesus was wrapped in strips of cloth, which were actually death wraps. He was born to die.

In Jesus' day, the poor weren't able to afford what we would call today fancy diapers. They used "swaddling clothes," a wrap that was used for mummies. And myrrh was used for burial, except that poor people didn't get myrrh. Poor people just got buried. The wise men gave Jesus very expensive gifts because He was a very important person.

But there's another reason. Look at Matthew 2:13:

> Now when they had departed, behold, an angel of the Lord appeared to Joseph in a dream, saying, "Arise and take the Child and His mother, and flee to Egypt, and remain there until I tell you; for Herod is going to search for the Child to destroy Him."

Joseph and Mary were "dirt poor." They didn't have any money to go to Egypt or to live there until Herod died. That is, they didn't until the wise men came with their gifts. God met their needs in an unusual way. He became their sufficiency. God also protected Joseph and Mary by sending the wise men home a different way, so Herod never found out where Jesus was.

God's Judgment

One other thing happened at the incarnation: judgment. Look at verses 16–18:

> When Herod saw that he had been tricked by the magi, he became very enraged, and sent and slew all the male children who were in Bethlehem and in all its environs, from two years old and under, according to the time which he had ascertained from the magi. Then that which was spoken through Jeremiah the prophet was fulfilled, saying, "A voice was heard in Ramah, weeping and great mourning, Rachel weeping for her children; and she refused to be comforted, because they were no more."

This is a quote from Jeremiah 31:15. Rachel was considered the mother of Israel—and interestingly enough, she was buried near Bethlehem. Rachel cried out one day, "Give me children lest I die," because she was barren and wanted children. So God gave her children.

Why then was Rachel pictured as weeping for her children? Because she took so long to have children, and now they were dying because in Jeremiah's day, the Babylonians either killed the children or took them captive to Babylon. In other words, Israel's children were undergoing the judgment because the nation had rejected God.

Matthew says that this was fulfilled in Jesus' day. Why did those babies die? Because the nation was rejecting God. Israel was ignoring the incarnate Christ. And whenever you ignore Jesus Christ, you pay a price, not because God is mean or vengeful, but because when you reject Christ, you remove the protection.

The Bible says, "If we go on sinning willfully after receiving the knowledge of the truth, there no longer remains a sacrifice for sins" (Hebrews 10:26). Protection ceases to be available. Jesus Christ protects you as you carry out His will so that nothing can happen to you outside of His plan. Judgment ensued because the incarnate Son of God was rejected.

We need to understand that the incarnation is far more than a baby in a manger. It is "God with us." God became a man, died for us, and rose again to live and reign forever. He demands our allegiance. The incarnation is serious business!

Responding to the Incarnation of God

When God became a man in the Person of Jesus Christ, all the rules for understanding and relating to God changed. The incarnation is not only a watershed event of history, it is at the heart of our salvation and day-to-day walk with God. Let me take the four lessons I outlined above and help you put "handles" on them:

1. How costly is your worship? What price are you willing to pay to worship God: the time involved, the mental and spiritual discipline of prayer, study, and meditation, the determination to give God your best? Test your "Worship Quotient" (WQ) today, and renew your commitment to make worship a top priority.

2. Any sincere Christian would say, "Yes, I want God to guide me every step of the way." That's fine, but let me repeat the question I asked above: Are you doing what God has already told you to do? Try this simple experiment to help focus your thinking.

On a piece of paper, write down the area where you need God's guidance the most right now. State it as the goal you have in mind: "I need a job." "I need God's wisdom on whether to move my family across the country or stay where we are." Now ask yourself: What has God shown me so far about this matter? Have I acted on what He has revealed? Am I really ready to take the next step if He were to show it to me today?

3. Don't expect any "wise men" to show up at your door with gifts to meet your needs. But the God who supplied in that day remains the same today. It's hard to talk about God's sufficiency without sounding like a televangelist, promising a blank check from God. God does not write blank checks for you to fill in with your own agenda, but God is sufficient! Let me suggest another side of this issue for you to think about: Often, God's provision doesn't arrive until the need arrives. If you're not seeing God's sufficient supply in some area, consider the possibility that you may be running ahead of Him a bit.

4. We'd rather put off dealing with the idea of God's judgment. But the incarnation of Jesus Christ has drawn the line in the sand. I want to urge you again: Don't reject the virgin-born, crucified, and risen Son of God. Make sure you know Jesus as your Savior. The back of this book even has an address that you can write to for help.

PART THREE
THE KNOWLEDGE
OF GOD

17
THE RESPONSE TO GOD

A s we begin the third and final section of this book, I feel a little bit like Job's "friend" Zophar, who asked Job, "Can you discover the depths of God? Can you discover the limits of the Almighty? They are high as the heavens, what can you do?" (Job 11:7–8a).

Zophar was thinking about who God is, much as I have tried to do in the preceding chapters. But he realized his subject was so big he couldn't handle it: "Its measure is longer than the earth, and broader than the sea" (v. 9). Even though I have addressed the major characteristics of God's nature, what I have said in these few pages wouldn't fill a thimble compared to who our awesome God really is.

We have become sophisticated today. We use all the theological phrases and the technical data, but the bottom line is that we have a big God! And when we come to that conclusion, we have to respond. If God is God, how can we ignore Him? How can we skip over Someone like this?

We can't. That's why I want to take these last four chapters to deal with the critical issue of what to do with what we know about God. This study was never intended to be merely an intellectual exercise. The knowledge of who God is should cause those of us related to Him to respond to Him.

If you hang around radioactive material, it's going to do something to you. If you hang around God, it ought to do something to you. One commentator said, "The study of God is so vast we get lost in its immensity and so deep our arrogance is obliterated in its infinity."

We're often like the writer of Psalm 73. He looked around and saw the wicked getting away with their wickedness. He saw the righteous getting hammered. It drove him to deep despair until he went into the sanctuary and got a new vision of God. Then he looked at himself in the mirror and said, "I was senseless and ignorant; I was like a beast before Thee" (v. 22). Most of our problems can be traced to our perspective on God. I want to go over five ways we should respond to God.

A GREATER DESIRE TO KNOW HIM

What we have learned about God should create in us a greater desire to know Him. In other words, knowing Him a little should make us want to know Him a lot. If you and I are satisfied with what we already know about God, we are of all people most miserable. We have hardly begun to explore what it's like to know God.

In fact, as I said earlier, the essence of heaven is the uninterrupted knowledge of God. What will make heaven so wonderful is that there will always be something new to know about God. And we have so much to learn, and this knowledge will come at such supersonic speed, that we will not have time to sleep.

To begin I want to go back to the Scripture we started with, Jeremiah 9:23–24:

> Thus says the Lord, "Let not a wise man boast of his wisdom, and let not the mighty man boast of his might, let not a rich man boast of his riches; but let him who boasts boast of this, that he understands and knows Me, that I am the Lord who exercises lovingkindness, justice, and righteousness on earth; for I delight in these things," declares the Lord.

God says, "If you can't brag that you know Me, don't talk about your education, your money, or your power. If you can't talk about Me, it's better to keep quiet. I created you to know Me, and when all is said and done, that will be the only thing worth bragging about."

When the doctor tells you that it will soon be over, your bank account won't help you. Who you are or who you know won't help you then. Where you went to school will be irrelevant. The only issue on the floor will be your knowledge of God. God wants to rule our lives by relationship. He wants the driving motivation of our lives to be a deep desire to know Him, not just, "Yeah, I'm a Christian. I'm supposed to do this."

Knowing God Brings Power

Yes, the Christian life has rules, but God wants the driving force to be that you know Him. And because you know Him, you obey Him. Because you know Him, you follow Him. Because you know Him, you submit to Him. Knowledge can be a very powerful thing. In fact, the Bible says that "people perish because of the lack of knowledge" if you hold back information that would benefit them.

If you've ever been to the circus, you may have noticed something very curious. Go outside where the elephants are kept, and you'll see each of them standing with one foot chained to a tiny stake hammered in the ground. These huge, powerful animals, weighing several tons, are controlled by a stick in the ground. All they have to do is decide they don't want to stand there any longer, and that stick will be ripped out.

But those elephants don't even try to pull their pegs out of the ground because when they were babies, they were lied to. The trainer taught them to believe that as long as a chain on their leg was attached to a stake, they were utterly helpless to get loose. The trainer drums this into the elephant's mind all day long by hitting his leg when he tries to move it, and thus enslaving the elephant to wrong information.

That circus elephant will die never knowing he could have been free, never knowing he had the power to move the stake. Many of us never understand that if we know God, no little stake can hold us down. We have the power to pull it out. That person who's holding you back, that little circumstance that's controlling you, can't tie you down when you know God.

In fact, the Bible says that the knowledge of God holds a wealth of benefits for us. Daniel 11:32 puts it this way: "The people that do know their God shall be strong, and do exploits" (KJV). When was the last time you did an exploit, something no one can explain? The knowledge of God can do it!

Knowing God Brings Peace

"Grace and peace be multiplied to you in the knowledge of God" wrote the apostle Peter (2 Peter 1:2). The more you know God, the more at peace you should be. Yes, negative circumstances do come, and they can throw you off kilter. I mean that if you are not at peace, if you do not experience a growing sense of inner peace, it's because your knowledge of God is not increasing.

WHEN YOU LACK THE ASSURANCE AND CONFIDENCE THAT COMES FROM KNOWING HIM AND WHO YOU ARE IN HIM, YOU CAN BECOME A SLAVE TO WHAT PEOPLE THINK, TO CIRCUMSTANCES, TO YOUR EMOTIONS, TO OTHER PEOPLE'S RULES AND EXPECTATIONS— TO ALMOST ANYTHING.

When you know God, He can make you sleep in troubled waters. When you know God and you have no money, you know it's not the last word. When you know God and your enemies move against you, you understand that they will not make the final decision. When you know God and people reject you, you can say, "No, never alone." The knowledge of God comforts the heart, because He dictates the final circumstances.

Knowing God Brings Wisdom

Knowing God also gives us wisdom. Paul prayed for the Ephesians "that the God of our Lord Jesus Christ, the Father of glory, may give to you a spirit of wisdom and of revelation in the knowledge of Him" (1:17).

The better you know God, the better the decisions you will make. The book of Proverbs is all about making the right choices because we know the God who is the source of wisdom. Our ability to make the right decisions has to do with our knowledge of God, and if our knowledge of God is lacking, our choices won't be right.

Knowing God Brings Growth

The knowledge of God brings growth and productivity to our spiritual lives. Here's Paul at prayer again, this time for the Colossians:

> For this reason also, since the day we heard of it, we have not ceased to pray for you and to ask that you may be filled with the knowledge of His will in all spiritual wisdom and understanding, so that you may walk in a manner worthy of the Lord, to please Him in all respects, bearing fruit in every good work and increasing in the knowledge of God. (1:9–10)

Apple trees bear apples. Oranges trees bear oranges. The more you know God, the more you will produce the fruit of His Spirit. And when you are producing sweet spiritual fruit, other people will get hungry for what you have and get the benefit of it. Fruit isn't designed to feed on itself.

When you know God, other people want to be like you because they see that what you have is tasty and well worth having. When was the last time someone looked at your walk with God and decided that you were the kind of person worth following? That's what the knowledge of God can do.

Knowing God Brings Freedom

The knowledge of God does something else, the Bible says. In Galatians 4:8, Paul makes a very interesting statement: "When you did not know God, you were slaves to those which by nature are no gods."

The lack of the knowledge of God brings slavery. When you lack the assurance and confidence that comes from knowing Him and who you are in Him, you can become a slave to what people think, to circumstances, to your emotions, to other people's rules and expectations—to almost anything.

Don't miss this, because many unhappy Christians walk around moaning, "Yeah, I'm a Christian, which means I can't do this and I can't do that and I can't go here and I can't go there. Christianity is a boring life." Anyone who thinks that has been sold a faulty, enslaving definition of God. An unhappy Christian is an uninformed Christian.

But knowing God brings freedom. All those other things that look like freedom are really shackles. Check out what Paul calls them in the next verse: "weak and worthless elemental things" (v. 9). We've got to have a right view of God to understand that the heart of being free is living as God wants us to live. If we are going to respond properly to God, we must get to know Him better.

A GREATER MOTIVATION TO WORSHIP HIM

The knowledge of God's character should give us all the motivation we need to worship Him. You've probably noticed by now how often worship keeps coming up in these pages. And I've reserved chapter 19 to explore the nature of worship.

It's no accident that we keep returning to this subject. Worship is always in order as we respond to God. The key to worship, of course, is the inner reality, not the outer rituals. Malachi 1 helps us see this crucial distinction. The Israelites of Malachi's day had the ritual, but no reality.

They were showing up for worship basically because it was time to go to the service. Their bodies were present, but they weren't worshiping God. So He asked them a penetrating question:

> "A son honors his father, and a servant his master. Then if I am a father, where is My honor? And if I am a master, where is My respect?" says the Lord of hosts to you, O priests who despise My name. But you say, "How have we despised Thy name?" (Malachi 1:6)

They didn't even know what God was talking about. They were saying, in effect, "What's the problem? We're here, aren't we?" They thought all was well.

Leftover Worship

But God says, "You are presenting defiled food upon My altar. . . . When you present the blind for sacrifice, is it not evil? And when you present the lame and sick, is it not evil? Why not offer it to your governor?" (vv. 7–8).

Here's the test of worship. Does God get less than you give to people? Some Christians worship God with lame excuses. Some of His people show up at church on Sunday with sick attitudes. We wouldn't treat our bosses this way—or at least we'd hide it at work. We would fake it, we would cover up. Why? Because we don't want our supervisor writing us up for a bad attitude. Well, God is writing us up for having bad worship. He says, "Try giving your leftovers to the governor."

Some of us are nonchalant about worship. We don't come to God's house with energy. We don't expend any effort of heart or mind to engage Him in prayer and praise.

Come to Dallas on some late fall or winter Sunday afternoon, and you'll see a real worship service! Tens of thousands of eager "worshipers" will come hours early, walk for miles, open their wallets until it hurts, scream and wave their hands, and bow at the altar of "Cowboyism."

If you don't think this is a worship thing, you should walk the streets of Dallas at Super Bowl time. Everyone is talking about "Da Boys." They are talking Super Bowl. People can't wait to share what they know about their team.

Well, I'm here to tell you Someone is greater than "Da Boys." God says, "They don't have anything on Me." I submit that if sports fans can do all of this, you ought not be ashamed to be called a Christian, to give God your best. If God isn't worth worshiping above anyone or anything else, only one thing is left to do. God says in verse 10, "Oh that there were one among you who would shut the gates."

That is, lock up the church! Imagine God looking at His people's worship and saying, "I wish someone would just go ahead and cancel the service, because I'm not listening. You give Me your leftover energy, your leftover time, your spare change. You don't take me seriously. You give Me less than you give your boss on Monday."

When it comes to church, it doesn't matter what time we arrive. But when it comes to work, we get there early. Give your boss your leftover effort and see what he says. Make that your habit at work, and see how it goes at your next annual review.

Tiresome Worship

God was saying to the people of Malachi's day, "You obviously don't know Me." Then He says in verses 11–12: "For from the rising of the sun, even to its setting, My name will be great. . . . But you are profaning it, in that you say, 'The table of the Lord is defiled.'"

How were the people profaning God's name? They said, "My, how tiresome [worship] is!" (v. 13). They looked at their watches and said, "Time to go home. Kickoff is at 12:00 sharp. Hurry up and finish the message. Don't sing another song. This is so tiresome. Same old thing, week after week!"

Maybe if those same people went to bed earlier on Saturday night, they wouldn't be so tired. Maybe they wouldn't give God their leftover energy. Maybe His worship wouldn't seem so tiresome.

Accursed Worship

It gets worse. God has another complaint in verse 13: "You disdainfully sniff at it . . . and you bring what was taken by robbery, and what is lame or sick; so you bring the offering! Should I receive that from your hand?" On the contrary. "Cursed be your flawed worship!" (see v. 14).

Ignorant Worship

When the people complained that God's table was "defiled," they were talking about the bloody mess of offering sacrifices when the lamb's throat was slit and its blood was drained. The priests got their hands all messy and bloody—and to borrow a modern-day expression, they were saying, "Yuck." But what they didn't know was what that bloody sacrifice was doing for them!

I DON'T CARE HOW MESSY IT GETS, YOU NEED TO WORSHIP GOD AND INTRODUCE PEOPLE TO JESUS CHRIST, FOR HE GAVE HIS LIFE FOR US.

These Israelites were like the girl who was ashamed of her mother because the whole side of her mother's face was contorted. She never wanted to introduce anyone to her mother because her mother was not a pretty sight.

On one occasion, when the girl was too embarrassed to introduce her friends to her mother, the mother asked, "Honey, why won't you ever introduce me to your friends? You're ashamed of how I you look, aren't you?" The girl nodded.

Tears welled up in the mother's eyes and she said, "Honey, come here and sit down. When you were just a baby, I was outside working in the garden one day. I looked up and saw the house on fire. I ran into your bedroom and picked you up, but on my way out, one of the beams fell and hit me on the side of my face.

"As it hit me and was about to knock me down, I was able to throw you through the door so you wouldn't get caught in the fire. I thought you might want to know that the reason my face is scarred is because I was saving your life."

We are here because Jesus Christ threw us to safety. His blood has cleansed us from our sins. Because of "the table of the Lord," you and I get to go to heaven, and we've been delivered from "the wrath that is to come." I don't care how messy it gets, you need to worship God and introduce people to Jesus Christ, for He gave His life for us.

Consuming Worship

A boy was on his way to Sunday school with the two quarters his mother gave him. She had said he could spend one quarter and put the other one in the offering at Sunday school. He was running when he tripped and fell. One quarter rolled out of his hand. He tried to get it, but it went into the sewer. He looked up and said, "Well, God, there goes Your quarter."

Why is it always God who loses out? We wouldn't like God to say, "Oops, there goes your air!" The author of Hebrews tells us:

> Therefore, since we receive a kingdom which cannot be shaken, let us show gratitude, by which we may offer to God an acceptable service with reverence and awe; for our God is a consuming fire. (12:28–29)

Since we have all of this, we ought to be lined up before the church doors open, saying to God, "I know You deserve to be number one."

A GREATER WILLINGNESS TO TRUST HIM

The knowledge of who God is should make us more willing to trust Him. In Proverbs 3:5–6, Solomon says:

> Trust in the Lord with all your heart, and do not lean on your own understanding. In all your ways acknowledge Him, and He will make your paths straight.

The Hebrew word for *trust* means "to lie down on, to stretch out on." When you go to bed at night, you lie down on your mattress. That is, you put the weight of your body on the mattress because you believe it is strong enough to hold you up.

315

Trusting God

God says, "Lie down on Me. I can hold you up. I can sustain you. But don't lean or lie down on your own understanding."

Watch out every time you say, "Well, I think." God says not to lean on your understanding because it can't hold you up. The writer contrasts this phrase with the previous phrase: "Trust in the Lord with all your heart." "Lie down on Me, not on yourself, because you can't hold yourself up. And if you don't believe it, look at how many times you've fallen flat on your face. But I can hold you up."

The phrase "your ways" covers anything having to do with your life. It's an umbrella statement. The concept of acknowledging God means to have an awareness of Him. Bring God to bear on all of your ways. God says, "Whatever you do, put it through the grid of your relationship with Me. Allow Me to be the criterion by which you judge every decision you make, everything you do. Allow Me to be the grid through which you pass every decision."

Straightening the Path

When we do this, God promises to make our paths straight. This wording is more accurate than the King James rendering, "He shall direct thy paths." God does direct our paths, without a doubt. But *straightening* has the idea of turning the path, redefining it as we go. God builds new roads ahead of us. He straightens the deadly curves, puts a bridge over the valley, and cuts a path through the mountains.

Therefore, even though life has a turn here and a turn there, those roads wind up going in a straight direction. The old axiom says, "The shortest distance between two points is a straight line." But when you are in the will of God, your life heads in a straight line no matter how the road curves. He will get you to the destination He has for you regardless of the crooks in the road of life.

A song says, "Follow Jesus, ain't no chance of getting lost." He knows the end from the beginning, the start from the finish. He knows where you are supposed to be, how you are supposed to get there, and what route you are to take. Sometimes, He even leads you backward to take you forward.

A GREATER DETERMINATION TO OBEY HIM

The knowledge of God's character should give us a greater determination to obey Him. Deuteronomy 8 is one of the great chapters of the Bible. The second generation of Israelites is going into the land. Moses says to them in verses 1–3a:

> All the commandments that I am commanding you today you shall be careful to do, that you may live and multiply, and go in and possess the land which the Lord swore to give to your forefathers. And you shall remember all the way which the Lord your God has led you in the wilderness these forty years, that He might humble you, testing you, to know what was in your heart, whether you would keep His commandments or not. And He humbled you and let you be hungry . . .

The Test of Obedience

Have you ever had trials like this in your life? "He let you be hungry. . . ." God tests obedience through trials. He tries you in order to test you. He tries me in order to test me. You see, it's not enough for God just to hear us say "Amen" in church.

When the benediction is over God is going to test us. He wants to see whether the "Amen" out of our mouths is also the "Amen" of our feet. He wants to know, when things go against us, do we believe Him enough to obey Him? Do we trust Him enough to follow Him?

The Provision of Obedience

Moses says something interesting at the end of verse 3: "Man does not live by bread alone, but man lives by everything that proceeds out of the mouth of the Lord." In other words, you don't live just by food, but by the Source of your food.

God provided manna in the wilderness to show His people where their daily bread was really coming from. In verse 4 Moses reminds them, "Your clothing did not wear out on you, nor did your foot swell these forty years." God miraculously provided when no clothing stores were around.

This is a great principle of obedience. When you obey God, He can take what little you have and make it last. Conversely, when you don't obey God, you can keep buying new stuff and it won't last. When you obey God, you can do more with less money. When you disobey God, you may get more money, but you'll do less with it.

God has the ability to keep what *little* you have from wearing out. But He also has the ability to take the *lot* that you think you have and cut holes in it so you don't even know where it went.

Whenever I think about this, I go back to my seminary days. I don't know how we made it on $350 a month. I cannot explain it other than to say that for those four years, God did not let what we had wear out. He sustained us by His grace. The trials of life are designed to prove our obedience. He says, "If I'm God and you trust Me, will you also obey Me?"

A Caution to the Obedient

Moses also tells the people that times are going to get better. But when they do, be careful:

> When you have eaten and are satisfied, you shall bless the Lord your God for the good land which He has given you. Beware lest you forget the Lord your God by not keeping His commandments and His ordinances and His statues which I am commanding you today; lest, when you have eaten and are satisfied, and have built good houses and lived in them, and when your herds and your flocks multiply, and your silver and gold multiply, and all that you have multiplies, then your heart becomes proud, and you forget the Lord your God who brought you out from the land of Egypt. (vv. 10–14)

Isn't that the danger? Think back to when you were poor. You never missed church, you had time for God, you gave thanks for the jalopy. Why? Because you knew that to get that car going anywhere, you needed the grace of God. You knew if you were going to have anything to eat, it would be by the grace of God. Hot dogs and baked beans were a blessing back then.

Oh, but now you've traded in the jalopy for a new car. Two of them, in fact, and you've got room in the garage for a third one. God has blessed you with that great job, that exciting opportunity —only now you're too tired from hobnobbing with the upper crust to have time for God. You are too uppity to be with God's people. You are too big to get your hands dirty serving Him.

God says, "Watch it. I remember where you came from. I know the road I used to get you out, and I also know the way to get you back! Be careful not to forget Me."

Why was God so concerned about what would happen to His people when they got comfortable? Look at verse 17: "Otherwise, you may say in your heart, 'My power and the strength of my hand made me this wealth.'" That would never happen to us today, would it? Just might! So God says, "In the midst of your trials, obey Me. And then when I bless you, don't forget Me."

A GREATER PASSION FOR HIM

The knowledge of God's character should increase our passion to love Him.

Go back to Deuteronomy 6:4 and you'll find the great *Shema* of Israel. *Shema* means "to hear." Every orthodox Jew recites the *Shema* every day. They did back in Jesus' day, and they do today. "Hear, O Israel! The Lord is our God, the Lord is one!"

What a great use of Hebrew names for God here. Moses says, "Hear, O Israel! Jehovah is our Elohim. Jehovah is one!" *Elohim* refers to the power of God. *Jehovah,* of course, is the great covenantal name of God. In other words, "Our covenant-keeping God and our powerful God is one!"

The Command to Love

"You shall love the Lord your God with all your heart and with all your soul and with all your might" (v. 5). Jesus adds in Matthew 22:37 "and with all your mind." Our love for God is to be all-consuming.

But notice also that it's a command—and not just a command for you to do, but a command you teach to your children (v. 7). How can love be "commandable"? Because love involves more than your affections. Love includes your will. You can choose to love.

Your affections may not immediately be there when you decide to love, but the decision must precede the affections. Now don't get me wrong. Love certainly includes more than the will. But love never excludes the will. So whenever you feel emotional about someone, but that emotion does not affect your choices, it's not biblical love.

Moses says, "I want you to love the Lord your God. I want you to make a decision with your will that you are going to seek the glory of God. I want you to passionately pursue the knowledge of God, because you will develop a love affair with Him when you do."

I think about the way many guys got their wives. He looked at her and decided to love her. He didn't know her. She didn't especially want to get to know him. He was just another smooth-talking dude who was trying to lay out a line. But he decided to love her and after a while he won her affection. It didn't happen until he exercised his will—and she had to exercise her will too, by the way. Marriage is not a one-sided decision.

Complete Love

Moses says, "You shall love the Lord your God with all your heart and with all your soul and with all your might." This is a complete love.

The *heart* speaks of devotion. Be devoted to the Lord. To love Him with your heart is to love Him sincerely and to give Him your affections.

The *soul* speaks of self-authentication, self-awareness. The reason you know you are here is because you have a soul, a sense of "I." So to love God with your soul means to love Him with the core of who you are. When two people have become "soul-mates," they have developed a oneness with each other. God says, "Develop an intense oneness between your inner being and Me."

I CHALLENGE YOU TO RESPOND TO GOD, TO GET TO KNOW HIM. IT'S GOING TO BE SOME WORK.

We are also commanded to love God with all of our might or strength. You do not love where you do not work. There is no such thing as lazy love. Imagine a husband telling his wife, "I love you, baby, but I'm not going to work. I can love you and stay in bed. I don't have to work to prove I love you."

Lady, if he's not going to work, don't marry him. Before God gave Adam a wife, God gave him a job. Love always demands your strength. Love has energy. Love requires work. God says, "Love Me to the point that you serve Me, that you expend energy for Me, that it costs you something to love Me. This is the kind of love I want."

Love is hard work. I'm a living witness to that. (Don't ask Lois to testify.) A man is only told to study two things—his Bible and his wife—because both require interpretation. A woman puts out a lot of signals, especially as she goes through certain stages of life. If you don't read those signals right, Lord have mercy.

As a married couple, you've got to work through all that. And I won't even attempt to imagine what a wife has to work through when her husband has his midlife crisis or whatever. Don't let anyone tell you love doesn't involve work.

If we put that kind of effort into loving other people, then loving God deserves much more. I love the story of the little boy who kept riding his bicycle around the block. Finally, a police officer stopped him and said, "Son, you keep riding around this same block. What are you doing?"

"I'm running away."

The officer replied, "You're running away? How can you be running away and keep going around the same block?"

The little boy answered, "Because my mommy told me I couldn't cross the street."

God wants us to love Him so much that even when we run from Him, we stay on the same block. We don't cross the street because we want to obey Him. We love Him so much we don't ever want to be foolish enough to go very far from home.

One day a little girl complained to her mother, "Mommy, I love my dolls, but they won't love me back!"

I think that's how God feels sometimes. "I love My kids, but they won't love Me back." I challenge you to respond to God, to get to know Him. It's going to be some work. You may need to get up a little earlier so you can spend time in His Word and time on your knees. You'll need to spend time with His people and time in His presence, because our great God deserves a response.

Responding to God

In one sense, this whole chapter, and this whole final section, are one big application of the truth we've been learning. But I still want to give you some specific ideas you can use along the way. So let me take four of the areas we discussed in this chapter and give you an applicational idea for each one to help you in getting to know God:

1. At your next family meal, discuss this question: What things would we as a family miss if we didn't go to church for an entire month? List them all, the tangible and the intangible. Does your list include a lot of good reasons to be worshiping God? Or does it reveal something else? Close your time by asking God to make worship a priority for you.

2. What's your biggest fear? What's the one thing in your life that you are most reluctant to let go of and trust God with completely? Write it on a 3 x 5 card, and put the card where you'll see it every day. Make that area of fear, doubt, or unbelief a matter of special prayer until you can say, "Lord, I trust You completely with this"— and mean it.

3. Since we're making lists and writing things down, list all the reasons you can think of for why children should obey their parents. Now take the role of a child and look at your list again from that viewpoint. Are you obeying God for these same reasons? Example: Children should obey their parents because good parents have their children's best interests at heart. You can obey God because you *know* He has your best interests at heart.

4. We saw that the Bible commands us to love God. Jesus commanded us to love God. That means you can choose to love. It also means you can *learn* to love God with all your being. If you feel your love for God growing a bit cold these days, go before Him and make a decision to increase your love for Him. Don't expect a lot of warm fuzzy feelings or tears when you do that, but decide anyway. Tell God that you want to love Him more deeply, and that you're willing to give it all you've got. He will be pleased, and the emotions will come.

18
THE PASSION
FOR GOD

A n airplane is meant to fly, a car is built to be driven, and clothes are designed to be worn. You would have very little use for a plane that would not take to the skies, a car that would not move, or clothes that could no longer be worn.

Why? Their purpose is not being realized. In fact, it's a great frustration to have things that are no longer useful. God must feel that way about us sometimes. We were designed to know and worship Him, not simply to have a good or comfortable life. We were not created just to get married and have children. We were not created just to have a successful business career, grow old, and enjoy a comfortable retirement. Those are some of the benefits of life, the side dishes, not its purpose.

LIFE'S PURPOSE

The tragedy today is that we have taken life's benefits and tried to make them the purpose. As a result, we often find the benefits very unsatisfactory. Before Eve took the forbidden fruit, Genesis 3:6 says she "saw that the tree was good for food."

Now that tree had been in the garden all the time. But when Eve looked at it in light of the benefit Satan promised her—to be like God—she decided it was right for her. She turned what was meant to be God's benefit, abundant fruit, into her purpose for living. But notice that she lost both the purpose *and* the benefit.

Do you know why people are not married in heaven, for example? Because the purpose of life is not to get married. Marriage is a benefit. That's why at the end of Ephesians 5, after all that Paul has written about husbands and wives, he sums it up this way: "This mystery is great; but I am speaking with reference to Christ and the church" (v. 32).

That's amazing. We would have expected Paul to say something final about marriage to tie it all together. But he doesn't. He says, "If you think I've been talking only about husbands and wives, you missed my point. I'm talking about Christ and the church." Why? Because marriage has more meaning than just two people living happily ever after. Marriage gives us a model on earth of the relationship between Christ and His church, so that when we all get to heaven, we won't go through culture shock.

A Foretaste of Eternity

You see, God wants to give you a microcosmic experience in time of what eternity will be like. Let's take marriage as an example, since we're on the subject. Back in Genesis 1:27, God said He made man in His own image, and created them male and female. Then Moses gives us an extended description of creation in chapter 2 to explain marriage. The key to understanding this is that God created man in His own image.

One of the fundamental truths about God is His Tri-Personhood. That is, He exists as three co-equal Persons who are distinct in their personal identity, yet one in essence. The Father is not the Son, and the Son is not the Spirit. Each is distinct, yet all three are one.

So God said He was going to create man in His image. But in order for us to experience what God is like in His Person, He had to give us something here on earth that would help us understand how three distinct persons can share one essence. So after God created Adam, we find in chapter 2 an extended discussion of how Eve came onto the scene.

This detail is important, because Adam already lives in the Garden of Eden. He has a good job, and he has every provision for living. But God says something is "not good" (Genesis 2:18), because Adam has no companion, no one like him. Naming all of the animals only underscores Adam's need, because every zebra has another zebra and every gorilla has another gorilla. So God cuts open Adam's side, takes out part of his personhood, and with it creates a woman.

Now Adam is only half the man he used to be. Half of him has gone into making the woman. She now shares his essence—bone of his bone and flesh of his flesh. Eve puts her hand in God's hand, and God brings her to Adam. Now in order for Adam to get back what he lost and be complete, he's got to take all of Eve. And Eve needs to reconnect to Adam, from whose side she came.

This reconnection will ultimately come in their sexual relationship. That's why chapter 2 ends by saying they were not ashamed. They came together in a one-flesh relationship. These two people are now one. Remember, we're talking about marriage as an illustration of God's triune Person. We've got two-thirds of the triune experience here, but we need a third entity.

The Bible teaches that the Son of God proceeds from the Father, and the Spirit proceeds from the Son. That's a theological point, but it's also important because of how marriage reflects this procession. Eve proceeds from the rib of Adam. The two become one, and Cain and Abel proceed from their union. These three, father, mother, and child, are distinct in person yet one in essence.

TO GLORIFY GOD MEANS TO MAKE HIM LOOK GOOD, TO PLACE HIM ON DISPLAY SO THAT WHEN OTHERS SEE YOUR LIFE, THEY STAND IN AWE OF YOUR GOD.

So for mankind to have a foretaste of what God enjoys in heaven in His triune Person, He created a male, took part of his essence and created a female, then took the female back to the male so that their two essences could come together and create a new essence. Marriage and family are designed to model eternity. God never meant the benefits of life to become our reason for living, but to drive us back to Him as the reason for living.

Reflecting God's Glory

If the purpose of life is not marriage, success, happiness, or any of that, what is it? What were we created for? Answer: We were created to know and worship God. That's it. So Paul can say, "Whether, then, you eat or drink or whatever you do, do all to the glory of God" (1 Corinthians 10:31).

The word *glory* means to put something on the mantle where it can be admired by onlookers. A woman seeks glory when she decorates her home in such a way that guests say, "Wow, where did you get that?" She puts a special treasure on display so that when people see it, they are in awe.

That's glory. To glorify God means to make Him look good, to place Him on display so that when others see your life, they stand in awe of your God. You're to do that even in the most mundane activities of life, Paul says. Even in the everyday stuff, your goal should be to make God look good.

GETTING TO KNOW GOD

The question is, how do we get to know God at this level, where He becomes our reason for living? I think Paul answers the question for us Philippians 3, where he tells us how God came to be *his* reason for living.

To understand why Paul brings up his personal experience in chapter 3, we need to remember the situation at Philippi. Personality conflicts had erupted (see 4:2). The believers were also concerned about Paul, whether he was going to live or die. On top of all that, the Judaizers were coming along behind Paul, trying to discredit everything he was teaching.

So the apostle begins chapter 3 by saying:

> Finally, my brethren, rejoice in the Lord. To write the same things again is no trouble to me, and it is a safeguard for you. Beware of the dogs, beware of the evil workers, beware of the false circumcision; for we are the true circumcision, who worship in the Spirit of God and glory in Christ Jesus and put no confidence in the flesh, although I myself might have confidence even in the flesh. If anyone else has a mind to put confidence in the flesh, I far more. (vv. 1–4)

Not by Human Effort

The Judaizers had been telling the Philippians, "If you really want to know God you've got to put forth greater effort. You've got to try harder to keep the Mosaic law. You've got to be better 'Old Testament Christians.'"

Paul knew better. He knew that if human effort, fleshly striving, flawless commitment, and boundless religious zeal could bring a person into an intimate relationship with God, no one should have been closer to God than he. Nobody had more going for him than Paul did. If you wanted to name the "Man of the Year" in religion, Paul was the choice. No one could outdo him.

But Paul knew that all of his pre-conversion effort and zeal was how *not* to get to know God. If the Judaizers were going to try to enslave the Philippians to human effort, Paul would use himself as an example of the futility and danger of that approach.

Paul had learned to put "no confidence in the flesh." Absolutely none. Then he says, beginning in verse 4, "My beloved Philippians, pay attention. Here's how I learned that lesson." We'd better sit up and listen closely too.

First up, Paul had the right start. He was born into a good family. We know that because he was "circumcised the eighth day" (v. 5). His parents were serious about their Judaism. It's like saying your dad and mom took you to church every Sunday. By having Paul circumcised according to the law his parents showed that they were committed to the Old Testament faith.

But probably a lot of Jews could say they had been circumcised the eighth day. "That doesn't put you in any special category, Paul" they might have said. But he was just getting started. He was also "of the nation of Israel" (v. 5). He was not an immigrant Jew, but part and parcel of the nation.

Paul's detractors would come back, "So you had good Jewish parents and you're living on Jewish soil. That's fine. But so are thousands of other Jews. No big deal."

But wait a minute, Paul responded. He was also "of the tribe of Benjamin" (v. 5). Now he has narrowed this thing down a whole lot. This little statement may not mean much to you and me, but to the Jews, it meant a lot.

Paul is giving a short history lesson. He's saying, "You'll remember that after the kingdom split, ten of Israel's twelve tribes forsook the Lord completely. The northern kingdom didn't have even one king who followed the Lord. You did your own thing until God judged you.

"But the two tribes in the south, Judah and Benjamin, had two things going for them. First, they had some faithful kings. And second, Benjamin was considered the faithful tribe. Whenever there was trouble, the Benjamites always went out to battle first. Well, I'm a Benjamite. I'm one of the faithful ones."

Well, perhaps a member of the Judaizers in Philippi could say, "I'm still with you, Paul: good family, native Israelite, tribe of Benjamin. You've got nothing on me so far." So Paul laid out another of his human qualifications. He was "a Hebrew of the Hebrews" (v. 5). That means "Superjew."

What Paul meant was that while other Jewish young men were immersing themselves in the Greek culture of the day, studying Socrates, Aristotle, and Plato; while they were out playing Greek games with their Greek neighbors, he was studying the Old Testament. He was immersing himself in Jewish thought, learning the law and traditions of his people so that he became an expert on Jewish law and affairs.

Then another Judaizer stood up and said, "So what? I'm an expert too. I got A's in Aramaic and Hebrew." But Paul had a few more block-busters left. How about this one? "I am a Pharisee" (v. 5).

That eliminates just about everybody because there were only a limited number of Pharisees in the history of the Jewish nation. To become a Pharisee, you had to memorize the first five books of the Bible. These guys were dead serious. They were dead wrong, but dead serious. A Pharisee dedicated his whole existence to keeping the law. Everyone was in awe of the Pharisees.

Do you remember how much trouble Jesus had trying to get something to eat on the Sabbath? It was because the Pharisees had hemmed the Sabbath in with so many minute laws that no one could do anything. The Pharisees would probably kill a hen for laying a egg on the Sabbath because she worked!

To say that the Pharisees prided themselves on their righteousness is like saying the Atlantic Ocean has a fair amount of water in it. Paul was one of these guys. He was the best of the best, the cream. He was zealous for the law and traditions of the Jews.

But let's give the Judaizing crowd in Philippi the benefit of the doubt one last time and assume a Pharisee among them could say to Paul, "Hey, hotshot. Here's my card. I'm a Pharisee too. I'm just as zealous for the law and traditions of the Jews as you are."

So Paul dropped his knockout punch: "as to zeal, a persecutor of the church" (v. 6). When the Sanhedrin, the Jewish ruling council, decided to move against this growing threat called Christianity, they needed someone who would lead the charge—someone who would hate Christianity so much and love Jewish history so much that he wouldn't stop until this new sect was wiped off the face of the earth.

They needed a volunteer. Paul said, "You're looking at him." Nobody could kill Christians like him. Nobody would follow orders like him. Paul said, "I was known as the Persecutor. No one was on fire for the religion of our people like me."

And just for good measure, Paul threw in one last qualification: "as to the righteousness which is in the Law, found blameless" (v. 6). What does it mean to be blameless? It means every time Paul did something wrong, he had the right sacrifice nearby. Whenever he blew it, the lamb was ready. He always atoned for his errors.

Nothing but Christ

That's an impressive list. It's unbeatable. No one could keep up with Paul, humanly speaking. He is telling the Philippians, "When I said I had plenty of reasons to put confidence in the flesh, I wasn't kidding. If any human effort could make you right with God, I would be there."

Swept Away

"But whatever things were gain to me, those things I have counted as loss for the sake of Christ" (v. 7). With one sentence, Paul swept it all off the table and into the trash can. Please note the verb: count*ed*. It's a past activity. He is referring to his Damascus road experience.

You remember it. Paul was on his way to Damascus when Jesus Christ confronted him one-on-one and said, "Saul, Saul, why are you persecuting me?" (Acts 9:4). He looked up, being blinded by the light, and said, "Lord." That was it. From that day forward, Paul considered his credentials worthless.

I believe you agree with me that we are not saved by works. We can't get saved by going to Sunday school, by being good people, being philanthropists. We have to count it as worthless when it comes to salvation. If you bring any works to the table of salvation, you have nullified it. You have said *Jesus paid most of it, but He needs a little help from me.*

The reason God does not accept our works for salvation is that they are an insult to the price He paid. Jesus said, "It is finished," paid in full. You may wonder, *What does that have to do with me? I'm already saved.*

Now THE QUESTION BECOMES, WHAT MUST I DO TO KNOW CHRIST? YOUR MOTIVATION MUST CHANGE.

It's got everything to do with you. Why? Because Paul not only counted everything prior to salvation as a loss. "More than that," he says in verse 8, "I count. . . ." The difference between the verbs in verses 7 and 8 is that the tense has changed from past perfect to present.

Paul is saying, "I dropped all my human effort when I met Jesus for salvation." But more than that, he still counts all things "to be loss in view of the surpassing value of knowing Christ Jesus my Lord, for whom I have suffered the loss of all things, and count them but rubbish in order that I may gain Christ" (v. 8).

Fellowship with Christ

This verse is critical. Paul says that just as human works could not give him a relationship with Christ, human works could not give him intimate fellowship with Christ. The "counting" of human effort as useless with Christ must be carried over from the past tense, salvation, to the present tense, fellowship with Christ. Many Christians have the mistaken idea that although works didn't get us saved, they are necessary to maintain fellowship with Christ.

Paul says no. God rejects purely human effort, whether before or after the cross. You remember Paul's struggle in Romans 7. He says he had a passion to do good, but every time he reached out to do good, evil took over. Paul was trying to retrain the flesh to please God, but in the flesh we can never please God.

KNOWING CHRIST

This raises an important question. If works have nothing to do with knowing our Christ, why all these commandments about how we should live as Christians? It has to do with our motivation. God foreordained us to good works (Ephesians 2:10). The key is our motivation, the *why* of what we do.

In other words, good works are only good when the knowledge and glory of God motivates those works. Paul says that the motivation in life must be to know Christ. He was not counting on good works as an end in themselves. He was counting on knowing Christ as his means toward a spiritual end. Good works are a tangible means of expressing our love for Christ and desire to know Him.

The Proper Motivation

Now the question becomes, what must I do to know Christ? Your motivation must change. Many Christians study their Bibles every day not to know Christ, but because somewhere along the line somebody told them that a verse a day keeps the devil away. Others study their Bibles not to know Christ, but because all good Christians are supposed to have devotions, and they feel guilty if they don't.

That's why so many people say Bible study is boring. Their motivation is not "that I might know Him." Others go to church merely because it's Sunday, or they do good things for people out of sheer duty with little or no devotion.

Paul worked for Christ, but his motivation wasn't the acclaim it might bring him. His motivation was to know Christ. His service was important, but he counted it as loss because what motivated him to work was not piling up credits. Paul does not say he didn't work, he just says he didn't *count* the work as worth anything compared with knowing Christ.

When your passion is to know Christ, Bible study becomes important because it's a Word from His heart to yours. You pray, but not because you're supposed to. You desperately need to talk to Him! You need to obey and to work, but work isn't the goal. You must count the work as loss because the moment you start adding up your "service points," you lose Christ.

Just as the unbeliever loses out on salvation if he brings works to the table, so the Christian loses out on fellowship when he brings works to the table. You can't say, "Lord, I ought to know You by now. I've been having devotions for five years." You just lost His fellowship because you made human effort your motivation. The husband who says to his wife, "You ought to cook for me, you're my wife," has wiped out her motivation, because now it's not an act of love but of duty.

The Proper Righteousness

Paul has more to say in Philippians 3 on this matter of knowing Christ. "[I want to] be found in Him, not having a righteousness of my own derived from the Law, but that which is through faith in Christ" (v. 9). He's speaking as a saved man now. When he hit verse 8, Paul left his old unsaved days behind.

He says, in effect, "I don't want a righteousness that comes because I'm keeping the Ten Commandments, as every good Christian should, but that which is through faith in Christ alone." Salvation and spirituality both come from faith, even as good works must be "faith works." We get saved by trusting Christ, and we grow by trusting Christ. Good works after salvation are designed to show that we love and trust God enough to obey Him.

Works don't provide merit in either case. A lot of things we have done will burn up at the judgment seat of Christ (1 Corinthians 3:10–15). Some of it may even be good stuff. At the judgment seat of Christ, some of my sermons will burn up. I will not be rewarded for them, even though people may have been saved as a result.

I say that because in 1 Corinthians 3:13, Paul says, "Each man's work will become evident." That word means everything we've done will be turned inside out so we can examine its inner core.

In other words, at His judgment seat Christ will not be impressed with what is seen. When He shows us our works on the screen of heaven and we look at them with Him to determine our reward, what we might applaud is not necessarily what Christ looks at.

He won't be looking at my sermons to see how many people came down the aisle. He is going to turn them inside out so we can see the core and ask the question, why were these sermons preached? I have no doubt that Christ is going to point out some sermons that were not preached for His glory but were designed to get the preacher a pat on the back. Those sermons will burn.

That's why Jesus said of the Pharisees who loved to show off and pray in public, "They have their reward in full" (Matthew 6:5). No credit will be given in heaven for showy prayers. God wants you to have works, but for the right goal.

The Proper Measure of Faith

Faith is simply trusting God. It is dependence on Him. Some Christians say, "If I just had a little more faith, I could do better. I just don't seem to have enough faith." Yes, you do! You've got more than enough faith. Jesus said even "mustard seed" faith can move mountains (Matthew 17:20).

He was saying that the issue is not how much faith you have. If you're saved, you've got the full measure of faith. The issue is how much of *God* you have. Far too many Christians have a God who is too small, so they experience very little of Him in their lives, for who wants to put confidence in a little God?

I was once scheduled to preach at a conference in a church in Iowa. The pastor called and said a pilot in their church had a little twin-engine Cessna airplane. To make it more convenient for me, this man would just fly down, pick up Lois and me, and bring us back to Iowa for the conference.

Now you must understand my wife. She doesn't even like to fly on Delta and American. So when she heard that some guy she didn't know was going to fly this little four-seater down to Dallas and take us back to Iowa, her faith died. Her faith died because when it comes to flying, the size of her faith is directly proportional to the size of the airplane. Small plane, small faith.

For some reason, those plans got canceled and we had to fly on a major airline. When Lois found out, her faith grew. Her faith grew because the size of the airplane grew about ten times.

The issue today is not how much faith you have, but the size of your God. If you've got even a little bit of faith in a huge God, you've got all you need. But if you have a huge amount of faith in a tiny God, you're in trouble. You study your Bible and pray and worship and obey, not to chalk up points in heaven, but so the "size" of your God will grow and your faith can begin to work.

WHERE TO BEGIN

Time for another question. How do we get this thing going; where do we begin in getting to know God like this? It begins with desire. Look at Philippians 3:10–11: "That I may know Him, and the power of His resurrection and the fellowship of His sufferings, being conformed to His death; in order that I may attain to the resurrection from the dead." In other words, Paul says, "I want what Jesus had."

Getting the Desire

Jesus got up out of the grave and lived a new resurrected life. I want spiritually, Paul says, what Jesus had physically. I want that power. But I also want to know Jesus in His sufferings. I want to share in what He suffered so I can know Him in a greater way, with a deeper intimacy.

I said this earlier, but God only feeds hungry people. "Blessed are those who hunger and thirst for righteousness, for they shall be satisfied" (Matthew 5:6). People who are full of themselves or anything else don't feel hungry. If you're not hungry, it's no wonder you're not being filled. You can always tell a hungry person because he's looking for food.

Feeding the Desire

So if you want a spiritual appetite like Paul's, hang around food and you'll start to get hungry. Begin to snack and you'll get even hungrier. Then once the hunger comes, let God feed you. As He does, you will get up to have your devotions not because you're supposed to, but because you're starving for a word from Him. You'll pray because your spiritual stomach is growling for a good prayer feast. You'll obey God because of the joy you find in bringing Him joy by your obedience.

Bible study is fun when you are desperate to know the mind of Christ about a matter confronting you. You're facing a decision and you say, "Lord, what is Your mind on this?" Now you're looking for God to feed you with His will. Once you're ready to obey His will, you'll know it. God will not waste good information on people who aren't going to do anything with it.

Connecting to the Power

I remember as a kid in Baltimore, Maryland, there was one thing I could not figure out, and that was how fire hydrants worked. I just couldn't understand it. We used to play in the fire hydrants when the fire marshal would come around and turn them on to flush them out.

What puzzled me about that fire hydrant was how all that water could come out of a three-foot pipe. I'd see water gushing out of this thing for hours. How did the fire department get all that water into that little pipe? That bothered me until one day somebody finally explained it to me.

You know the answer as well as I do. That pipe has absolutely no water of its own. But underneath the ground a hookup leads to another pipe which leads to the dam. And the dam is chock full of water. It has got more water than you'd ever know what to do with. That three-foot pipe only delivers to the hydrant what is contained in the dam.

If something goes wrong underneath the ground so that the pipes become disconnected from the dam, you can open the hydrant as far as it will go but nothing will come out, because the dynamic of the hydrant is its connection with the dam.

Of course, you can't see the connection from the street. You're not supposed to. This is exactly how the Christian life is meant to be lived, except that people are supposed to be able to see our "power source" when they look at our lives. You're the hydrant, but you can't pump water unless the hookup is right, unless earth has laid hold of heaven. Heaven has everything earth will ever need. All that you need in your life is contained in the dam of heaven.

So the question is not how much heaven has, or how small your hydrant is. Rather, how good is your connection? If you get hooked up right, anything that needs to be pumped out will come out.

Struggling to Bear Fruit?

This is why Jesus likened Himself to the vine and likened us to the branches (John 15:5). We need only to abide in Him to bear fruit. Some of us strain to bear fruit! We struggle so hard. But if these words of Jesus mean anything, they mean that if we get connected to Him, what we need will be able to flow from Him.

The abundant Christian life is called the "fruit of the Spirit." Fruit is not responsible for fruit. If the fruit is connected to the right kind of tree, it will grow.

It is my conviction that if "Greater is He who is in [us] than he who is the world" (1 John 4:4), then no craving of the flesh can fail to be contained by the power of God alone working through us. That includes drug addiction, immorality, smoking, or any other addiction or habit.

Suppose that I as a Christian go with an unbeliever to one of these secular treatment centers together to stop smoking, and the treatment works for both of us. What difference did it make that I have the Spirit of God in me? The unbeliever does not, but we got the same results.

If some treatment center is the world's way of helping a person get over a fleshly habit, and if "Greater is He who is in *me* than he who is in the world," should I not be able to break that habit without the help of a center? I believe so.

To me, the issue is whether the power of God is greater than the methods of the world. If I overcome my problem in the power of the Spirit without going to the center, that gives me a stronger testimony. So I am of the conviction there is no habit which cannot be broken by the application of the knowledge of God in the spirit of a man or woman, enabling him or her to overcome the cravings of the flesh.

This doesn't necessarily mean that a Christian has to go off in a corner and overcome the problem alone with no help or encouragement from other members of the body of Christ. God can and does use the spiritual gifts of others to help us overcome our struggles and sins. But that's precisely the point. It should be the work of the Holy Spirit through the person and through other believers, not the techniques of the world, which brings about the victory.

I know most people are not used to hearing this, and you may think I'm off base. But I had a chance to see my "theory" proved with a young lady who had been through all kinds of programs trying to quit smoking. Then she heard me preach through Romans 6, which talks about the fact that we were buried with Christ and raised with Him to a brand-new way of life. The "old man" has been crucified.

One Wednesday night, the young woman stood up in the service and told how she had been hopelessly addicted to smoking. Then she heard the teaching of God's Word on who she is in Jesus Christ. "The new me has now come out," she said. "The caterpillar has turned into a butterfly, and what good is a butterfly doing hanging around the cocoon?

"So I just looked up to God and thanked Him for making me a brand-new person in Christ. I said, 'Greater is He who is in me than he who is in the world,' and in the name of Jesus Christ I declared victory over my smoking." She went on to say she flew away from her "cocoon" of smoking and has not moved back since!

I believe that what that young woman did can be duplicated on a regular basis in the lives of God's people, because the Spirit can overcome any deed of the flesh.

TO KNOW HIM

So the question in this matter of knowing God becomes what kind of hook-up do you have? You ought to have devotions each day *to get to know Him.* You ought to pray *because you want to know God.* You ought to be under the teaching of His Word *because you want to know Him.*

This is the motivation for everything. This is what you were created for, to know God. This is your purpose in life, but when you know God you also get all the benefits that come with knowing Him.

My kids enjoy certain benefits because they have a Christian father who is committed for life to their mother, who doesn't drink, and who doesn't take drugs. They also get a lot of benefits because they have a godly Christian mother who loves them and loves their father.

Knowing god is the goal of the christian life. if you fall short of that, your hard work won't mean a thing.

One time my brother decided he didn't like the way my father was running things. My brother was a big guy: football star, wrestling champ in the unlimited heavyweight division, about 240 pounds back then. He announced that he didn't like the way my father was running the house, and he said, "I'm tired of all these rules."

My father said, "OK. I'll help you pack. Good-bye."

So my brother packed a bag and walked out. Two days later he was on the porch, pleading to come home. Do you know why? Because he found out that when you leave the fellowship of the father, you lose the benefits of the home.

The Christian life has some rough spots in it because your flesh will always want to do things you shouldn't do. Your flesh will try to get you to pack up and leave. But let me tell you, the benefits of the Father's home far outweigh the pull of any fleshly desire. Get to know Him, no matter what!

Responding with a Passion for God

I hope you've gotten the message by now: Knowing God is the goal of the Christian life. If you fall short of that, your hard work won't mean a thing. Make it your purpose to know God intimately, and come on in to the Father's house. Here are some ideas to help you get off the porch and in to the dinner table:

1. Search your heart and life and make sure you haven't switched around the purpose of life and its benefits. One way to check up on yourself is to get a pencil and paper and figure how you spent your time over the past week or so. If your habits reveal a preoccupation with the "benefits," take whatever steps you need to get things back in perspective.

2. Maybe you're one of those extra-conscientious Christians who is working hard to please God. Only you and the Holy Spirit can call this one, but if you are working *for* God's approval rather than out of gratitude for His approval in Christ, stop and take a hard look at what you're doing. A close Christian friend can be a real help here. Talk it over with that person soon.

3. Sometimes we as Christians can get the idea that living by faith is "ABC" stuff, and we're looking for the advanced course. Just by way of reminder, read Colossians 2:6 and answer these two questions: 1. How did I come to Christ? 2. How am I to "walk in Him"? (Hint: the answer comes in verses 5 and 7.)

4. What would happen if, like Paul, you lost all of your earthly credentials—everything that marked your place in life and helped you know who you were and where you came from? Would Christ alone be enough? Could you still be content? These kinds of questions take some serious thought, so at your next opportunity take a quiet walk where you can meditate on this issue.

19
THE WORSHIP
OF GOD

I n the preceding chapters, the subject of worship has come up in a variety of contexts. We shouldn't be surprised, because worship pervades the Scriptures and helps to define our relationship with God.

In this chapter I want to pull together the threads of this subject that run throughout the book and see if we can come to a fuller understanding of what worship is all about.

ARE WE WORSHIPING YET?

Worship is one of those activities every sincere Christian knows he ought to be doing, and even wants to do. But we're not always sure how to go about it. Like the puzzled party-goer who asks, "Are we having fun yet?", Christians sometimes try hard to worship but feel like asking, "Am I worshiping yet?"

To help us get a handle on a big subject, I want to turn to John 4, the familiar story of Jesus and the Samaritan woman at the well. It's appropriate that the setting for this great chapter on worship is a well, because I believe the reason many Christians run dry is that they have not learned how to worship.

Worship is the pump that keeps the water flowing so that the well of living water (John 4:14), which never runs dry, does not *feel* like it is running dry. Many of us go through the rhetoric of worship. We know the words of the hymns and the right phrases to say at the right times.

The Dry Zone

But far too many believers harbor a "dry zone" deep down inside. For some, it has been there for quite a while. For others, it has only recently become a way of life. No matter where you fit on the continuum, you can get the inner spring of your life flowing only by establishing a relationship with Jesus Christ and by learning to worship.

That's what Jesus told the Samaritan woman, who thought she was just going for a bucket of water. The early verses of John 4 set the familiar scene, but I want to focus on verse 16. It brings us to the turning point when Jesus Christ tells the woman, "Go, call your husband, and come here." Her response sparks this interchange, which leads to the issue of worship:

> The woman answered and said, "I have no husband." Jesus said to her, "You have well said, 'I have no husband'; for you have had five husbands, and the one whom you now have is not your husband; this you have said truly." The woman said to Him, "Sir, I perceive that You are a prophet." (vv. 17–19)

Where to Worship

After this observation, the woman jumps immediately into the subject of worship, a section that climaxes with Jesus' great pronouncement in verse 24. The word *worship* in one form or another is found no less than ten times in this short passage. The woman gets the ball rolling when she brings up a hot discussion topic of the day relative to worship: "Our fathers worshiped in this mountain, and you people say that in Jerusalem is the place where men ought to worship" (v. 20).

"Our fathers" refers to the woman's Samaritan ancestors. "You people" were the Jews. The religious and social gulf between Samaritans and Jews in Jesus' day was incredibly wide. Let me give you a brief bit of history to help you understand why, because it is important to our subject of worship.

Way back in 722 B.C., God judged the ten tribes of the northern kingdom, called Israel, by allowing the heathen nation of Assyria to conquer the land. Many of the Israelites were carted off as captives to Assyria, although some were left behind. At the same time, the Assyrians resettled many of their own heathen people back in Israel.

You can imagine what happened as decades and then centuries passed. The heathen people and the Jews in Israel intermarried, producing a culture of people who were half-Jew and half-Gentile. These people came to be known as Samaritans, and the Jews in Galilee and Judea despised them.

From that time to the day of our text, there had been deep antagonism between the pure-blooded Jews and these Samaritan "half-breeds." The Jews called them "dogs."

Separate Worship

The Samaritans had developed their own system of worship because they weren't welcome at the temple in Jerusalem—and this was the key to Jesus' conversation with the woman. The Samaritans only accepted the Pentateuch, the first five books of the Bible, as Scripture, and they established their own temple on a mountain called Gerizim.

So when the woman says, "Our fathers worshiped in this mountain," she is saying, "My people have their place of worship on this mountain right behind me. You Jews go to your temple in Jerusalem. Now I've got a question: Which one of us is right?"

TRUE WORSHIP

Her question is the first-century equivalent of a question people in our culture ask every day. "Should I go to Such-and-Such Baptist Church down the street, So-and-So Methodist Church around the corner, or This-and-That Bible Church a few miles up the road? Which church is the right one?"

Which Church?

This woman wants to know which "mountain church" is the right one, and Jesus' response to her contains the meat of our subject. Therefore, I want to proceed deliberately, because my goal is to help you understand what worship is all about. In verse 21 Jesus says, "Woman, believe Me, an hour is coming when neither in this mountain, nor in Jerusalem, shall you worship the Father."

Please don't misread that. Jesus didn't choose either of her options. He said that *neither* mountain was the place to worship because a new "hour" was coming. "It's on its way," Jesus tells the woman. "In fact, it's standing right in front of you," meaning He Himself was going to usher in this new hour.

In other words, Jesus was saying, "I am going to inaugurate a new basis for worship that has nothing to do with either Gerizim or Jerusalem. And woman, as far as you're concerned, this new hour has already come."

Jesus was referring to the cancellation of the Old Covenant, the approach to God that He had made available to people in the Old Testament. If you wanted to worship in those days, you had to go to the tabernacle. God built a tabernacle in Israel that had the sole purpose of serving as the place of worship.

As we saw earlier, this tabernacle was a huge tent put right in the middle of the camp. All twelve tribes of Israel were gathered around the tabernacle. It was the centerpiece of the nation. The problem with the tabernacle was that you could not go directly into the presence of God. You could go past the first curtain into the large inside area where the altar was. But a veil covered the entrance to the Holy of Holies, where the ark of the covenant rested and God's presence dwelt.

IF YOU LIMIT WORSHIP TO WHERE YOU ARE, THE MINUTE YOU LEAVE THAT PLACE OF WORSHIP YOU WILL LEAVE YOUR ATTITUDE OF WORSHIP BEHIND LIKE A CRUMPLED-UP CHURCH BULLETIN.

Any Israelite who went to worship God had to go through the priests, and even then the high priest could enter the Holy of Holies only once a year. As an Israelite, you never got to meet with God directly. Later, the temple contained the same divisions as the tabernacle, and the same restrictions applied.

If you and I were living in Old Testament days, we would have to become part of Israel in order to worship God. It used to be fashionable for certain Hollywood stars and entertainers to say they had become Jewish. They were saying that they had embraced the Jewish faith, and they did understand it rightly according to the Old Testament way. If you accepted the Jewish faith, you had to become part of the Jewish people. Gentiles who did this were called "proselytes." They had identified with the Jewish way.

People do much the same thing today, only they say, "I am a member of Such-and-Such Baptist Church or So-and-So Methodist Church." I'm not condemning these statements. I'm just saying that many people attach worship to where they are.

Canceled!

Jesus was telling this woman, "The old system has been canceled. Under that system, worship was tied to where you were. You had to be part of Israel, gathered around the tabernacle or temple. But from now on, worship will be not tied to where you are, but *who* you are. I am inaugurating a new means of worship called the New Covenant."

TEMPLES OF GOD

Worship has less to do with where you go on Sunday morning than who you are in touch with all week long. Jesus was teaching here in John 4 what Paul later spelled out in 1 Corinthians 6:19: "Do you not know that your body is a temple of the Holy Spirit?" God's presence is no longer centered in the temple at Jerusalem, or on any mountain. He now lives inside His people.

Individual Temples

So where can you worship? Anywhere! It's not where you are, it's who you are. You are the temple of the living God. He now lives within you. Does this mean we don't have to go to church anymore to worship God? Not at all, and I'll show you why in a few paragraphs.

I am saying that if you go to church thinking you are now going to *the* place of worship, you've missed the message. If you limit worship to where you are, the minute you leave that place of worship you will leave your *attitude* of worship behind like a crumpled-up church bulletin.

That's why we have a group of people who can worship on Sunday and then do their thing Monday and the rest of the week. They do not understand that they carry worship around within them instead of just going to a place of worship only. Is the church a place of worship? Of course it is. But it's not the sole extent of our worship.

Hebrews 10 has some powerful things to say about this new way of worship Jesus inaugurated. Here the author quotes Old Testament prophecies which describe the work of Jesus. Even though the terms are different, this is basically what Jesus tells the Samaritan woman:

> For it is impossible for the blood of bulls and goats to take away sins. Therefore, when He comes into the world, He says, "Sacrifice and offering Thou hast not desired, but a body Thou hast prepared for Me; in whole burnt offerings and sacrifices for sin Thou hast taken no pleasure." (Hebrews 10:4–6)

Then the writer, again quoting prophecy, says in verse 9, "Behold, I have come to do Thy will." That is, Jesus Christ has come to do the will of His Father in inaugurating this new way of approaching God. That's why the writer of Hebrews goes on to make these strong statements about the Old Covenant system and to issue a wonderful invitation:

> Every priest stands daily ministering and offering time after time the same sacrifices, which can never take away sins; but [Christ], having offered one sacrifice for sins for all time, sat down at the right hand of God. (vv. 11–12)

> Since therefore, brethren, we have confidence to enter the holy place by the blood of Jesus, by a new and living way which He inaugurated for us through the veil, that is, His flesh . . . let us draw near with a sincere heart. (vv. 19–20, 22a)

Where can you go today? Directly into the presence of God! You don't need a priest. You don't need a confessional booth. You don't need another brother or sister. You don't even need a preacher to go before God for you. You can come straight into His presence and say, "Let's talk a while."

In the Old Testament, you couldn't do that. Those people needed an earthly priest, but now we have Jesus Christ as our heavenly High Priest. He is located in the heavenly temple, and we are now God's earthly temple. We do not need to go to another earthly temple to worship and approach God.

Do you understand who you are? God is saying, "Just as the temple was the place to worship Me in the Old Testament, you are My temple in the New Testament because I live within you." The Bible says our High Priest, Jesus Christ, is at the right hand of the

Father, ready to take us to Him at any time. That's why for us today, worship is a way of life, not a once-a-week event.

The Corporate Temple

Now the Bible does not leave this thing on the individual level only. We are not only temples of God individually, but the corporate fellowship is also His temple. Here's the answer to the question, "Do I have to go to church to worship God?" People who ask that aren't really interested in worship.

You see, people who balk at worshiping collectively are not worshiping privately. You show me a person who debates coming to church, and I will show you a person who is debating whether to have daily devotions.

Private temple worship, *me,* always leads to corporate temple worship, *the body.* If you are worshiping in private, you can't wait to worship in public. If you don't care about private worship, you'll debate whether you need church.

Some people will argue, "I don't have to go to church to worship God. I can worship right here in my bed (which means they don't want to get up). I can worship God anywhere." That's true, but the issue is *do* they worship God when they kill the alarm and pull the covers back over their heads? I doubt it!

Whenever anyone tells you that, the person has just served you notice that he or she probably never worships. How can I prove that? Because the same chapter (Hebrews 10) which tells you that you don't need anyone else to help you into the very throne room of God goes on to say this:

> Let us consider how to stimulate one another to love and good deeds, not forsaking our own assembling together, as is the habit of some, but encouraging one another; and all the more, as you see the day drawing near. (vv. 24–25)

The writer is saying, "If you are worshiping in the temple of God in private, you know you've got to worship in public also. You want to share your private temple with the corporate temple. You can't help it."

So those who debate corporate worship are spiritually anemic privately. They have not learned that worship is a way of life. We do not go to church to worship God, but we go because worship is what we've been doing all week, and we can't help but join with others who have been worshiping all week. We worship corporately because it has become a way of life privately.

You are the temple of God. That's why the Bible says you cannot do whatever you want with your body. How many people would plan to commit immorality in the church building? Not many. Most people would never think of stealing or cursing in church because, well, it's God's house.

But God says, "Wherever you sin, you've done it in My house. Wherever you have done it, you have done it in My church, for that is who you are. If you sin, you might as well sin in the pulpit, because you are My temple individually and collectively."

So we come back to Jesus in John 4. He is telling this woman, "Worship is no longer a place. It's not where you are, it's who you are. You are the temple."

THE HEART OF TRUE WORSHIP

A great event happened when Jesus died. They killed Jesus on the cross, but when they went back to the temple, guess what they found? The huge veil covering the holy place was torn (Matthew 27:51). This veil, which separated the people from the very presence of God, was torn in half because the death of Jesus Christ gave His people permission to walk right on inside.

So Jesus says, "Woman, the hour is coming when a place makes no difference at all." Then He continues in verse 22: "You worship that which you do not know; we worship that which we know, for salvation is from the Jews." As I said earlier, in the Old Testament, you had to come through the Jews. You were saved by identification with Israel and Israel's God.

That's why Ruth said to her mother-in-law Naomi, "Your people shall be my people, and your God, my God" (Ruth 1:16). Ruth understood that if she were going to move to Bethlehem with Naomi, she had to move all the way. "Salvation is from the Jews," Jesus says. The great respect we have for the Jewish nation is because it is through them that you and I were redeemed.

Now Jesus drives home His point even more particularly:

> But an hour is coming, and now is, when the true worshipers shall worship the Father in spirit and truth; for such people the Father seeks to be His worshipers. God is spirit, and those who worship Him must worship in spirit and truth. (vv. 23–24)

The Focus of Worship

Let's make a couple of observations. For true worshipers, the focus of worship is God: not just His name, but His person. We say we go to church to worship God, but our focus is not always on Him. To worship God, He must be the focus. What do we mean by the focus? Jesus says, "To worship God is to worship the Father."

Y*OU CANNOT WORSHIP PROPERLY WITH JUST YOUR BODY. IF ALL GOD HAS OF YOU ON SUNDAY MORNING IS YOUR BODY, YOU ARE NOT WORSHIPING.*

To appreciate what this means, we must understand the idea of God the Father from two vantage points. First, He is our Father. Second, He is the Father of the Lord Jesus Christ. That is, the Father and the Son share equally in the same essence as God, as we learned earlier. So if you try to worship God the Father and you bypass Jesus Christ, you have not worshiped God. People will say, "We can worship any god."

I say, "No, you can't."

Some people say, "Just worship one God. You may take that road and I may take this road, but we'll all arrive."

I say, "No, the God we are talking about is the Father of the Lord Jesus Christ. If the God you are talking about is not the Father of Jesus Christ, you are not worshiping God."

By this criterion, a Muslim does not worship God. A Buddhist does not worship God. A Hindu does not worship God. They may worship a supreme being, but they do not worship God, for the God we must worship is the Father: our Father, but also the Father of the Lord Jesus Christ.

Closer to home, a Jehovah's Witness does not worship God, because to the Jehovah's Witness, Jesus Christ is not equal in essence to the Father. The Mormons are even further off from the truth, because in their system man becomes a god.

We are not called to worship Mary. We are not called to worship the saints. We are called to worship God the Father, the Father of the Lord Jesus Christ. If we worship something less than this, we do not worship God.

God is spirit. He is the "invisible" God (1 Timothy 1:17). So if you are trying to pray and see God, you will wait a long time. We don't worship an object we can see.

IF YOU SIT IN CHURCH THINKING ABOUT MONDAY NIGHT FOOTBALL, WORRYING ABOUT YOUR PROBLEMS, OR EVEN COUNTING YOUR BLESSINGS, YOU ARE NOT WORSHIPING.

In Isaiah 40:18, the prophet asks, "To whom then will you liken God? Or what likeness will you compare with Him?" Nothing in the physical universe can give you a vision of God. The only flesh and blood understanding of God you are ever going to get is in the Person of Jesus Christ, who came to reveal the Father. But there is no way you can picture God. He is a Spirit so vast that He encompasses the whole universe.

Worship and Your Inner Self

Among other things, this means you cannot worship properly with just your body. If all God has of you on Sunday morning is your body, you are not worshiping. If you get up to have your private worship and your body is the only part of you present, that's not worship. If you don't want to be there, if you're thinking about work, if you're in a hurry, you have wasted your time, because you cannot worship a Spirit in body only.

Jesus said so, in fact. Those who worship the Father must worship Him "in spirit" (v. 24). If you are going to make contact with God, you've got to make contact with Him in your spirit, because that is His nature.

The spirit refers to your inner person, the immaterial part of you. Physical death occurs when the body no longer functions and the spirit is separated from the body. But you can die spiritually too. You are spiritually dead when your spirit does not function, when it does not respond to God. All of us are *born* spiritually dead.

When Jesus said He came to give life (John 10:10), He was talking to people who were already alive physically. But He was not saying, "I've come to give you more bodily function." Instead, "I've come to quicken your spirit so that your inner person becomes functional."

Fellowship with God occurs when God's invisible Spirit and your invisible spirit get together with one another, when they commune and communicate. If God has your body, but He does not have your invisible spirit, you cannot worship the God who is Spirit. You can clap to the songs. You can sing with the choir. You can say "Amen" to the words, but unless the spirit has kicked into gear, you cannot worship.

So the question is, how do you kick your spirit into gear with God's Spirit so that your spirit is worshiping His Spirit?

The Holy Spirit

The ministry of the Holy Spirit is to act as liaison (see 1 Corinthians 2:10–16). The Spirit knows the mind of God, so His work is to link your human spirit with the God who is Spirit. Therefore, if you want to worship God, you must be yielded to His Spirit. You must come to worship collectively or privately with the attitude, "Lord, I am depending on the Holy Spirit to bring me in contact with You."

Your Thoughts

In addition, your thoughts, your mind must be centered on God. If you sit in church thinking about Monday night football, worrying about your problems, or even counting your blessings, you are not worshiping. How about if you are so tired you can't hold your eyes open? If you stay up late every Saturday night and go to church so tired you wish you were home, you are in no condition to worship God.

God wants your undivided attention in worship. He does not want to be competing with other things for your mind. The object of worship is God. Period. That may mean moving your bedtime up on Saturday so you can get the sleep you need to worship God.

Prayer

Worship always begins with the proper attitude. That's why prayer is so important. Prayer is simply communicating with God. But it involves much more than just saying words, since God rejects communication with the lips that doesn't include the heart (Isaiah 29:13). Prayer connects the heart and mind of man with the heart and mind of God, whether it be verbal or nonverbal.

This is why Paul can exhort Christians to "pray without ceasing" (1 Thessalonians 5:17). When prayer is understood to bring God to bear on every aspect of our lives, then we can be in a constant attitude of prayer because we live with a perpetual God-consciousness. This consciousness may regularly give rise to verbal prayers, but it should be ever-present. Prayer then is not a position of the body or a carefully arranged set of words to express religious sentiments. It is first and foremost an attitude of the heart and mind that seeks to make contact with God.

Meditation

Fixing your heart and mind on God is called meditation. Meditation is a fixation on one subject for an extended period of time. The problem with Eastern religions is not that the people meditate. They have the wrong *object* of meditation, the wrong god.

As they sit and hum by the hour, they are trying to get to the spiritual man. They try to get beyond the physical to the spiritual. They meditate to get inside of themselves, which is doing the right thing with the wrong subject. Eastern religious practitioners meditate, but not on the Father of the Lord Jesus Christ.

So in your devotion time, if all you do is read a passage of Scripture and rattle off a few prayer items, you do not worship. Worship includes yieldedness to the Holy Spirit and a fixation on God. That means you cannot worship and watch television at the same time. It would be better to delay your devotions for another time, because the goal of worship is total fixation on God.

Is it any wonder sometimes that our spirits seem so dead? God can't get our undivided attention to talk to us. The Holy Spirit will not compete with the distractions around us. You may say, "But all of us come to church with problems and other things on our minds."

I understand that. That's why most churches have a "Call to Worship." The idea is to take a few minutes before the service begins to clear our minds for worship. It doesn't mean God doesn't care about our needs. It's that we can't rush into His presence tired and frustrated and expect to worship Him "in spirit and truth." We can't do that because we have not prepared ourselves to worship.

Believe me, I know how much we need that time of getting settled and clearing our minds and setting our focus on God. I'm not telling you anything that's not a problem in the Evans house too. Lois and I know what it's like to be trying to get the kids ready and do something about Sunday dinner and it's getting late, and so forth.

But there has to be a time when we stop, when we pull our spirits together and prepare for undistracted focus on God. When the choir is singing, we may enjoy the sound, but our focus needs to be on God.

Nothing is wrong with spirited worship, with praises in song. But to be authentic worship it must be combined with truth.

I realize that what I have just said means that a large segment of people who call themselves Christians are not worshiping. They go to church, but they don't understand that church attendance in itself is not worship. They don't understand what Jesus told the Samaritan woman: "God is spirit, and those who worship Him must worship in spirit."

Spirit and Truth

Notice that in verse 24 Jesus goes on to say, "God is not only spirit, He is truth." Worship must be in spirit *and* truth. It's not either/or, but both/and. Some groups really get high on worship. They shout praises and sing and clap and feel good. The tears are running down their cheeks and they're shouting, "Hallelujah!"

But worship involves more than an emotional experience. Nothing is wrong with spirited worship, with praises in song. But to be authentic worship it must be combined with truth. The people may be shouting, but what is the preacher saying?

On Mount Gerizim, where the Samaritan woman worshiped, they had a lot of spirit but no truth. Down in Jerusalem where the Jews worshiped, they had a lot of truth but no spirit. It was dead orthodoxy. That's how a lot of churches are today.

When they choose a church, some people will say, "I like that church because they are really alive when they worship. They have a great spirit."

Others will say, "I like this other church because they teach the Bible. They are really strong on the truth."

But we shouldn't have to choose between the two. We need both spirit and truth. True worship is when my innermost being, having received the proper information about God, explodes with joy at the very thought of such a great God being mine!

That's why the core of a church service is the Word of God. That's why when you come to church, you've got to have your Bible with you because the issue is truth. In many churches, you don't ever need your Bible because you never evaluate truth. The question there is, did the preacher sound good and did the choir jam? The question is not, was my inner being exposed to God?

This means you must deal with another issue if you are going to worship God in spirit and truth: the absolute authority of His Word. This makes some church people uncomfortable because they don't want anybody—the preacher, not even God—messing in their business.

But the Bible tells pastors and leaders to mind the business of God's people. I'm not talking about being nosy and pushy and authoritarian, trying to tell everybody what to do. But if God's Word is going to be our absolute authority, we have to preach it, teach it, and obey it.

Some people want to live any old way they please. Now I know that people struggle with problems. I realize issues exist in all of our lives that God is still helping us to work through. And I know that things don't get solved in a day.

I'm referring to people who want to have the privilege of worship and the freedom to sin at the same time. But no one can have it both ways. God is holy. We can't come spiritually dirty before a holy God.

If I came to church all sweaty and smelly, you would say, "How can you come in here smelling and looking like that?"

Well, God looks down on our worship and says, "How can you come to church with that spiritual dirt all over you? How can you come to your private worship time smelling and looking like that?" This is what confession of sin is all about (1 John 1:9). We dare not approach worship with the attitude, "It will make no difference in my life."

God wants to get into your business. Why? Because He's into truth. My commitment as a pastor and the commitment of the other leaders of our church is to tell it like it is. Sometimes, our people will like it and applaud. Other times, they won't like it. They may even get mad. But that's all right, because the issue is truth.

GOD SEEKS WORSHIPERS

In the course of this tremendous teaching on worship, Jesus makes one of the most awesome statements ever recorded. Did you notice it at the end of verse 23? God is looking for worshipers! The great God of the universe hunts for folks who want to worship Him.

THE ESSENCE OF WORSHIP IS THAT YOU COME BEFORE THE GOD WHO IS THE FATHER OF THE LORD JESUS CHRIST WITH YOUR INNER PERSON, NOT JUST YOUR BODY, RESTING ON THE TRUTH OF GOD.

God is saying, "Dallas, Texas (or your hometown), are there any worshipers down there? I see lots of churchgoers in Dallas. The churches are filled, but I'm trying to find people who will link up with Me in spirit. I don't need more bodies, I need some spirit. I want people who are willing to align their lives with My truth. Is anyone down there like that?"

What a stunning thought, that God is searching for worshipers. Volunteers ought to be lining up by the millions. But can you believe it, He's having a hard time finding them. Do you know that God once had a whole nation of people called Israel, but very few worshipers? So He says, "I'm still looking for worshipers."

Are you ready to volunteer? Do you understand the essence of worship now? The essence of worship is that you come before the God who is the Father of the Lord Jesus Christ with your inner person, not just your body, resting on the truth of God.

That's worship. Nothing else is!

Responding to God in Worship

L et me come back to the question I asked above: Will you be one of the worshipers God is looking for? If so, I have some ideas for you that I think will help get you rolling:

1. Start by going to God right now and telling Him, "Dear God, I want to be one of Your true worshipers. I want to know You, fellowship with You, and learn Your ways. Help me to worship You in spirit and truth."

2. If you find that everyday worries and concerns are a real interference for you when you're trying to worship, try this little experiment. Before you enter your devotions, or in that time of quiet mediation before the church service, go ahead and worry about your worries. I'm serious. Write down the two or three things that may be weighing on your mind, and take a minute to think through them.

Take it all the way. Imagine the best and the worst that can happen in each situation. Play out the scenarios, then take a deep breath, crumple the paper, and thank God that He knows all about them. Now that you've given these things your attention, ask Him to help you lay them aside while you focus on Him.

3. Sometimes it's hard to explain a concept like worship to children and young people. Try this for a family discussion starter. Ask each member of the family to tell which worship activity at church means the most to him or her, and why. Be prepared to answer this yourself.

4. I really believe that eliminating hindrances to worship is about half the battle. Do some hard thinking about your daily routine with preparation for worship in mind. Maybe you need to go to bed earlier on Saturday night. Perhaps you need to lay the newspaper aside and keep the TV off until you've had your time with God. Pray that God will reveal to you anything that may be interfering with your worship—and resolve to do something about it.

20
THE GOSPEL
OF GOD

n these pages we have considered a lot of truths about God, about His character and attributes. We've talked about His perfections and the implications they have in our lives. And for the last three chapters we have been considering what God expects from us in terms of our response to who He is.

The point where all of this crosses our lives most directly is in the gospel, the good news of Jesus Christ. It's in the gospel that we see God's perfect standard applied to mankind, what that means for us, and what God did in love to rescue us. So as the capstone to our study, I want to review the gospel with two purposes in mind.

First, if you are saved, I want to remind you of the great grace of God that has been afforded to you, so that you might respond accordingly. I also want to give you a simple and easily reproduced plan or outline by which you can lead someone else to faith in Christ.

Second, for those who are not saved, I want to clarify exactly what the content of the gospel is, lest anyone be confused to his or her own destruction.

Paul the apostle wrote what has been called the *Magna Carta* of the church, the book of Romans. It is the great doctrinal statement of the Christian faith, and in this book Paul sets forth the gospel, the good news about Jesus Christ. I want to talk about five aspects of the gospel we find in Romans. To make it clear and easy to follow, each point in my outline will begin with the letter *P.*

OUR PROBLEM

To appreciate and really understand the gospel, we need to begin by seeing the magnitude of our problem. It's stated for us in clear terms in Romans 3:23: "All have sinned and fall short of the glory of God."

"All have sinned." Some of us may be better-looking sinners than our neighbors. Some of us may be wealthier sinners than the people who live on the other side of town, but sinners we are nonetheless. When God measures us, He does not measure by degrees. The murderer on death row is no different in the eyes of a holy God than the person who tells a little lie. All sin is an affront to His character. We have to understand that.

The Sickness of Sin

Jesus put it in these terms: We are sick, and He is the Great Physician who has come to people sick with the spiritual illness called sin to bring about spiritual healing (Mark 2:17). If you are ever going to be saved, or fully appreciate the salvation you already have, you've got to understand you are a sinner. Verse 10 of Romans 3 says it this way: "There is none righteous, not even one."

Every man and woman born into this world is born alienated from a holy God, because we are born in sin and "shapen in iniquity" (Psalm 51:5 KJV). The Bible makes clear that our whole nature is consumed by sin. But we try to hide our sin. We try to cover it up, dress it up, paint over it, and excuse it, but we can't get rid of it. So we call sin by other names.

But what we call accidents, God calls abominations. What we call blunders, God calls blindness. What we call defects, God calls disease. What we call chance, God calls a choice. What we label as errors, God labels enmity. What we call fascination, God calls fatality. What we designate as infirmity, God designates as iniquity. What we view as luxury, God views as leprosy. What we see as liberty, God sees as lawlessness. What we call a mistake, God calls madness. And what we call weakness, He calls willingness.

Different Standards

God's view and our view of sin are different! You and I cannot understand sin or communicate the gospel to those who need to hear it unless all of us clearly understand that God sees no degrees of sin. When He judges, He does so based on a *perfect* standard, which is His holiness.

I've often said what holiness is to God, clean is to my wife. She is a cleaning fanatic. Some people get high on drugs. Lois gets high on Lysol. One day when she had to go somewhere, being the wonderful husband that I am, I offered to oversee the cleaning. Not to *clean,* you understand, but to oversee the cleaning.

So I called the kids together and gave them their assignments. I supervised, and in my eyes we did a very good job—an excellent job, if I say so myself. When Lois came home, I expected a big hug and a medal for being such a supportive husband. But she came in and said, "I thought you were going to clean up for me."

I got a little frustrated. Now I'm a preacher so I don't get mad, but I got a little frustrated. She took me to some forsaken corner of the house and showed me a piece of lint. I'm talking about something an ant wouldn't have seen. "When I mean clean, I mean this too," she informed me.

The problem was that we were operating on two different standards. My standard was to hit the center and all is well. Lois's standard included the crevices and the corners. When God deals with us, He's dealing from a standard of absolute perfection. So even though we may look relatively clean, even though we may not have committed any crimes, we still fall short of the standard of a perfect God.

Missing the Mark

The word Paul uses for falling short in Romans 3:23 is an archery term that means "to miss the mark." It pictures a bowman who shoots at the target but misses. Sin is missing the target, and we've all missed it. "All have sinned." We may be better than someone else, but unless we are as good as God, we don't qualify!

What is the target? It's the "glory of God." We've come across this term before. The word *glory* means to show off. It means to put something on display in such a way that it embellishes you, makes you look good. When we talk about the glory of God in relation to our words and actions, we are talking about putting Him on display.

God's glory is such that if you or I fail even one time to display Him properly, we demonstrate that we are sinners. Anytime we fail to reflect God as He is, that's sin. People get upset because they think the whole human race was plunged into sin by one man eating a piece of fruit. "It's not fair of God to condemn all of us over a piece of fruit," they argue.

> YOU PASSED ON TO YOUR
> KIDS NOT ONLY YOUR LOOKS,
> BUT YOUR SIN NATURE,
> THE PROPENSITY ALL OF US HAVE
> TO OPERATE INDEPENDENTLY
> FROM A HOLY GOD.

No, that's not it. The world was plunged into sin over man deciding he was going to do his own thing by eating a piece of fruit. He was going to disobey what God told him, run his own life, be his own god. Anytime we act autonomously, we prove that we don't measure up to God's glory.

Just before I go to the dentist, I do the same thing you do. I brush my teeth real hard to fool him. But I can't fool my dentist because he makes me rinse with a red dye that sticks to any plaque on my teeth. By the time the dentist is through with me, my whole mouth is red! You see, I can deceive myself with Crest or Colgate, but I can't fool the dentist because he's using a much more thorough method to determine what's clean.

God judges us by His standard, not ours. He does not measure our standing in the community, what our parents say about us, or how we stack up compared to everyone else. His "target" is the glory of His own character, and we fall far short of it.

Sinners by Nature

We are born with the problem of sin. The Bible says we are sinners by nature, as well as by choice. That's why you don't have to teach your children how to lie. You don't have to enroll them in a course on how to be selfish. They pick that up all by themselves. That's because you passed on to your kids not only your looks, but your sin nature, the propensity all of us have to operate independently from a holy God.

When most people see an apple with a hole in it, they assume that a worm has bored its way into the apple and is still in it. We have this old joke: "What's worse than finding a worm in your apple?" Answer: "Finding *half* a worm."

But a worm does not bore into a ripe apple. The egg of the worm is laid on the blossom of the apple before the apple is ever formed. The apple actually grows up around the worm. So if you see an apple with a hole in it, it's because a worm has bored its way *out,* not in. The hole you see is simply the effect of something the apple was created with or grew with.

In the same way, the "larva" of sin is transferred from generation to generation, from parent to child, so that what comes out is what's already there. No matter where you run, you cannot run from the reality that God is offended by all unrighteousness. Until we understand that the gospel is bad news first, we can't appreciate the good news.

We spend so much time trying to make ourselves think we are OK that we never get around to admitting, "I'm a sinner." But Jesus only died for sinners. So let's make sure we understand the problem. All of us have sinned in God's sight, because His standard is perfection.

OUR PREDICAMENT

Our sin problem has led to quite a predicament. Here's how Paul describes it in Romans 4:4–5:

> Now to the one who works, his wage is not reckoned as a favor, but as what is due. But to the one who does not work, but believes in Him who justifies the ungodly, his faith is reckoned as righteousness.

Our problem is that we are sinners. Our predicament is that we can't save ourselves. Now most people will agree they are not perfect. They will admit to some degree of sin, but that's where the problem ends as far as they're concerned. Not many people want to admit they can't do something about it themselves.

Earning God's Favor

People want to work off their debt to God. It's the American way. "I'll pay my own way." Most people know enough about God to realize that He has some kind of standard. But "not knowing about God's righteousness, [they seek] to establish their own" (Romans 10:3) by trying to work their way to God. The most common misunderstanding of the gospel is this: I can work my way to a holy God. I can earn His favor by being and doing good.

So people set about doing this in a lot of ways. Some do it through religion. They think if they go to church enough, read the Bible enough, and pray enough, somehow these religious exercises will satisfy God. But they won't.

> *We CANNOT USE OUR RIGHTEOUS DEEDS TO CANCEL OUT OUR UNRIGHTEOUS DEEDS. . . . IF ANYTHING SHOWS UP ON THE BAD SIDE, YOU ARE OUT BECAUSE GOD IS PERFECT.*

Other people try to be as good as they can: be a model citizen, try to live right, keep the Ten Commandments, and so forth. I don't know of any greater deception than this last one—the idea that we can keep the Ten Commandments and thus please God.

Guilty of All

First of all, James 2:10 reminds us that if we break even one of God's laws, we are guilty of breaking them all. "That's an impossible standard to obey," someone will say. You got it!

Second, there's probably not a person on the topside of earth who has not actually broken all of God's commandments. Let's take "Thou shalt not commit adultery" as an example. Probably lots of people would raise their hands and say, "I haven't done that one, preacher. Move on to the next one."

But wait a minute. Jesus said, "Everyone who looks on a woman to lust for her has committed adultery with her already in his heart"

(Matthew 5:28). Now I have a question: Are there any adulterers out there?

Let's go on to "Thou shalt not commit murder." Again, someone will say, "I got you there, preacher. I have never killed anyone in my life." But Jesus also said, "Everyone who is angry with his brother shall be guilty before the court; and whoever . . . shall say, 'You fool,' shall be guilty enough to go into the fiery hell" (Matthew 5:22).

In other words, if you have ever been so angry at someone you wished he or she was dead, you have committed murder already in your heart. Question: Any murderers out there?

God's law says, "Thou shalt have no other gods before Me." You may not have any pagan idols in your house, but anytime you have chosen to do something other than what God would want, anytime you have put God second and yourself first, you have put the god of your own will and pleasure before Him. Any sinners out there by this standard?

A Perfect Standard

You see, God's standard is so perfect that it creates an awful predicament for us sinners. We can't get ourselves out of our mess. But that's part of the gospel message. Paul says salvation is "not as a result of [our] works" (Ephesians 2:9). Otherwise, we would strut and brag about it. But we can't earn it. We can't fix ourselves.

Imagine a man going before the judge for stealing. Just before he's sentenced, the man says, "Your honor, I just want you to know that I've never raped or killed anyone." He goes through a list of twenty-five bad things he's never done.

What will the judge say? "Well, that's nice, but it's irrelevant. While you haven't done those other twenty-five things, you did steal and that's why you're here. And I'm bound by the law to send you to jail."

We cannot use our righteous deeds to cancel out our unrighteous deeds. Most people think that God has a huge scale in heaven. When we get there, He's going to put the good we've done on one side and the bad on the other, and if the good outweighs the bad, we're in. If the bad outweighs the good, we're out.

No! If anything shows up on the bad side, you are out because God is perfect. Even one sin is an affront to His perfection. So all your striving and struggling and effort won't free you from your sin predicament. Again, that doesn't mean you can't be a good person, even better than your neighbor. It means you cannot satisfy the demands of a holy God.

OUR PENALTY

So we've got a problem: sin. We've got a predicament: We can't get ourselves out of it. We also we have a penalty. "The wages of sin is death," Paul warns in Romans 6:23.

Sin carries with it a price tag, a payoff, which is death. The proof that we are sinners by nature is that all of us are going to die. I don't care how healthy we are or how well we eat, we are going to die. In fact, we are going to die by appointment.

The Bible says, "It is appointed for men to die once and after this comes judgment" (Hebrews 9:27). You may be late for a lot of things in your life, but that's one appointment you will keep. Then everything you've accumulated will be left behind. I've never seen a hearse pulling a U-Haul. You don't get to take any of it with you.

Separation from God

In fact, the non-Christian will actually die twice, because in the Bible death means separation, not cessation. In other words, biblical death never means that you cease to exist. There is no such thing. Once you are born you will exist forever. The concept of death as the cessation of life, as annihilation, or as nothingness has no meaning to God.

Instead, physical death is merely the separation of the soul and spirit from the body. Another death is described in Scripture, a much more serious thing: eternal death, in which the soul is separated from God forever and ever. That's the death Paul talks about as the payment for sin.

So if you want to know how seriously God takes sin, look at death. Solomon advises us that if we really want to know what life is about, we're better off going to a funeral than to a party (Ecclesiastes 7:14).

The reason? At a funeral, you get the real deal, the real story. You see how everyone is going to wind up some day. But at a party, people will lie to you. At a party, you won't get the real story because everyone tries to cover up and pretend they don't have to face life. Physical life doesn't end with a party; it ends with a funeral.

Home with the Lord

But if you are a Christian, you are never going to die. That's not a contradiction to what I just said, because Paul tells us to be "absent from the body" (physical death) is to be "at home with the

362

Lord" (2 Corinthians 5:8). Less than one second after you die, you will open your eyes in the presence of God. That's why Paul asks, "O death, where is your victory? O death, where is your sting?" (1 Corinthians 15:55). Jesus Christ has taken the sting out of death.

It's like the two brothers who were playing in the yard when a bee stung one of them. He began to cry and hold his arm where he had been stung. The bee then began circling the other brother, who cried out, "Help! Help!"

But the boy who had been stung said through his tears of pain, "Stop hollering! That bee's not going to hurt you. All it can do is make a lot of noise. It only has one stinger, and it's already stung me. I've taken the stinger."

Jesus Christ took the "stinger" of death for those who trust Him, so that all death can do is make a lot of noise. It can't hurt you once you know Jesus Christ. That's why for the Christian, physical death is going to sleep and waking up "at home with the Lord." But those who don't know Christ must pay the awful price of eternal separation from God.

Eternal Judgment

It always traumatizes some people to think that God would banish someone from His presence for eternity. The old line usually goes, "I just don't believe a loving God would do that." Let's look at several serious problems with that line of thinking.

First of all, it reflects a terrible misunderstanding of the character of God. I won't spend a lot of time here, because we've already covered this argument. Suffice it to say that while God is loving, He's also just and holy.

Second, God never prepared hell for people. Hell was prepared for the devil and his angels (Matthew 25:41). But God allows you a choice, and if you don't choose Him, you get the repercussions of that decision: eternal separation from Him.

Why is this separation eternal? It couldn't be any less and be a payment for sin. When a man rejects God's *eternal* Son, who died on the cross for the sins of *eternal* men, he must pay the *eternal* price, which is *eternal* separation from God.

The Fear of Death

People don't like to talk about this because it scares them. Well, if you are not a Christian, you have every reason to be afraid. And if I can help you to be more afraid, I welcome the opportunity. I'm not being facetious. You don't want to be caught dead without Jesus Christ!

If you know Jesus Christ, however, you have no reason to fear death. The second the doctor says it's over, you will enter a blissful environment free of any contamination by sin and free of all the things that cause you pain here on earth.

OUR PROVISION

This brings us to our fourth *P,* the provision that God in His grace has made for sin: Jesus Christ.

Again we go to the book of Romans: "God demonstrates His own love toward us, in that while were yet sinners, Christ died for us" (5:8). Notice that it's not when we got better, not when we fixed ourselves, not when we came up with our own answers and our personal solutions. No, Jesus Christ died for us while we were still mired deep in our sins.

Our Great Salvation

God wants all the credit for your salvation, so He takes you just as you are. Some people say, "When I straighten out my life, then I will come to God." But if you could straighten out your life, you wouldn't need to come to God. He came to you because you are incapable of cleaning yourself up enough to come to Him. All God asks you to do is bring your sin to Calvary.

I'M GOING TO HEAVEN BECAUSE JESUS CHRIST'S BLOOD IS SUFFICIENT TO SATISFY THE DEMANDS OF A HOLY GOD— AND THAT'S THE ONLY REASON.

The Bible uses several words to explain the process of salvation because there's a lot to it. For example, God's holy wrath against sin had to be satisfied by a sacrifice. That's called *propitiation.* Your good works could never satisfy or appease God because they're all mixed up with the sin in your life. That's not good enough. God demanded a perfect sacrifice. Only His perfect Son could offer it.

Salvation also involves *justification;* that is, a legal declaration that the sinner is now righteous in God's sight. God can declare you righteous not because you are not guilty, but because your guilt has been dealt with by Christ.

Your sin also required *redemption,* or payment. Someone had to pick up the tab. That's what Jesus did when He said on the cross, "It is finished!" (John 19:30). In other words, "The debt is paid in full." That's a very picturesque word, drawn from the Old Testament. God delayed punishment for sin one year at a time in the Old Testament on what was called the Day of Atonement.

A Sacrifice for Sin

On the Day of Atonement, God accepted a substitute sacrifice for Israel's sin. The priest presented the animal to God on the altar, the animal's throat was cut, its blood was poured out as a payment for sin, and God counted that good for another 365 days.

Then the people would bring in the "scapegoat" (Leviticus 16:8), and the sins of the people were transferred to the goat. The goat was driven out of camp, signifying that the people's sins were now gone for another year. The only problem was that every now and then, the scapegoat would wander back in the camp.

So the Israelites had someone acting as a shepherd to look out for this goat. If the goat wandered back, this person would lead it to the edge of a cliff and shove it off. That goat would never come back again.

The Greek language had a word for that action: *lutrosis.* It meant that payment was made. But when they wanted to talk about a payment being made and never having to be made again, they added a prefix to this word to make it *apolutrosis.* When Paul describes the death of Christ as His "redemption" in Romans 3:24, he uses this word.

Over the Cliff!

Our sins were "shoved off the cliff," never to come up again! That's why you can't lose your salvation once you are saved. When I stand before God and He says, "Evans, why should I let you into heaven?", I'm not going to say a thing. I'm going to let Jesus do all my talking for me, because He paid the full price for my sins.

I'm going to heaven because Jesus Christ's blood is sufficient to satisfy the demands of a holy God—and that's the only reason. It's not because I'm a preacher or because I try to live right and do good things. None of that has anything do with my relationship to God. The only thing that will get anyone into God's heaven is that he or she is covered by the blood of Christ.

Not by Works

The Bible says that God saved us "not on the basis of deeds which we have done in righteousness" (Titus 3:5). Now I know that's not logical to us. We think if a person lives a good life, he ought to get some credit for it. But that's because we do not use God's standard of judgment.

Remember the kid in your class who always made A's? We had one when I was growing up. Every time we didn't do well on a test and we all wanted the teacher to grade us on the curve, this kid would make an A on the test and ruin the curve for everyone else.

We didn't like Mr. Know-It-All. He wasn't very popular. It wasn't because he did anything wrong. In fact, we didn't like him because he did everything right. He messed up our chance to get off easy. He ruined the curve.

Do you know why the people of Jesus' day didn't like Him and put Him to death? He broke the curve. Everyone was OK until He showed up. When the people measured themselves against each other, they came off looking good. But when Jesus came, He ruined the curve. We need a Savior, not someone like us. We need a pardon, not a curve.

OUR PARDON

To go to heaven, you must accept Christ's pardon. That's what Romans 10:9 is all about: "If you confess with your mouth Jesus as Lord, and believe in your heart that God raised Him from the dead, you shall be saved."

Pardon Accepted

As we have seen, the death of Christ satisfied the demands of God against the sin of all men for all time. But His death only benefits those who accept it. Salvation was provided for everyone, but it is only experienced by those who recognize their guilt and accept Christ's pardon.

In an earlier chapter, I told you about the man who refused a pardon for his crime and was executed. At least he acknowledged his guilt, unlike the late U.S. communist Victor Debs, who was imprisoned and later pardoned by President Warren Harding in 1921.

On his release, an unrepentant Debs declared, "It is the government that should ask me for a pardon." Debs's pardon did nothing to change his heart.

A Change of Heart

To be saved, you must accept the pardon Jesus Christ offers, but acceptance must be accompanied by an admission of guilt and a change of heart. That's why Paul says *you* must believe in your heart. Your mother can't believe for you. Your father can't accept your pardon for you. Your children can't get saved for you. This is a personal decision.

You must "believe in your heart." You must believe that Jesus is God, that He paid for your sins, and with a repentant heart—that is, a heart that wishes Him to address your sin—you come to Jesus Christ for pardon, believing that God has raised Him from the dead.

If Jesus Christ were still dead, He couldn't even be His own Savior, much less yours. If Jesus Christ were still dead, how could He deliver you if He couldn't even deliver Himself? But early on resurrection morning, just a little while before day, His grave turned up empty! God raised Jesus from the dead. Why? To testify to the world that Christ's payment for sin was accepted. God never asked us to put our hope in a dead man.

Our "Umpire"

Because of Christ's death and resurrection, then, God can grant a pardon to anyone who comes through Christ. Jesus Christ is the only Mediator between God and man (1 Timothy 2:5). Job was anticipating the Mediator, and I like the word he uses in Job 9:33: "I've got a problem. I'm a sinful man, and I'm trying to reach a perfect God. I need an umpire." In other words, Job needed someone who could bridge the gap between his humanity and God.

Job is saying, "I need someone who is a man like me and understands how I feel. But I also need someone who is like God and understands how He feels. If I had an umpire like this, He could take my hand and take God's hand and bring the two of us together."

That's what Jesus Christ is, our divine Umpire. He knows how you feel because He became a man. He knows how God feels because He is God. He is the God-man. So He can be for you and for God at the same time and bring the two of you together. He can offer you God's pardon and take your acceptance back to God and say, "Father, this person has trusted Me. He's under My blood. He's fit for heaven now."

Paying the Price

Let me pull all of this together with a familiar illustration. A young woman was caught going 100 miles an hour in a 55-mile-per-hour zone outside a small, out-of-the-way town. The policeman brought her into court, where the judge fined her $100. "But I don't have $100," she said.

"I'm sorry, but you will have to spend the weekend in jail," the judge told her. "You've been found guilty of speeding, and you owe the court $100. I know you don't have the money, but the law is the law."

She began to cry. "Your honor, I don't have $100, but I don't want to spend the weekend in jail. Have mercy on me."

The judge said, "I can't change the law. And the law says you either have to pay $100 or spend the weekend in jail." The young woman begged for mercy again—and to the surprise of the bailiff and the policeman, the judge did something very interesting.

He pushed his chair back from the bench, took off his robe, walked around to where the young lady was standing, pulled out his wallet and gave the bailiff a 100 dollar bill, went back to the bench, put his robe back on, and sat down.

Then the judge picked up his gavel and said, "Young lady, you owe the court $100 or a weekend in jail. But I see someone else has paid the price." He banged his gavel on the bench. "Case dismissed. You're free to go."

That's what God did for you and me. We stood before the bench of His justice, and He said, "You've been found guilty of going against My holy character. You've either got to pay perfection or spend eternity in the prison called hell."

But God the Judge also heard us cry out for mercy. He knew we had nothing to pay our debt with. So He stepped out of heaven, "zipped down" the independent use of His deity and put on the robe of humanity in the Person of Jesus Christ, reached into His pocket, and paid the price Himself on the cross. Three days later, He publicly displayed the robe of deity at His resurrection and ascended back to the bench of heaven.

Now He looks down and says to anyone who comes to Him and begs for mercy, "I can't change the law, but I can pay the price." You will never have to worry about heaven again if you will come to Jesus Christ.

Responding to the Gospel of God

I f you are still not sure of your relationship with God, I urge you to pray the prayer below. But if you can say, "I'm already a Christian; I know my price has been paid. I've repented of my sins and accepted Christ's pardon," that's great. Below are three things you can do about it:

1. If you are unsure of your salvation or want to come to Christ right now, tell Him so. Pray, "Dear heavenly Father, I acknowledge to You that I am a sinner and cannot save myself. I believe that your Son Jesus Christ died on the cross in my place for my sins and rose from the dead to give me salvation. I now accept the Lord Jesus Christ as my personal Savior, trusting Him alone to give me eternal life and a relationship with You. Thank You for saving me, and help me from this day on to live a life pleasing to You. Amen."

2. Be Christ's willing servant for the rest of your life. Why? Because that's how long you would have been dead if He hadn't saved you. I realize this one isn't very specific, but it's an important mindset to have. To make this more vivid, turn to Philippians 2:5–11 and make this great passage about Jesus Christ your prayer to the Lord.

3. Add to the power of your witness by committing Ephesians 2:8–9 to memory. Even though we did not discuss these verses in detail, they contain the real heart of what a person needs to understand and believe before he or she is ready to accept Christ's pardon and give up self-efforts at salvation.

4. Why not go back through this chapter with a pencil and paper and copy down the basic outline of the gospel I presented. It's a simple and effective way to communicate the truth, and I believe God will bless your use of it in witnessing. You may even want to write the outline in the front of your Bible for ready reference in witnessing situations.

EPILOGUE

I hope that as you have read this book, you have
been encouraged, motivated, and challenged to
know your God better and be transformed by
the reality of that knowledge. Knowledge with-
out application leads to pride, whereas application without the
proper context leads to empty emotionalism. Today we have far too
many Christians living at both extremes. Unless the knowledge of
God results in an encounter with God bringing about the proper
response to God, there will be no transformation by God. The in-
evitable result will be a fruitless, empty, and defeated Christian life.

On the other hand, when we are apprehended by the greatness of
God and apply the knowledge of that encounter to the realities of
daily existence, we begin to experience life as it was meant to be
lived. The knowledge of God and meaning in life are intrinsically tied
to one another. You can't truly have the latter without the former.

The German lyricist Joachim Neander expressed it clearly when
he wrote:

Praise to the Lord, the Almighty, the King of creation!
O my soul, praise Him, for He is thy health and salvation!

All ye who hear, Now to His temple draw near;
Join me in glad adoration![1]

God, the "King of creation," the architect of the heavens, and our "health and salvation" condescends even to speak to a human being. David articulated this same sentiment in Psalm 8:3–4:

> When I consider Thy heavens, the work of Thy fingers, the moon and the stars, which Thou hast ordained; what is man, that Thou dost take thought of him? And the son of man, that Thou dost care for him?

The very things that God created bore witness to David of His omnipotence. The fact of God's omnipotence must have informed David of his own insignificance. But what was so puzzling was why God attended to the needs of mankind with such special care and grace in light of man's insignificance.

So also when we consider God's prominence and virtue, we gain a new perspective on who we are and who we are not. For some reason we are special to God, although it's not because of our merit. The more we peer into His attributes, the more it becomes obvious that the portrait we are painting of God belongs on a larger and larger canvas, and the more we appear as but a speck in the picture.

This leads us to think that God must really love us to have anything to do with us. We are like babies, useless in terms of the pragmatic functions of life, but loved and cherished in spite of our lack of utility.

Babies do some of the strangest things. Their perception of the world is radically different from that of adults. Babies will do things like trying to reach out and touch the sun. The sun is so bright and its warmth so penetrating that the baby thinks this great ball of fire must be very close.

We adults are like babies to God. God is distinct because of His perfections, but He sends His rays so that we can feel His warmth. As any curious baby would, when we feel the revelation of God's rays we should naturally reach out for them; and when we do, we will experience the joy, awe, and splendor of basking in the rays of His love. May you reach out to God in childlike faith, and may the pursuit of God be your greatest passion and your most cherished desire.

---

1. "Praise to the Lord the Almighty" (German: "Lobe Den Herren"). Neander lived from 1650 to 1680. Translation to English by Catherine Winkworth.

INDEX OF SCRIPTURE

INDEX OF SUBJECTS

Moody Press, a ministry of the Moody Bible Institute,
is designed for education, evangelization, and edification.
If we may assist you in knowing more about Christ
and the Christian life, please write us without obligation:
Moody Press, c/o MLM, Chicago, Illinois 60610.